Prague

WHAT'S NEW | WHAT'S ON | WHAT'S BEST

www.timeout.com/prague

Contents

Don't Miss

Itineraries

Published by Time Out Guides Ltd
Universal House
251 Tottenham Court Road
London W1T 7AB
Tel: + 44 (0)20 7813 3000
Fax: + 44 (0)20 7813 6001
Email: guides@timeout.com
www.timeout.com

Managing Director Peter Fiennes
Editorial Director Ruth Jarvis
Business Manager Dan Allen
Editorial Manager Holly Pick
Assistant Management Accountant Ija Krasnikova

Time Out Guides is a wholly owned subsidiary of Time Out Group Ltd.

© Time Out Group Ltd
Chairman Tony Elliott
Chief Executive Officer David King
Group General Manager/Director Nichola Coulthard
Time Out Communications Ltd MD David Pepper
Time Out International Ltd MD Cathy Runciman
Time Out Magazine Ltd Publisher/Managing Director Mark Elliott
Production Director Mark Lamond
Group IT Director Simon Chappell
Marketing & Circulation Director Catherine Demajo

Time Out and the Time Out logo are trademarks of Time Out Group Ltd.

This edition first published in Great Britain in 2009 by Ebury Publishing
A Random House Group Company
Company information can be found on www.randomhouse.co.uk
Random House UK Limited Reg. No. 954009
10 9 8 7 6 5 4 3 2 1

Distributed in the US by Publishers Group West
Distributed in Canada by Publishers Group Canada

For further distribution details, see www.timeout.com

ISBN: 978-1-84670-133-7

A CIP catalogue record for this book is available from the British Library.

Printed and bound in Germany by Appl.

The Random House Group Limited supports The Forest Stewardship Council (FSC), the leading international forest certification organisation. All our titles that are printed on Greenpeace approved FSC certified paper carry the FSC logo. Our paper procurement policy can be found at www.rbooks.co.uk/environment.

Time Out carbon-offsets all its flights with Trees for Cities (www.treesforcities.org).

Prague Shortlist

The **Time Out Prague Shortlist** is one of a new series of guides that draws on Time Out's background as a magazine publisher to keep you current with what's going on in town. As well as Prague's key sights and the best of its eating, drinking and leisure options, the guide picks out the most exciting venues to have recently opened and gives a full calendar of annual events. It also includes features on the important news, trends and openings, all compiled by locally based editors and writers. Whether you're visiting for the first time, or you're a regular, you'll find the *Time Out Prague Shortlist* contains all you need to know, in a portable and easy-to-use format.

The guide divides central Prague into six areas, each of which contains listings for Sights & Museums, Eating & Drinking, Shopping, Nightlife and Arts & Leisure, with maps pinpointing all their locations. At the front of the book are chapters rounding up these scenes city-wide, and giving a shortlist of our overall picks in a variety of categories. We include itineraries for days out, plus essentials such as transport information and hotels.

Our listings give phone numbers as dialled from within the Czech Republic. To call from abroad, preface them with your country's access code and the country code, 420.

We have noted price categories by using one to four $ signs ($-$$$$), representing budget, moderate, expensive and luxury. Major credit cards are accepted unless otherwise stated. We have also indicated when a venue is NEW .

All our listings are double-checked, but places do sometimes close or change their hours or prices, so it's a good idea to call a venue before visiting. While every effort has been made to ensure the accuracy of information included, the publishers cannot accept responsibility for any errors that this guide may contain.

Venues are marked on the maps using symbols numbered according to their order within the chapter and colour-coded according to the type of venue they represent:

❶ Sights & Museums
❶ Eating & Drinking
❶ Shopping
❶ Nightlife
❶ Arts & Leisure

Map key	
Major sight or landmark	▬
Railway station	▬
Metro station	Ⓜ
Park	▬
Pedestrian zone	▨
Church	✚
Steps	▬
Area name	JOSEFOV
Tram route	—

Time Out **Prague** Shortlist

EDITORIAL
Editor Will Tizard
Deputy Editor Nicola Homer
Researchers Hela Balínová,
Kateřina Kadlecová, Helena Vančurová
Proofreader Jo Willacy

DESIGN
Art Director Scott Moore
Art Editor Pinelope Kourmouzoglou
Senior Designer Henry Elphick
Graphic Designers Kei Ishimaru,
Nicola Wilson
Advertising Designer Jodi Sher

Picture Editor Jael Marschner
Deputy Picture Editor Lynn Chambers
Picture Researcher Gemma Walters
Picture Desk Assistant Marzena Zoladz
Picture Librarian Christina Theisen

ADVERTISING
Commercial Director Mark Phillips
International Advertising Manager
Kasimir Berger
International Sales Executive Charlie Sokol
Advertising Sales (Prague) Michal Jareš,
Prague InYourPocket

MARKETING
Marketing Manager Yvonne Poon
**Sales & Marketing Director, North America
& Latin America** Lisa Levinson
Senior Publishing Brand Manager
Luthfa Begum
Art Director Anthony Huggins

PRODUCTION
Production Manager Brendan McKeown
Production Controller Damian Bennett
Production Co-ordinator Kelly Fenlon

CONTRIBUTORS
This guide was researched and written by Will Tizard, Jacy Meyer, Kateřina Kadlecová
and the writers of *Time Out Prague*. The editor would like to thank Czech Tourism.

PHOTOGRAPHY
All photography Jitka Hynkova, except: pages 12, 44, 51, 57, 121 Elan Fleisher; pages
29, 139 Peter Brenkus; page 30 Rudolfinum_CZćPra ské jaro–Zden k Chrapek; pages
43, 47, 151 Helena Smith; pages 50, 56, 68, 123, 129, 135, 141 Olivia Rutherford;
page 84 René Jakl; pages 89, 110 Will Tizard.

The following images were provided by the featured establishments/artists: pages 33,
34, 35, 36, 37, 38, 54, 64, 67, 71, 73, 75, 79, 80, 83. 102, 107, 126, 129, 152,
162, 167, 171, 175, 119, 148, 161.

Cover photograph: © Chris Coe/Axiom.

MAPS
JS Graphics (john@jsgraphics.co.uk).

About **Time Out**

Founded in 1968, Time Out has expanded from humble London beginnings into the
leading resource for those wanting to know what's happening in the world's greatest
cities. As well as our influential what's-on weeklies in London, New York and Chicago,
we publish nearly 30 other listings magazines in cities as varied as Beijing and
Mumbai. The magazines established Time Out's trademark style: sharp writing,
informed reviewing and bang up-to-date inside knowledge of every scene.

Time Out made the natural leap into travel guides in the 1980s with the City Guide
series, which now extends to over 50 destinations around the world. Written and
researched by expert local writers and generously illustrated with original photography,
the full-size guides cover a larger area than our Shortlist guides and include many more
venue reviews, along with additional background features and a full set of maps.

Throughout this rapid growth, the company has remained proudly independent, still
owned by Tony Elliott four decades after he started Time Out London as a single fold-
out sheet of A5 paper. This independence extends to the editorial content of all our
publications, this Shortlist included. No establishment has been featured because it
has advertised, and no payment has influenced any of our reviews. And, for our critics,
there's definitely no such thing as a free lunch: all restaurants and bars are visited
and reviewed anonymously, and Time Out always picks up the bill.
For more about the company, see www.timeout.com.

Don't Miss

Sights & Museums

Prague has entered its third decade of revitalisation following 1989 with a bold, classy move that adds significant lustre not only to the Prague Castle district of Hradčany but to the Czech Republic's vast (and all too often rarely seen) art collection. The opening of the former military museum, the Schwarzenberg Palace (p69), as the National Gallery's home for Baroque art would have been a major development even if the new venue was like the eight other collections of the organisation.

The 160 sculptures and 280 paintings that the museum contains, ranging from stirring stone saints by Matthias Braun and Maximilian Brokof to epic portraits by Karel Škréta and Bartholomeus Spranger, would surely impress on their own. The impact of seeing these works would have been heightened as they were finally awarded a dedicated home, having been freed from the confines of a wing another institution of the National Gallery.

But, after years of top-to-bottom retrofitting, the reopening of the Schwarzenberg Palace, which is something of a Baroque marvel in itself, complete with sgraffitoed walls lending an 18th-century 3D effect to its façade, has been nothing short of a triumph.

Aside from the stunning collection itself, showing off the developments of late Renaissance and Baroque art in Bohemia, and the bold marriage of high-tech modern lighting and infrastructure with 300-year-old palace walls, the gallery is infused with a new spirit. National Gallery staff, who normally seem either bored or a bit suspicious of visitors,

Charles Bridge p95

S H O R T L I S T

Best revamped
- National Technical Museum (p11)
- Schwarzenberg Palace (p69)
- Zoo Praha (p153)

Best Prague experience
- Charles Bridge (p95)
- Old Jewish Cemetery (p101)
- Prague Castle (p61)

Best views
- Astronomical Clock (p105)
- Old Town Bridge Tower (p105)
- Petřín hill (p82)

King of the castles
- Prague Castle's Old Royal Palace (p65)
- Vyšehrad (p140)

Best outdoor attractions
- Jazz Boat (p122)
- Wallenstein Gardens (p82)

Best architecture
- Church of St Nicholas (p78)
- House of the Black Madonna (p99)
- Municipal House (p103)

Best for kids
- Stromovka (p160)
- Výstaviště (p153)
- Zoo Praha (p153)

Best art stops
- Convent of St Agnes of Bohemia (p98)
- Karlín Studios (p151)
- Municipal Library (p104)
- National Gallery Collection of 19th-, 20th- and 21st-Century Art (p153)

Best historic
- Museum of Communism (p104)
- National Museum (p130)
- Old Town Hall (p105)

are welcoming here. Exhibits and displays have been rethought with the clear goal of capturing hearts and minds – mostly to great effect.

For once in a state collection, displays focus not just on the art but on the everyday workshop practice of the artisans who created it. Sculptural and painting sketches, models and workshop replicas introduce you to both the inspiration and the endless toil of the great Baroque artists who laboured in the court of Rudolf II and well before.

It has been said that reflecting on past glories is a common enough syndrome in small countries whose more recent history is far less glorious, but it seems that Czechs finally have a place to celebrate justly cherished works of masterful artistry and scope. The spirit seems to be spreading even to that other fusty state cultural organ, the National Museum (which also has multiple venues about town, as does the Prague Municipal Gallery).

Long the resting place of dusty mammoths, boxes of geodes and

www.treesforcities.org

Trees for Cities
Charity registration number 1032154

Travelling creates so many
lasting memories.

Make your trip mean something for
years to come - not just for you but
for the environment and for people
living in deprived urban areas.

Anyone can offset their flights,
but when you plant trees with
Trees for Cities, you'll help create
a green space for an urban
community that really needs it.

To find out more visit
www.treesforcities.org

Leave
Your
Mark

Create a green future for cities.

Prague Castle p61

busts of historic Czechs, the National Museum's crown jewel at the top of Wenceslas Square has also stepped up its creativity and relevance. The recent show charting untold stories from the 1968 Warsaw Pact-led invasion was an unqualified success – and seems a good indicator of things to come. The show grew out of a plea from the state television channel Czech TV for viewers to submit their photographs and stories of '68, which resulted in a flood of impassioned, never-before-heard tales. So much material turned up that the station was able to fill the halls of the National Museum with one of its most electric shows to date. What's more, it actually dared to raise the discussion and rethinking of recent and unquestionably historic events. Hopefully this will inspire some of Prague's other museums.

Home to 1.2 million, this city has more than a dozen significant museums and, for a time, had three military ones alone. Old Town itself is described as an 'open-air museum of architecture', and Old Town Square hosts four major art collections that feature Czech work: the National Gallery's Kinský Palace and House at the Stone Bell, the newly renovated House at the Golden Ring and Old Town Hall.

One of the most engaging museums, the National Technical Museum – which shows off countless examples of cunning 'Czechnology' in the form of planes, cars and inventions – is due to reopen in early 2010, and promises to be another exciting offering, especially for kids. Further glimpses of interwar Czechoslovakia can be found at the Museum of Decorative Arts (p144), which has benefitted from the added capacity of the Schwarzenberg Palace opening; its incredible collections of Baroque jewellery, ceramics, glass, textiles and clothing are grandly displayed at the new Hradčany venue.

Meanwhile, the city's other starring attractions, Prague Castle (p61) and the Old Jewish Cemetery, and the Jewish Museum (p101), are still worth visiting, although they are fairly traditional in their curatorial practice. However, the latter has been ramping things up with exhibitions such as 'Unknown', which displayed 700 archive photographs of Prague Jews who disappeared during the Holocaust, inviting the public to provide any clues as to their fates.

Long-standing State v Church turf battles, sadly, still affect St Vitus's Cathedral at Prague Castle, so you shouldn't be too surprised to hear of different areas being opened or closed off to the public, or admission fees to the church being waived and then reinstated. Meanwhile, Prague Castle's displays still consist mainly of dusty mimeographed illustrations, with Russian in prominent use. In any case, the interiors of Prague Castle have been largely absent of wonders for some time; the treasures that weren't carried off by the Swedes during the late Renaissance and were subsequently carted off by the Nazis and Soviets during the twentieth century.

The Old Royal Palace part, however, continues to improve, building on its renovated exhibition space with historically themed shows geared towards attracting international audiences. These exhibitions stretch out over a dozen rooms and feature insights into the lives that have occupied this unique space since 3200 BC (the roots of the castle itself extend back to a mere AD 900).

The Museum of Music (p82) on Karmelitská Street in the Malá Strana district is also worth a visit, for its colourful, noisy interactive displays. The kid-friendly Zoo Praha (p153), is also looking better than ever, with new programmes, a collection of rare gavials, a petting zoo and lion feeding times posted on the website.

Despite all these attractions, most people still experience the city mainly by walking its streets, which are conveniently compact (Old Town, with its Astronomical Clock, is just two kilometres across). These passages, thankfully, seem to be almost impervious to the economic fluctuations that occur through the centuries.

Tickets and information

The latest details about the city's main attractions, together with new exhibitions, are reliably posted on the Prague Information Service website (www.pis.cz). The Prague Tourist Card is a worthwhile investment if you're planning to see much more than Prague Castle, but note that it does not include entry to the Old Jewish Cemetry. However, it does cover three days of visits to dozens of other venues, for the 790 Kč, or 530 Kč for students, with public transit included for an additional 350 Kč. Pick it up at the Prague Information Service on Old Town Square or at the Čedok tourism office in Můstek metro (at the bottom of Wenceslas Square, Nové Město, 224 219 992).

Church of St Nicholas p78

U Vejvodů p115

WHAT'S BEST
Eating & Drinking

Economy gurus say that the Czech Republic has escaped the worst of the global financial meltdown for various reasons, one being that it has not yet entered the euro, another being its slightly more sensible banks. That may well be true, yet in the hospitality business, the downturn has been visible, with hotels offering bargain basement deals and upper-end restaurants in Prague often looking distinctly hushed, if not quite forlorn.

It's likely that more such ventures have been launched, often by ambitious venture capitalists to flesh out their portfolios, than such a small capital could support, even one with an influx of foreign visitors averaging well over 6 million annually.

Clearly, based on the marketing efforts, many new restaurants were aimed at the new Czech elite (it's handy to host a Parliament minister at a feast), and most of the customers on any given day at Sarah Bernhardt (p114) are locals. Besides, according to the apparent logic, if you're going to put all the wherewithal into setting up a restaurant in central Prague, why on earth would you target ordinary people who value great cuisine at reasonable prices?

So, the prevailing Prague trend during the past few years has been the splashy culinary shrine, complete with the obligatory chic designs, elaborate lighting and dinner dishes that simply must come in various forms of foam. Anything less would hardly impress the city's influential glossy magazine critics, who are guilty of fuelling all this excess.

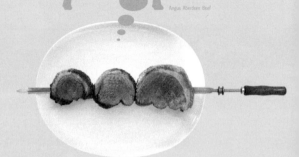

The secret is in the ingredients

Angus Aberdeen Beef

We believe that there is nothing mysterious about
good food; because all it takes are fresh, all-natural ingredients
and the use of well-proven techniques of hand preparation.

U Radnice 8, Praha 1, tel. 224 234 474
Na Příkopě 22, Praha 1, tel. 221 451 200

AMBIENTE°
RESTAURANTE BRASILEIRO

w w w . a m b i . c z

However, with the fine dining cannons firing so many duds, the smart money is on owners who exhibit a little more vision – enough to see that if you're after staying power, you can't beat the classics. Nineteenth-century Bohemian fare, with a fresh game, grilling and sauce focus, along with a complement of smoked meats and old-fashioned courteous service is proving to be consistently popular with visitors to the city.

Even the highest profile venture to start up at Prague Castle during recent years, the idyllic Villa Richter (see box p73), chose to invest substantial energy into training waiting staff and poaching some of the best traditional chefs around. The result is such offerings as a mouth-watering roast duck with the age-old Czech complement of white and purple sauerkraut, or *zelí*, as it's known to Czechs, which has garnered rave reviews. Of course, the chefs can whip up a caramel soufflé and a lamb carpaccio to impress the fussiest of diners – but, as often as not, visitors are content to have their favourite childhood meal cooked for them, evoking comforting memories of visits to granny's house, yet rendered with more flavour, aroma and texture than they've ever experienced.

The owners wisely took a leaf from the book of true blue, die-hard pubs such as U Medvídků (p112) and U Vejvodů (p115), the lofty Café Louvre (p132) and art nouveau shrine Café Imperial (p108), all of which have pedigrees dating back for a century and are usually bustling with patrons every night of the year, as well as most days.

Meanwhile, the fancy-pants dining gallery competitors have come and gone in droves. In early 2009, another old-time gem that had been shuttered since 1992

SHORTLIST

Best new
- Latin Art Café (p86)
- Noi (p87)
- Villa Richter (p74)

Best value
- Angel (p107)
- Bar Bar (p84)
- Café Louvre (p132)
- Dynamo (p132)
- U Malé Velryby (p86)
- Universal (p134)

Best cocktails
- Barego (p84)
- Hapu (p149)
- Tretter's (p115)

Best wine lists
- Monarch (p113)
- Sarah Bernhardt (p114)

Best classic pubbing
- Baráčnická rychta (p84)
- Bredovský dvůr (p132)
- U Medvídků (p112)
- Pivovarský dům (p134)
- U Vejvodů (p115)

Most characterful
- Alcron (p132)
- Blue Light (p85)
- Café Montmartre (p108)
- Cowboys (p85)

Best brunch
- Fraktal (p157)
- Jáma (p133)
- Radost FX Café (p134)

Best for romance
- Aromi (p149)
- Oliva (p134)
- Palffy Palace (p87)
- U Zlaté Studně (p88)

Best fast food
- Bakeshop Praha (p107)
- Bohemia Bagel (p107)

Get the local experience

Over 50 of the world's top destinations available.

rejoined the fold, continuing the revival: Myšák (see p133). The famous old Czech confectioner, which was established in 1904 and moved into a neo-Renaissance building along Vodičkova street seven years later, was founded by the celebrated sweets master František Myšák, who brought in an avant-garde architect in tune with the most progressive inter-war styles to create a Rondo-cubist façade in 1922. The fine confectioner rose to near-legendary status, attracting sweet-toothed customers from far and wide. It not only re-emerged after World War II, but carried on well into the communist era – even though the store was so badly neglected that part of the building collapsed in 2006, leaving only the exterior wall standing.

The loving, modern-day reconstruction carried out by Jan Špaček, complete with original mosaics, ceiling paintings, marble staircase and wooden alcoves, has brought back to life a two-storey sweet shop with the kind of character that only a First Republic Prague icon could manage. Best of all, Myšák cups, the trademark caramel sundaes from the original incarnation, are back on the menu these days (along with delicious new additions such as chocolate mousse with Cointreau).

Concentrate

If you look closely, you will find a number of venues that are a world away from the ubiquitous *cukrárna* shops, as contemporary Praguers know them: uninspiring places that all serve the same sugary cakes, most of which have been mass-produced and trucked in.

The lesson: focus, people. Czech restaurants can do brilliant work when they stick to a clear goal and it need not be Bohemian at all.

Angel p107

In the city, you'll discover excellent international cuisine. Thai places like Zen-like Noi (p87) in Malá Strana and the relaxed Modrý Zub (p133) in Nové Mesto have won over their respective districts, while Sofia Smith leads the local team at Angel in Staré Město (p107) to Asian-tinged fusion delights. Brasileiro (p108) slices off prime cuts of excellent South American beef and grills it expertly, as does El Barrio de Angel (p90).

For vegetarian delights, check out Lehká Hlava (p112), and for a teahouse fantasy, visit Dahab (p109). The ideal wine bar is personified by Monarch (p113), which does much to restore the tarnished image of Czech vintages that were badly neglected until the mid-1990s.

Tretter's at the high end of the scale (p115) and Hapu at the dive bar end (p149) make cocktails like nobody's business – without, thankfully, feeling the need to throw every bottle, shaker and ice cube over their heads as legions of 'flare'-obsessed Prague bars do.

Tipping and etiquette

At pubs and beerhalls, tables are often shared with patrons who, like you, should ask '*Je tu volno?*' ('Is it free?') and may wish each other '*dobrou chut*' ('Bon appetite!') before tucking in. Prague dines with a relaxed dress code and reservations are necessary at upmarket spots.

Many waiters still record your tab on a slip of paper, which translates at leaving time into a bill. Pay the staff member with the folding wallet in their waistband, not your waiter ('*Zaplatím, prosím*' means 'May I pay, please?').

A small cover charge and extra for milk, bread and the ubiquitous accordion music are still in practice at many pubs, as is tipping by rounding the bill up to the nearest 10 Kč. At fancier places, 10-15% tips are now expected. Although you should have little trouble making a telephone reservation in English at modern establishments, at other places it might be easier to book in person.

El Barrio de Angel p90

Big Ben Bookshop p116

Shopping

It sometimes seems as if every Praguer who dreamed of entrepreneurship before 1989 went out and opened a shop. And why not? Czechs are supremely practical and handy, and are tireless workhorses when building their savings. Unfortunately, a lack of exposure to many shoppers up to that revolutionary year resulted in some unrealistic expectations.

It appeared that, no matter how much Jan Novak loved both flags of the world and house paint, no one was willing to patronise a venture that proudly displayed both. So, although it would be tempting to blame the waves of small business failures on competition from global giants and the severe economic downturn, it would be more realistic to say that retail is clearly something you have to keep up on. Being out of practice from 1948 to 1989 sets you a bit back.

What's more, a culture of state stores selling cheap but low-quality, no-return merchandise creates some bad habits that are hard to shake. Fortunately, the vision and the customer service are better than ever and a number of successful Czech retailers have begun to multiply and inspire others. Dr Stuart's Botanicus (p116) is a good case in point, and it seems to have spawned a wave of little places specialising in affordable, unusual and enchanting crafts, such as this year's coolest ceramics entry, La Lagartija (p150).

Fashion, meanwhile, has always been a Czech forte (hardly surprising in a land with more supermodels per capita than anywhere else), and every year sees more designers hanging out their shingles. Several with lines worth a look are Atelier Tatiana (p116), Boheme (p116) and Pavla & Olga (p117), while vintage

WHEREVER CRIMES AGAINST HUMANITY ARE PERPETRATED.

Across borders and above politics.
Against the most heinous abuses
and the most dangerous oppressors.
From conduct in wartime
to economic, social, and cultural rights.
Everywhere we go,
we build an unimpeachable case
for change and advocate action
at the highest levels.

HUMAN RIGHTS WATCH TYRANNY HAS A WITNESS

WWW.HRW.ORG

HUMAN
RIGHTS
WATCH

fans will find much to sort through at Toalette. These boutiques cluster in the Stare Mesto district, where their bold cuts, muted colour palette and touch-me textures seem to have been inspired by the grand, stony architecture. Shopping is actually a pleasure at such places, whether you buy anything or not.

Style and design extend well beyond couture in the Czech tradition, as a visit to the Museum of Decorative Arts (p114) will reveal, and it's reassuring to see how the classics seem to be surviving and thriving, economy, come what may. In Old Town alone, Alma Mahler, Antik v Dlouhé, Art Deco and Artěl (p116) make for a hell of an A list, with the latter having revived bespoke crystal making via the work of classically trained Bohemian glass artists. Another find for design lovers is the Kubista shop (p117), with unique porcelain creations contained in a building that is itself a shrine to Cubism.

Czechs are taking to active sports more than ever before, and their deep need to tinker and customise has resulted in a few busy local sport clothing and gear chains, such as Rock Point (p117). These carry not just all the international brands you'd expect but also competitively priced local ones that put their insignia on backpacks, rain, snow and climbing kit that's given the acid test by the company owners before it lands on the shelves.

For those who prefer aesthetics to athletics, this city remains a treasure trove of little neighbourhood shops, where you'll find the weird, yet still (mostly) affordable trinkets from the past, whether it's antiquarian books or Victorian-era brooches. What's more, you're likely to be dealing with the owner (or a family relation), rather than an obviously bored and miserable employee, as you may be on the high streets.

S H O R T L I S T

Best new
- La Lagartija (p150)
- Pour-pour (p150)
- Rock Point (p117)

Best designs
- Artěl (p116)
- Boheme (p116)
- Kubista (p117)
- Pavla & Olga (p117)

Best souvenirs
- Bazar Antik Zajímavosti (p136)
- Beruška (p136)
- Manufaktura (p117)
- Truhlář Marionety (p88)

Best retro
- Antik v Dlouhé (p116)
- Art Deco (p116)
- Hamparadi Antik Bazar (p137)

Best decor
- Le Patio (p137)

Best food/wine
- Bakeshop Praha (p107)
- Cellarius (p136)
- Monarch (p113)

Best reads
- Antikvariát Kant (p136)
- Big Ben Bookshop (p116)
- Globe Bookstore (p137)
- Trafika Můstek (p118)

Best specialists
- Foto Škoda (p137)
- Dr Stuart's Botanicus (p116)
- Terryho ponožky (p137)

Best museum gift shops
- DOX (p160)
- Havel Library (p78)
- Kampa Museum (p81)
- Museum of Decorative Arts (p104)
- National Gallery (p153)
- Prague Castle (p61)

Head down any narrow side street, even in the old centre of town, and you'll find amazing knick-knacks, 'junque' and artefacts, from gorgeous maps with engraved illustrations to vinyl recordings of forgotten Czech pop stars.

If you're under strict orders to bring home traditional Bohemian crystal or an old-fashioned puppet – and there are good reasons the country is famous for both – then just about any of the dozens of highly visible shops selling these will do (although the artists at Truhlář Marionety, p78, create the puppets of dreams and nightmares). As for the more conventional glass shops, there's very little difference in quality or price, at least in central Prague, and goods can generally be shipped home safely and reliably.

English is spoken, if somewhat begrudgingly, at just about all shops in the centre of Prague. Credit cards are in widespread use, though – to reiterate – you'll probably find welcoming smiles and offers of 'How may I help you?' fairly rare.

Shops also have longer opening hours now than those you'll find outside the touristy areas.

The average Czech salary is still low compared to those of other European countries and, even with a strong crown, retailers often price accordingly, which means that you can pick up some bargains. If you do want to try swimming with the locals, leather goods are another safe bet in Prague. Also excellent value is local music, particularly classical recordings on the respected Supraphon label. These sell for about half the price they do in Western Europe and are available at most music shops. (Bontonland on Wenceslas Square has the most comprehensive collection, with listening stations.)

When entering a shop, the salesperson will ask '*Máte přání?*' ('Do you have a wish?'). While ringing up your purchases, they may ask '*Ještě něco?*' ('Anything else?') or '*Všechno?*' ('Is that all?'). Try saying '*Kolik to stojí?*' to find out what something costs.

Pour-pour p150

and Czech art titles. The *bazars* (second-hand shops) are also fun for browsing. The Globe Bookstore (p137) is a good spot to refuel after a stocking up on paperbacks. For folk crafts with local colour, try Manufaktura (p117); at first sight, it seems touristy, but it's worth a second look for natural soaps, old-fashioned homewares and herbal essences. Art is an excellent buy, and it needn't be from a vendor on Charles Bridge. Many galleries offer serious bargains on rare items, as do gift shops in museums such as Prague Castle (p81), or the National Gallery (p153). Of course, never underestimate the power of Czech alcohol. The liqueur Becherovka, bitter Fernet, plum brandy Slivovice, or beloved beer Pilsner Urquell will keep the Prague memories flowing.

Garnets and fashions

Every jeweller worth his weight in carats offers garnet gemstones in Prague, but those businesses with distinctive settings are worth noting. Garnets and amber are impossible to miss, featured prominently among the crystal and nesting dolls lining the tourist shops. The fashion dates back to the Renaissance days of Emperor Rudolf II, who collected many garnet-encrusted pieces, as did Russian tsarinas in the 1800s.

Nowadays, garnets come set in gold-plated silver, sterling silver, 14- or 18-carat gold. The Granát facility is the only legal mining operator in the country, so always ask for a manufacturer's certificate. True Bohemian garnets will be marked with G, G1 or G2.

For book lovers, the city abounds with *antikvariáts*, fusty places that are full of old Czech tomes, ornate Bibles, photos, maps, magazines and postcards. Palác Knih Luxor on Wenceslas Square (www.neoluxor.cz) has a great selection of English books

Shopping areas

As in most cities, avoid the central shopping areas unless you're rushed or need classic souvenirs. This especially applies to Hradčany and the area around Prague Castle. Many of the backstreets contain rewarding second-hand junk and bookshops. High fashion and high prices can be found on Pařížská, along with inviting outdoor cafés. Mall central, as well as many other chain stores, is along Na příkopě. Wenceslas Square can pretty much be skipped for shopping, because there's nothing especially unique here. But the streets on either side of the square are great for a wander. Beware of some shady characters, however, especially in the evening. Souvenir seekers should stroll any of the streets leading out from Old Town Square, as well as the Malá Strana area near Charles Bridge. Moving further out to Smíchov and Holešovice will pay off for antique junkies; Prague definitely rewards the adventuresome.

Retro Music Hall p145

Nightlife

Clubbing mavens in the Golden City have been noticeably glum of late, with the inevitable plateauing of night spot openings. For many years, they had been popping up (and, just as often, closing after a few months) in every district in every shape, form and genre. Old-school places with well-worn carpets and pre-1989 habits, such as black light effects and vintage Czech pop playlists, became fashionable again with young crowds that possessed a keen sense of irony.

Over-the-top clubs would launch with improbable themes, such as alchemy or James Bond flicks. The fates of these were all too predictable, although a few managed to hang on for longer than expected, especially considering the well entrenched Czech custom of giving freebies to all your friends from your employer, which put a strain on the creative accounting of barmen.

Make no mistake about it, a steady stream of would-be 'concept' places continue to come down the pike. However, they usually turn out to be little more than a name, with the club stocking the same liquor, employing the same bottle-juggling bar staff and tossing in the occasional naughty beefcake party especially for the ladies.

Those looking for memorable nights out in Prague remain fairly frustrated. The irony is that, for a city that has become an icon for partying, the pickings remain pretty lean unless you're smashed out of your head and unaware of your surroundings. It's very likely the city has been the victim of its own reputation, with what seems like every other American university now offering semesters abroad

DON'T MISS

here. This kind of demand for party space doesn't do much to force the issue of originality or sophistication.

Of course, there are bright spots: the Retro Music Hall (p145), for one, has been evolving its programme, with international DJs and fresh live acts, who know how to create momentum. For a floating barge party, try the cosy club U Bukanýra (p118). A night out in Prague is a worthy pursuit, in part because of the challenge and the inevitable funny tales that you'll be able to add to your spiel after dealing with Neanderthal doormen only to get into lame and teen-packed venues.

The trick, says one veteran of the clubbing scene, is to keep an eye on party websites like www.techno.cz and seek out the one-off events. Tim Otis, who still plays at Radost FX Café (see box p134) after 15 years, points out that Carl Cox, and half a dozen other DJs on his level, still do Prague nights and they go down grandly here.

As in many areas of city life, folks are gaining an appreciation for the classic clubs, which still

Cross Club p158

deliver heartfelt shows and where, after a few visits, everyone knows your name. Aside from Radost FX Café , there's Mecca (p158)and, on fun nights, Nebe (p138). Younger ventures are reaching a pleasant stage of maturity, offering that rarest of qualities in Prague: consistent good times. Popocafepetl (see box p89) and Cross Club (p158) have attracted much respect since opening a few years back.

Venues like the Roxy (p121) and Akropolis (p150), which are officially civic organisations, still relish the status they have earned by dragging Prague into the most creative and exotic realms of sight and sound. The Roxy, installed in a former movie house with the seats ripped out, has pedigree stretching back more than 15 years and still satisfies the demands of clubbers young and old with a crumbled kind of sophistication. These personify Prague's greatest nightlife quality: funkiness. Folks who used to party here in illegal venues without heat have a special appreciation for these shrines.

Be advised, there is also an atmosphere of 'anything goes' when clubbing in this city: drug laws exist, but they're rarely enforced and sexual mores are as loose as ever. Getting roaring drunk is still considered cool, despite recent cover stories on national magazines that dare ask whether the Czech Republic's high alcoholism rate might be storing up problems for its population.

Alas, Prague nightlife draws many visitors for its decadence, and one thing that's not in dispute is the city's reputation for sleaze. Even though Wenceslas Square is home to the popular club Duplex (p138), which overlooks it from a dizzying height, the area also features neon, drug hawkers and touts for half a dozen adult clubs.

The ubiquitous sex clubs and the legions of stag parties they attract have boosted the economy, but at what price? Hot Pepper's (p138), one of the few such places in which lap dancing is as far as the action goes, is competing with more *noční*, or 'night' clubs than ever, many brazenly offering rooms with girls by the half-hour.

Prostitution is not legally proscribed in the Czech Republic, whereas pimping is, which means that night clubs operate openly but categorise the girls as independent contractors – a handy loophole. How many are truly working for themselves and how many may have been trafficked from the East, no one actually knows.

Most run the standard entrance scam (the first drink or even entry is free, but another drink is required for around ten times the usual cost).

U Bukanýra p118

Gay clubs

Many of the best-run clubs – and certainly those with the best soundtracks – are, not surprisingly, gay clubs. Even though these venues are fairly few in number, the trade-off is they are concentrated around the old centre and most are quite welcoming to anyone.

Valentino (p145), in Vinohrady, is a state-of-the-art venue with three floors for mad clubbing, whereas the casual gay bar Saints (p145) has a small but amusing dance space, and serves excellent cocktails. The American-style Friends (p120), located on a quiet street in Staré Město, is as amiable as its name, with a grown-up, intimate quality, great sounds and 200 square metres of dancefloor that will keep you entertained all night.

Le Clan p145

Managing it all

A time-honoured strategy for Prague clubbing is to start pretty much anywhere in the old centre and move on to other venues to check if you've missed anything, stopping off at any number of late-night bars and pubs along the way to refuel. U Medvídků (p112) has a bar on one side that's open until 3am, N11 (p120) is open all night and a vast number of holes-in-the-wall spots will present themselves as you migrate.

Hot tips and information tend to be available in free pocket-sized 'zines that come and go like the seasons. *Prague in your Pocket*, a 150 Kč investment available at the Globe Bookstore (p136), is usually plugged in. Other useful English sources are the expat websites that you can turn to for amusing forums on dating, laundry and many other sundry concerns regarding Prague life, namely www.expats.cz and prague.tv. The *Prague Post*'s website (www.praguepost.com) has food and drink listings, along with good coverage of music, film and festivals, but there's no systematic clubbing coverage.

Note that the Prague metro shuts down at midnight, but don't fret: the city centre is small, mostly walkable and by-and-large safe. Otherwise, taxis – at least the reputable ones like AAA (14014) – are still cheap and night trams run till 5am on all the main routes from the centre to outlying areas. Hopping aboard one of these booze-loving Prague is an experience that you're unlikely to forget in a hurry, though a clothes peg for your nose or being in a high state of intoxication might be the best preparation.

The other option is to stay up with everyone else in the city: regular tram and metro services start up again at 5am.

State Opera p139

Arts & Leisure

Prague's reputation as the conservatory of Europe seems assured for the time being, with more world-class musicians performing Dvořák, Mahler, Smetana and Martinů on any given night at more chapels and concert halls than you can imagine. The biggest event of the year is still the Prague Spring classical music festival, for which opening night seats are invariably sold out. The crowds, dressed in their best evening attire, recently thrilled to Japanese violin prodigy Midori at the art nouveau shrine Municipal House, which usually draws the attention of the Czech president for the gala on the first night in May.

However, the country's star orchestra, the Czech Philharmonic, which resides a few blocks away at the other end of Old Town, in the stately Rudolfinum, a pillared 19th-century pile looking out upon the Vltava river and Prague Castle, has not been as tranquil as its setting of late. Following the sudden resignation of chief conductor Zdeněk Mácal, Israeli maestro Eliahu Inbal has taken over the post, winning rave reviews. A new managing director, Vladimír Darjanin, has stepped in, with the hope of lifting morale at the storied orchestra – recently, the poorly paid but highly respected musicians have gone rogue, some even refusing to perform contemporary classical pieces not to their taste.

While the reshuffle cost the Czech Philharmonic a bit of its dignity, at least before the dust settled, the group has managed, along with the city's own counterpart, the Prague Symphony

Rudolfinum p122

Orchestra, to keep staffing and budgets relatively healthy. The programmes of Prague's two opera companies, at the State Opera and National Theatre (p139), have been nothing short of ambitious. An avant-garde interpretation of Leoš Janáček's *The Makropulos Case*, set in a 1920s legal office in the eastern Czech city of Brno, has impressed audiences at the latter with its engaging staging and high level of acting chops – something to which local opera fans aren't always treated. Artistic direction at the National Theatre, which also has a ballet facet, seems to be well on track following previous intrigues not unlike those at the Czech Philharmonic.

Suspense on screen

The Prague film world, by contrast, has been a mixed bag lately. Filmmakers themselves have fared well: emerging movie moguls have been uniformly upbeat at the recent news that the main funding body, the Czech Cinematography Fund, was flush – so much so that there was scarcely a film treatment that it wouldn't back (including several it really shouldn't have). Local filmmakers, who create features for around what a Hollywood trailer would cost, have thus been busy, and Czech film is fast developing, reviving and sometimes surpassing its great pre-1989 tradition. Documentaries are a strong suit, with Helena Třeštíková setting the standard and winning festival prizes around the globe for her chronicle of a Czech writer and career criminal *Rene*.

One of the few positives about the bad old days of communism, besides the great public transport system, was robust funding for the arts – that is, as long as you stayed away from polemics – and the Czech New Wave of the 1960s produced not just the likes of Milos Forman and Ivan Passer, but counterparts who chose not to emigrate to Hollywood as they did, such as Oscar winner Jiří Menzel and the bold and ironic Věra Chytilová.

Now a new generation is seizing the day, including a younger Oscar winner, Jan Svěrák, and others who have shown distinctive visions; Petr Zelenka's *The Karamazovs* has won critical attention, while the late Pavel Koutecký's *Citizen Havel*, which was filmed over 13 years using rare, behind-the-scenes footage of the playwright president, has led a revival in non-fiction film.

And what of Prague's long and lustrous reputation as the backlot of Europe, attracting hordes of foreign film productions eager to use the city as the ultimate setting? Here too the global economy has caught up with the city, making it clear the salad days are over. Sure, *Wanted* and *GI Joe* shot at Barrandov studios, as did *Paris 36*. But these days Hungary offers better incentives, along with a host of new state-of-the-art studios, while Bulgaria and Romania are now far cheaper and their crews have more experience than ever, so competition has heated up. Still, the Czech lead in filmmaking was established by smart and savvy players – thus, you'll still see their fingerprints on many international feature films (and television series, such as HBO's *John Adams*, for one), but possibly not the city itself.

Local technicians, engineers and entrepreneurs have excelled at digital post-production, winning a steady stream of international clients with films that need pumped-up colours or other special effects. Animation, always a strong suit in Bohemia, is as vibrant as ever, whether through the films of surrealists such as Jan Balej, whose *One Night in One City* is a hip update of the proud Jan Švankmajer tradition, or the

SHORTLIST

Best travelling shows
- Galerie Rudolfinum (p99)
- Wallenstein Riding School (p83)

Best arias
- National Theatre (p139)
- State Opera (p139)

Best rock
- Akropolis (p151)
- Archa (p122)
- Rock Café (p138)

Best jazz
- AghaRTa (p121)
- U Malého Glena (p90)
- U Staré Paní (p121)

Best symphonies
- Municipal House (p122)
- Rudolfinum (p122)

Best of the fests
- Febiofest (p37)
- Prague Spring (p39)
- United Islands (p39)

Best cutting-edge galleries
- Galerie Jiří Švestka (p99)
- House at the Golden Ring (p99)
- Leica (p129)
- NoD, Roxy Club (p120)

Best film venues
- Evald (p138)
- Kino Lucerna, Lucerna Pasaz (p130)
- Světozor (p140)

Best state collections
- Convent of St Agnes of Bohemia (p98)
- Museum of Decorative Arts (p104)
- National Gallery Collection of 19th-, 20th- & 21st-Century Art at the Veletržní palác (p153)

popular comic hit *Goat Story – The Old Prague Legends* by the talented Jan Tománek.

Indie filmmakers from abroad, who are able to work on a Prague budget, using their creative resources to achieve a Cadillac look for a Škoda price, are still drawn to the city. One such writer/director, Carl Haber, recently won TV audiences of more than a million by writing in parts for Czech characters in his mistaken-identity romantic comedy *The Wrong Mr Johnson*. The film was a success with both Americans and locals because it featured the up-and-coming Prague actress Klára Issová, along with fresh faces from the West, and a hip, original jazz soundtrack. It turns on the misunderstandings that the city is famous for – especially among those under its magic spell.

Native filmmakers are coming into their own, such as Zdeněk Tyc, whose story of Roma family struggles, *El Paso*, tugged heart strings at the Finale Festival of Czech films, and Václav Marhoul, who has won praises with his war film *Tobruk*. Maria Procházková's chilling fairy tale *Who's Afraid of the Wolf* won the event, boding well for the future of art on screen.

Although it's doubtful as to whether the state can continue to run the deficit spending that it has got used to in recent years, including more backing for Czech film, it's clear that film festivals, which rely more heavily on private sponsors, are hurting. Prague's biggest festival, Febiofest (see box p37), had to cut back heavily in 2009 (though, fortunately, programming director Stefan Uhrík was already retooling the 16-year-old event to focus more on quality than quantity).

Such festivals, which act as showcases for all the independent, non-blockbuster fare that Czech audiences adore, are invariably packed with film lovers young and old from all over the country. That's likely because most local cinemas these days feel they must book mainly action films, comedies and animated hits to survive.

However, even with droves of loyal fans, Febiofest and the documentary festival One World have seen key sponsors withdrawing, citing the pressure from the global financial crisis to cut back on non-essential investments.

Visual arts

It was a bit cringe-worthy for many Praguers when bad boy visual artist David Černý publicly admitted to conning his state sponsors after being granted some 75,500 euros to create a piece of public art to commemorate the Czech Republic's turn at the presidency of the European Union.

The artwork, a sculpture christened *Entropa*, turned into a PR debacle. Černý depicted each European Union member country as a piece of a plastic model kit of the kind that a 10-year-old would build a fighter plane from. Except that this one measured 16 metres by 16 metres in size, weighed almost 8 tons and employed national stereotypes. The artist argued that it was stereotyping itself that he was sending up, but Bulgaria, having been depicted as a collection of squat toilets, did not buy that and complained loudly. (The UK was absent from the work, which was apparently a statement about the general lack of enthusiasm with which most Brits regard the EU.)

Černý agreed to cover up the Bulgaria part of Entropa and to return his funding to the state, admitting that he hadn't used artists from each of the EU member countries as he had pledged to do. But, although the sculpture was

Archa Theatre p122

considered by some to be a humorous break from Brussels' usual pomposity, many Praguers did not feel the episode did much to establish respect abroad for the work of Czech visual artists.

However, they also have much to celebrate, with the opening of the DOX contemporary art exhibition space in Holešovice (p160), which intends to rival the Rudolfinum as a major venue for large travelling shows, and the dynamic homes for the art photography shrines Leica Gallery (p129) and Galerie Fotografie Louvre at the Café Louvre (p132). Another positive sign for visual arts in the Czech capital is a change in the main venture of the National Gallery Collection of 19th-, 20th- and 21st-Century art (p153) – its biennale is now a triennale, dubbed the International Triennale of Contemporary Art (ITCA), to keep it from directly competing with the popular, privately run Prague Biennale (www.praguebiennale.org). The main winner of this all is the public, which is benefiting from more diversity in the contemporary arts than ever before.

Tickets and information

Many box office clerks only have a basic command of English, so you are better off purchasing tickets via one of the central booking agencies. These accept credit cards, you can book via their websites or by phone in English and there are numerous outlets across Prague. Bohemia Ticket International (Malé náměstí 13, Staré Město, 224 227 832/ www.ticketsbti.cz) is the best agency through which to make advance bookings for performances at the National Theatre, the Estates Theatre and the State Opera.

Ticketpro at Old Town Hall (Staré Město, 224 223 613/www. ticketpro.cz) sells tickets for some events. Ticket touts cluster at many, so you can often get into sold-out (*vyprodáno*) performances, although for a price. Wait until the last bell for the best deal. For the latest art, film, theatre and dance listings, pick up a copy of The Prague Post www.praguepost.com), drop into your nearest branch of the Prague Information Service or check out its website at www.pis.cz.

Rene p31

Calendar

Prague Writers' Festival p39

There are a generous 12 public holidays in the Czech Republic. Except for Easter Monday, the dates are fixed, with the sliding holiday concept not employed – that is, when they fall on a weekend day, the following Monday is a normal business day.

Public holidays are highlighted here in **bold**.

January

1 New Year's Day/Prague New Year's Concert
Rudolfinum, p122
www.czechphilharmonic.cz
Czech Philharmonic's annual concert.

February

Mid-Feb (7th Sun before Easter)
Masopust
Various venues in Žižkov
www.palacakropolis.cz
A weekend of street parties, concerts and feasts.

Mid-Feb (7th Sun before Easter)
Carnevale
Various venues in Staré Město
www.carnevale.cz
The streets of Old Town fill with carnival spectacles in the glitziest pre-Lent celebration.

Feb-Mar **Matějská pouť**
Výstaviště, p153
www.pis.cz
St Matthew's Fair marks the arrival of warm weather with cheesy rides for the kids at a run-down funfair.

March

Mar **Febiofest**
Palace Cinemas, Anděl
www.febiofest.cz
The city's biggest film fest is strong on world cinema. See box p37.

Mar **One World**
Lucerna cinema, p138, and Světozor cinema, p140
www.jedensvet.cz

The year's best documentaries and their authors from around the globe appear for this film festival.

Mar-Oct **Prague Jazz Festival**
Various venues
www.agharta.cz
Prague's hottest jazz fest brings in the likes of John Scofield. Mainly at Lucerna Music Bar (p138).

April

Early Apr **Days of European Film**
Various venues across Prague
www.eurofilmfest.cz
Ten days of flicks from across Europe, many with English subtitles.

Mar/Apr (date varies)
Easter Monday
Staré Město
www.pis.cz
Men whack women on the backside with sticks; women douse men with water and give them painted eggs.

30 **Witches' Night**
Petřín hill, map p58
Halloween and Bonfire Night in one.

Old Town Easter Markets

May

Mid-May (2009 onwards)
Prague Biennale
Karlín Studios p151
www.praguebiennale.org
This upstart modern art exhibition has knocked the local gallery scene on its ear. The show is traditionally held in the Karlín Studios, a hulking former factory. Check the biennale website for the latest details.

1 **Labour Day**
Letná park, map p154

1 **May Day**
Petřín hill, map p58
Czech lovers of all ages kiss in front of the statue of Karel Hynek Mácha.

8 **VE Day**
Letná park, map p154
Czechs now celebrate the Allied victory more openly, with American Jeeps joining the memorials to the Red Army.

May **Prague International Marathon**
Across Prague
www.pim.cz
Those not up to the full 42km (26mile) race can try their foot at the more palatable 10km run.

May **Four Days in Motion**
Various venues across Prague
www.ctyridny.cz
This excellent festival of international dance and visual theatre takes place at unusual venues.

May **Khamoro**
Various venues across Prague
www.khamoro.cz
Concerts, seminars and workshops on traditional Roma culture.

May **Prague Fringe Festival**
Various venues across Prague
www.praguefringe.com
The city's newest theatre festival fills venues such as Vyšehrad with many different performances, ranging from cabaret to multimedia.

Screen on the world

Prague's Febiofest is a watchword for art house film.

Like scores of other cultural events now on Prague's cultural calendar, the city's biggest film festival, **Febiofest** (p35), has fought to win over sponsors despite them reigning in budgets as a result of the global economic downturn.

Film fans from around the country, not just those in the capital, are rooting for the underdog organisers – respected Slovak documentary filmmaker Fero Fenič and his programming team, Štefan Uhrík and Hana Cielová. If Febio were to go down in flames, so would the only opportunity for thousands of Czechs to see edgy, art house film – from home and abroad – which would otherwise be absent from Prague's big screens.

Uhrík and Cielová, founders of the Forum of Independents event at the Czech Republic's annual Karlovy Vary International Film Festival – have been a particular boon to Febio. The Slovak couple not only have connections to emerging filmmakers from their homeland, they have built up relationships that result in the screening of genuine film gems, with the chance for audiences to be inspired by rebel filmmakers.

Years ago, it was these two who brought Joel and Ethan Coen to the Czech Republic for the first time, where they were peppered with questions by youthful crowds on every aspect of their distinctive, absurdist film noir style.

More recently, they have brought Alan Parker to Febio – but also lesser-known innovators such as Kadri Kousaar, an Estonian writer whose first film, *Magnus*, won the top prize. Based on the true story of a young man's long-planned suicide, an event that seems strangely accepted by his dysfunctional family, her film has caused a stir in her home country, with the hero's father played by the real father of the boy who inspired the film.

Fearless, smart programming like this, plus Febio's screenings of the boldest international films, would be a loss indeed if funding fell through. Fortunately, it seems, more and more converts are won over every year.

Prague Biennale p36

Mid-May **Czech Beer Festival**
PVA Letňany Exhibition Centre
www.ceskypivnifestival.cz
For ten days, the biggest brewers and
best butchers and delis in the republic
show off their goods. Free entry.

Mid-May to early June
Prague Spring
Various venues across Prague
www.festival.cz
The biggest and best Prague music
festival draws a sparkling array of
international talent.

Last weekend in May
Mezi ploty
Around the Psychiatric Hospital,
Bohnice
www.meziploty.cz
Events put on by professional, amateur
and mentally or physically disadvan-
taged artists over two days.

June

June **Prague Writers' Festival**
Various venues across Prague
www.pwf.cz
Czech and international literati gather
to read and hobnob.

June **Respect**
Various venues across Prague
www.respectmusic.cz
A celebration of world and ethnic music,
throughout June.

June **Tanec Praha**
Various venues across Prague
www.tanecpraha.cz
A top-flight international gala of modern dance with recitals in Prague's
major theatres.

June **United Islands of Prague**
Střelecký ostrov, Žofín
www.unitedislands.cz
Popular weekend of rock, jazz and folk.

July

5 **Cyril & Methodius Day**

6 **Jan Hus Day**

July **Prague Proms**
Various venues in Staré Město
www.pragueproms.cz
Classical, opera and jazz concerts.

July **Summer Old Music Festival**
Various venues in Staré Město
www.tynska.cuni.cz
Renaissance and Baroque music on
period instruments, in historic settings.

August

Mid-Aug **Letní Letná**
Letná park, map p154
www.letniletna.cz
Theatre, music and circus festival
attracting Czech and European talents.

Mid-Aug **String Quartet Festival**
Bertramka, p93
www.bertramka.com
Prague's best quartets perform in an
idyllic setting.

September

Sept **St Wenceslas Sacred
Music Festival**
Various venues across Prague
www.sdh.cz
Sacred music festival, held at half a
dozen chapels, churches and cathedrals.

Sept **Tina B**
Various venues across Prague
www.tina-b.com
An acronym of This Is Not Another
Biennale, showcasing contemporary art
in surprising locations around Prague.

Mid-Sept **International
Aviation Film Festival**
Various venues across Prague
www.leteckefilmy.cz
A week-long festival of war and action
films, with famous pilots and war heroes.

Mid-Sept **Tesco Night Grand Prix**
Staré Město
www.pim.cz
An offshoot of the Prague Marathon
(p36), despite the confusing name, with
a 5km women's run, a 10km men's race
and a 3.8km health run.

Sept-Nov **Strings of Autumn**
Various venues across Prague
www.strunypodzimu.cz
A festival of world-renowned classical talents, based around theatres and churches in Old Town.

Late Sept **Burčák arrives**
Various pubs across Prague

28 Czech Statehood Day
Cloudy, half-fermented, early-season wine from Moravia is served from jugs during this month-long festival.

October

Mid-Oct **Festival of Amateur & Professional Puppet Theatre**
Various venues across Prague
www.pis.cz
Innovative puppetry festival.

Mid-Oct **Prague International Jazz Festival**
Various venues across Prague
www.pragokoncert.com
A mix of local and international jazz masters perform at some of the city's top clubs, over several days.

28 Anniversary of the Birth of Czechoslovakia
Various venues across Prague
Fireworks and a public holiday celebrate Czechoslovakia's independence from the Habsburg state.

November

Nov **FAMU Festival**
Academy of Performing Arts
www.famufest.cz
FAMU students' best work is screened.

2 All Souls' Day
Olšany Cemetery, p148
Czech families say prayers for dead loved ones.

Mid-Nov **Alternativa**
Archa Theatre, p121
www.alternativa-festival.cz
Underground film, music and stage performances.

17 Anniversary of the Velvet Revolution
Wenceslas Square p131,
and Národní třída, map p124,
Nové Město
Flowers are laid at the foot of the equine statue, with a memorial to the student protesters.

19-25 **French Film Festival**
French Institute
www.ifp.cz
Indie and pop French movie overload, some with English subtitles.

December

Early Dec **International Festival of Advent & Christmas Music**
Various venues across Prague
www.orfea.cz
Choirs and choruses ring in the season.

5 **St Nicholas's Eve**
Staré Město
www.pis.cz
Trios dressed as St Nicholas, an angel and a devil grill children about who's been naughty and who's been nice.

Mid-Dec **Christmas Markets**
Wenceslas Square, p131, and Old Town Square, map p96
www.pis.cz
Stalls with crafts and Czech Christmas food and drink spread the cheer.

24 Christmas Eve/Midnight mass
St Vitus's Cathedral, p69
www.hrad.cz
The finest Christmas observance in Bohemia fills the (cold) Gothic church; bring your thermal underwear.

25 Christmas Day

26 St Stephen's Day

31 **New Year's Eve**
Wenceslas Square, p131
'Silvestr' sparks off a plethora of fireworks and flying bottles. Be prepared to be bombarded by firecrackers, bangers and general high spirits; bring your helmet along.

Itineraries

Veletržní Palace p45

First Republic Walk

Czechoslovakia between the wars was no bastion of peace, prosperity and national security. Fascist agitators were facing off with communist sympathisers, the world was enduring the throes of the Great Depression and the new state was still foundering over stark ethnic and economic divisions. Nevertheless, most Czechs reflect fondly on the brief period known as the First Republic and relish the chance to revisit the sophisticated art, music and literature that emerged from those turbulent times.

This walk through the icons of interwar Bohemia takes about four hours, presuming that you'll be willing to invest one hour in each of the historic galleries on this itinerary (the dazzling collection of art up to 1930 at the National Gallery Collection of 19th-, 20th- and 21st-Century Art at Veletržní Palace is worth more in-depth exploration if you have got the time to spare).

Start your time travel at the Nové Město riverside embankment downstream from the Jirásek bridge, where you'll discover the **Galerie Mánes** (p128), easily spotted by the nearby water mill from 1489 with a distinctive onion dome. Named for one of the great Prague artists of the 19th century, Josef Mánes, this functionalist gallery by Otakar Novotný has always been, ironically, a hotbed of the kind of art that left his in the dust of time. Avant-garde painting and sculpture, and social debate were on the programme of this seminal art gallery during the interwar years, and Praguers flocked to see Picasso, Munch, Chagall, Klimt and Braque here. The management, with an acute sense of history, usually hosts a well-curated, unconventional show, so you should seize the opportunity to have a wander inside. Try to imagine the bohemians of the Jazz Age gathering amid thick smoke and cocktails to discuss the relationships between Einstein's theories and popular art. In clement weather, the terrace at the back of the gallery is a fine place to sip a coffee and watch life on the water – don't miss the groundbreaking architectural features, such as the glass-walled section that extends over a Vltava river lock.

From here, stroll downstream to the ornate **Legionnaires' Bridge**. It's an appropriate spot for pondering what might have been, had Czech society been allowed to continue to blossom after the end of World War I brought the collapse of centuries under the old Habsburg order. The bridge, by Antonín Balšánek, is dedicated to the Czech legions who fought for the Entente nations in the hope of winning their support for a free Czechoslovakia, then marched back to Prague behind a man who was to be the first head of state, Tomáš Garrigue Masaryk.

From the bridge (which also crosses Střelecký island, a place that has fostered contemplation by unconventional sorts, along with a good bit of merrymaking), stroll east down Národní, dominated by the soaring National Theatre. Continue past it to the second block, where you'll come to the **Café Louvre** (p132). This storied kavárna, which still features chandeliers, frescoes, high windows, vested waiters and a poolroom at the back, has been a gathering point for artists, scribblers, students, philosophers and political theorists since its opening in 1902. Among the past characters who have fuelled up on its creamy coffees are Einstein himself, the seminal Czech writer Karel Čapek, most of his literary contemporaries, and his artist brother Josef, who helped advance Cubism. Untold surrealists have also made the Louvre a second home, including

Café Louvre

the sexually liberated Toyen and a long string of French artists who inspired the Czech modernists.

From here, continue east towards Jungmannovo náměstí, taking note as you pass the Tesco that this contructivist glass building was also a remarkable modernist achievement back in a day when department stores were thought to be the height of urbane fashionability (under communism, it was named for the revolutionary month of May, or Maj, and carried truck wheels but nothing of popular interest).

At Jungmannovo náměstí, head to the south-eastern corner of the square on the north side of **Our Lady of the Snows** (p130) to spot the world's only cubist lamp-post. Although it looks a bit forlorn these days, it represents a movement in revolutionary visual representation that Czechs took up with unique enthusiasm, which was inspired by the work of Picasso. Prague was the only place in the world, in which designers tried to extensively infuse architecture with the multi-plane style, often to incredible effect.

Lucerna shopping passage

From here, locate the entrance to the Franciscan Gardens on the south side of the square and make your way through this little park. You'll discover another glass constructivist wonder, the **Baťa building**, which has always sold shoes by the greatest Czech footwear mogul, Tomas Baťa. They're still a good bargain, even though some have reported that they don't last like they used to. Pass out the south-eastern corner of the park and go through the Světozor shopping passage south to Vodickova street.

Next, turn right to **Myšák** (p133), the recently reopened sweetshop. Another historic gem that personified Czech style and frivolity between the wars, this gorgeous rondo-cubist building got its façade thanks to the pen of a trendsetting architect, who was also, no doubt, as fond of Myšák's caramel sundaes as any other Praguer.

Now cross Vodičkova into the **Lucerna shopping passage** (p123). This arcade, filled with faux marble, wide staircases, balconies, glass and brass, is owned by the Havel family, which may explain why it has escaped the developers and still hosts two resident theatre companies, among a dozen other charming little ventures and characterful cafés.

Now exit the passage on the north side onto Wenceslas Square. The broad boulevard, which is, as you'll notice, not even remotely square-shaped, is a showcase of art nouveau and modernist architecture from top to bottom. A particular highlight is Ludvík Kysela's **Lindt Building** at No.4, an early showpiece of constructivism. If you follow the square south-east to its top end, you'll find, just next to the equine statue of St Wenceslas by Josef Myslbek, the Museum entrance to the metro.

Get a ticket from one of the machines at the entrance and take the red line north to the Vltavská stop in the Holešovice district. From here, it's a five-minute walk to the **National Gallery Collection of 19th-, 20th- and 21st-Century Art** (p155) housed in the **Veletržní Palace**, a soaring marvel of early 20th-century architecture and design by Oldřich Týl and Josef Fuchs. Inside, the permanent collections are arranged around thecruise-ship lines of its five-storey, glass-topped atrium. These include an extensive display of the sculpture, art, decoration, technology, architecture and stage designs that personified Czechoslovakia's heady, if abortive, first era of independence. Some are almost painful to behold, such as an ambitious design for a vast National Gallery building in Malá Strana, a project that was never to be.

Czech Airlines propellers, art deco ceramics, glass art, and ground-breaking bronze sculptures, such as Otakar Švec's 1924 Sunbeam futurist motorcyclist bending into a curve, provide a tantalising taste of what was brewing in the Czech lands up until the dark day when the Nazi invasion of the country put out the lights from October 1938 to March 1939. They were not to burn that brightly again until after the Velvet Revolution in 1989.

A good place to process everything that you encounter is the counter of the streamlined **Bohemia Bagel** (p153), across the street on the next block north. Amid the Czechs, Brits and Americans cavorting there, you'll discover an appreciation for the destiny that may have been delayed but couldn't be denied. Czechs are as much a part of progressive Europe now as any other EU member. A toast!

Astronomical Clock p49

Magical Mystery Tour

Y ou're not imagining things
when a chill creeps up your
spine while walking through a
dark lane in Malá Strana. Nor is it
chance when, of all people, you run
into your best friend from primary
school on the **Charles Bridge**
(p95) right after you thought of
them for no reason after 30 years.
Prague has strange and mysterious
vectors of energy – and seems
pretty adept at warping time and
space too. Even before the obsessive
Rudolf II gathered cosmologists and
alchemists to Prague to set about
divining the mysteries of the
universe, Czech kings took the
subject of magic seriously.

This walk, which transports
you from the spaces where royal
retainers set about seeking the
Philosopher's Stone at Prague
Castle to the city's greatest occult
object on Old Town Square, will
take you about three hours at a
leisurely pace, factoring in time
to poke about the sights, or four

hours if you stop to power up at
an old pub of the kind favoured by
the city's seers over the centuries.

The **Belvedere** (p63) or Summer
Palace in the Royal Gardens, just
north across the Stag Moat from
Prague Castle, is not only known
for Paulo della Stella's marvellous
Renaissance form, dating from
1538, which suggests the structure
of an overturned ship. In fact,
a lot more than kingly trysting
went on in this elegant, terraced
edifice. It was here that the
alchemists hired by Rudolf, the
only Habsburg king to locate his
court in Prague, not Vienna, set
about their experiments.

The Holy Roman emperor no
doubt felt the city's power, as
reports of his childhood visit in
1562, for his father's coronation,
attest. Occasional exhibitions
honour the Belvedere's mystical
role in the Czech court set up in
Hradčany in 1583 but, unless you
catch one of these, few visible signs

St Vitus's Cathedral

remain of the building's dark arts. Some have reported that they can still feel the energy, however.

From here, exit the west end of the Royal Gardens, turn left and go over the bridge across the Stag Moat, and enter the Prague Castle grounds. Head for **St Vitus's Cathedral** (p69) and enter the nave (no ticket is required for this area). As you face the apse, you'll notice the small entrance to the **Chapel of St Wenceslas** in the right transept. Work your way through the tour groups to get to the door. Entry is not permitted because of the delicacy of the agate-covered walls, but this chapel, built in 1345, has a small chamber door leading to the treasury. It contains the crown jewels and the skull of Wenceslas himself, which is covered in a fine, spiderweb-like veil. They are only taken out on major state occasions (the end of communism merited such an outing, but little has since).

It's said that the jewels, protected by a papal bull, carry a curse for anyone who disrespects them. A scoffing Nazi Reichsprotektor,

Reinhard Heydrich, tried on the crown and was assassinated by British-trained Czech patriots shortly thereafter. Lesson anyone?

Sadly, you can't really see the chamber door, for which there are seven keys, each held by a top church or state official. So head out of the cathedral now and make your way to the south end of the Third Courtyard, which takes you to the entrance of the Old Royal Palace. Rather than go in, notice the stairway to its right, delineated by Egyptian-looking golden forms. They are one of several occult touches marking the **Prague Castle** complex (p61). Now descend these stone steps, known as the Bull Staircase, and venture out into the Paradise Gardens, taking note of the odd obelisk a few metres to your left.

This marks the spot where, according to the official Church record, at least, angels descended from heaven in 1618 to carry the Catholic councillors gently to the ground after they were tossed out of a palace window by a Protestant mob. The Czech Protestants, of course, say the lucky councillors

Prague Castle p47

survived only because they landed in a dung heap – but then they would, wouldn't they?

From here, head back up the Bull Stairs, turn left and enter the Castle's second courtyard, and continue west through the **Mathias Gate**. Turn left and then right, go down the Ke Hradu steps to Nerudova street and take your first right, descending along Jánský vršek to No.8, U Magistra Kelly (257 217 770). This pub, built in a medieval hall where one of Rudolf's unlucky consorts once stayed, is filled with alchemical symbols and tools of the trade, and exudes a suitably dark and musty atmosphere. Edward Kelly, along with his mentor, John Dee, worked on deciphering the language of the angels for the court, among other things, but fell out of favour, resulting in prison for the former.

Once refreshed, continue on down Nerudova to Malostranské náměstí, turning left onto Tomašská. Head north and turn right into the first parking area, and walk through the Czech Parliament courtyard entrance into the **Wallenstein Gardens** (p82). The megalomaniacal general Albrecht von Wallenstein, a key player in the Counter-Reformation, was a serious subscriber to numerology and, although he had been awarded vast treasures, including the palace surrounding this garden, he was fearful of the fates. He thus pestered Rudolf's court mathematician, Johannes Kepler, to read his star charts. Kepler wasn't told the data was for Wallenstein and predicted a violent death caused in large part by the raging ego of a man talented at creating enemies. Wallenstein was slain by Scottish and Irish assassins on the very day Kepler predicted: 25 February 1634.

Consider cosmic justice as you meander through this dignified garden, then make your way back to Malostranské náměstí and turn left down Mostecká to the Charles Bridge. Few of the millions of visitors here know that this bridge, arguably the most important infrastructure development for medieval Prague, was also planned for good auspices. After consulting with his numerologists, Charles IV chose a date and time for laying the founding stone that's perfectly symmetrical: 9 July 1357 at 5.31am. In digits, the number could be read as 135797531. If you happen to ascend **Old Town Bridge Tower** (p105) at dusk on the Summer Solstice, you'll notice the sun sets directly over the point of St Vitus's Cathedral under which Charles's tomb lies. The king made use of similar alignments in laying out the streets of New Town.

Now head west into Old Town and ramble up Karlova street towards Old Town Square. The plaza's centrepiece, the Orloj, or **Astronomical Clock** (p95) has on its face, or *cifernik*, a complex set of dials, hands, astrological symbols and rings. Books have been written on how to read them all, but a good indicator of the importance of cosmology in Prague's history is the clock face's function as an astrolabe, or instrument used for calculating the positions of the sun, moon and stars at any given time. The dials not only show these in relation to the horizon, but the time of day and hour at which the sun will set and rise for any time of year.

All that you have to watch out for is that no sleight-of-hand magician pulls a disappearing act on your wallet as you take in these mysteries. Consider mulling them over at the **Angel** restaurant (p107) nearby. Surely, John Dee and Edward Kelly would.

Laterna Magika p54

Century Shuffle

Prague's architectural feast is visible in some form in just about every quarter, with the odd tenth-century rotunda popping up in even modern urban grids. But a good sense of the progression (and sometimes regression) of the centuries is afforded right in the Staré Město district, in the area once bounded by fortress walls – the city's oldest and most historically intact quarter has survived fairly well the onslaught of nightclubs and neon-lit crystal shops. The district forms a compact, easily manageable collection of an incredible expanse of building forms, styles and eras.

To tour this history of Bohemia written in stone in chronological order, you'll need about two hours if taking the walk at an easy strolling pace, not counting breaks for fortification of your own batteries (an even greater variety of options are on show for that). Note that some backtracking is

required to move through the centuries in order.

Start with a simple structure that thousands of visitors pass by without much notice, but which is the oldest standing building in Staré Město. The innocuous nature and lack of pretence of the 11th-century **Rotunda of the Holy Cross**, or Rotunda svatého Kříž in Czech, at the corner of Konviktská and Karoliny Světlé streets, speak to the values of early Christian worshippers. Little is known today about what inspired its Byzantine style, which sets it somewhat apart from the two other remaining rotundas in Prague, St Longinus in the Nové Město district and St Martin in Vyšehrad, but it's a cherished site, to which the celebrated nationalist artist Josef Mánes added the hammered iron lattice work. It is said that the structure marks the location where a cross spontaneously arose on the site of a martyred Christian girl's

Prague Castle

demise but the building likely functioned as a private chapel for some earthly Middle Age merchants.

Older structures are, of course, still visible in other parts of the city, although they are no longer intact: for a glimpse of the oldest ruins on show in the city, seek out the foundations of the rustic **Church of Our Lady**, established by Prince Bořivoj some time before 885. They don't look like much more than pits and walls through the glass of the north passage between **Prague Castle**'s second courtyard and the north-west corner of the grounds. In the Castle's Third Courtyard, behind the grille on the south side of **St Vitus's Cathedral** (p69), the foundations of the 11th-century Chapel of St Maurice are just visible, but are frustratingly limited in their signage and access. Nearby, in a part of the **Old Royal Palace** (p65) that's inaccessible, the remains of humble single-room houses from tenth and 11th centuries have been unearthed, as well as nearby Bronze Age graves and dwellings. Findings from the site

are displayed in the Old Royal Palace permanent exhibition, 'The Story of Prague Castle.'

From the Rotunda of the Holy Cross, make your way to an unlikely site of some of the best preserved Gothic structures excluding St Vitus's Cathedral: the **Old Town Square**. Head north-east up Konviktská, then continue north up Husova and Jalovcová to Malé Náměstí, thence to Old Town Square proper.

By now, you will be in the heart a Gothic and Renaissance treasure trove. Old Town Hall, built out of a private house that the civic authorities bought in 1338 before adding the improvement of a wondrous clock tower, provides only a hint of what used to stand here, thanks to the Nazis and their artillery during the Prague Uprising in 1945. The Czech resistance had made use of medieval tunnels under the hall to cache weapons and ammunition and the Germans responded to the discovery by blasting much of the hall down. However, the spindly **Týn Church** (p95), across the

Old Town Square p51

square, is a fine Gothic showpiece that is still remarkably intact, particularly its original tympanum, which rises above its Renaissance façade. The golden chalice there, the symbol of Czech protestant Hussites, was cast from the melted down cross that adorned the church up until the end of World War I and the collapse of the last remnants of the Habsburg empire.

The **House at the Stone Bell** (p101), just to the north of the church across the tiny lane, is another excellent, if weathered, original Gothic sandstone structure, with a 14th-century façade harkening back to the dark days of the square's once-fetid market. A calming patio and café is hidden within, making for a surprisingly handy oasis just feet from the normally tourist-jammed square.

The next-door **Goltz-Kinský Palace**, finished by Anselmo Lurago in 1755 after a design by the Baroque master Kilian Ignatz Dientzenhofer, shows how harmoniously a different architectural age can be integrated into a space like the Old Town Square, which features variegated structures spanning six centuries. Such fanciful chocolate-box palaces and churches are to be found throughout the city, ushered in during the Counter-Reformation in the hope that cherubs and marble would help dispel the troublesome Protestant movements led by the followers of **Jan Hus**, whose mournful bronze likeness dominates the square. Ladislav Šaloun's gloomy 1915 bronze work, which has been restored, is inscribed with the motto 'Truth will prevail', a slogan adopted by dissidents during the Velvet Revolution. For a time, Hus stared down a Marian column that had stood in front of the Old Town Hall since 1650, in commemoration of the Catholic

armies' victory over the Czech protestants at White Mountain, but it was toppled during an independence rally in 1918. Near where it stood, crosses are still marked in the cobblestones for each of the Czech nobles who was executed on this spot following their loss in the pivotal White Mountain battle.

From the square, walk four blocks north-west up Kaprova to one of Staré Město's finest riverside sights and the former home of Parliament, the grand, neo-classical **Rudolfinum** (p122), built during 1875-84 by Josef Zitek and Josef Schulz. The warm-coloured sandstone walls of this concert hall and art gallery are a common feature of many Prague buildings (and one theory behind the origin of the city's nickname Golden City). It's a building intended to personify the Czech nationhood movement and that legacy has been carried out by its many civic purposes, especially its current role as home to the Czech Philharmonic Orchestra. The return of Czechs to world culture is celebrated in its exhibition halls, where Asian art shows are a particularly strong suit. A bronze statue of Dvořák is another recent nod to the Bohemian passion for the fine arts.

After standing before the Rudolfinum, walk over to the Vltava river for another blast of patriotism. The **Mánes Bridge**, another nationalist shrine, was completed in 1914 and features reliefs by two of the country's best sculptors of the period, František Bilek, who had a knack for spooky symbolism, and Jan Štursa.

Now head back to Old Town Square and east up Celetná for a look at where things progressed in the 20th century. At the end of this street is a reward that makes all the kitsch shops that line it worth enduring: the **Municipal House** (p102), a magnificent 1906-12 art nouveau structure that hosts one of Prague's most fabulous concert halls (and murals by the likes of Alfons Mucha, Mikoláš Aleš and Max Švabinský). It's also home to the Prague Symphony Orchestra and another well-curated gallery on the top floor. Pause for a drink in the Vienna-style coffeehouse here and it will be one you'll remember for years. Don't forget your order of *sachertorte*, best enjoyed as the grand piano tinkles away.

Back down Celetná, a block to the west, is the entrance to **Ovocný trh**, a plaza named for a fruit market that once stood here – but this wide open street signifies far more. At the far end stands another Baroque classic, the wedding-cake **Estates Theatre** (p122), while at the north end lies Czech modernism at its finest. Here, in the form of the angular **House of the Black Madonna** (p99), is one of the finest cubist structures anywhere, the 1911-12 former department store by Josef Gočár. Apart from the excellent art collection within, if offers prime balcony real estate for sipping or snacking, as an alternative to that of Municipal House.

If you continue across Ovocný trh now, past the Estates Theatre, down Rytířská, and then Martinská, turning left on Na Perstyně, you'll emerge onto the main drag of Národní. Here, just where things should have reached their peak of grace, is one of the last great monuments to the fate that ensnared this loveliest of cities in the 20th century. The fantastically ugly block of 1970s glass that is the **Laterna Magika** (p129), at No.4, was at least good for one thing. The plotters of the Velvet Revolution secretly met there in 1989 to plan yet again for Czechs to wrest control of their destiny from foreign occupiers. As a long-time home for theatre artists, it made the perfect hideout. Sadly, these days that legacy has devolved into tourist-targeted mime shows using black light effects.

As for the souvenir tat and corporate offices that followed after 1989, the less said the better, surely.

Municipal House

Prague by Area

St Vitus's Cathedral p69

Hradčany

PRAGUE BY AREA

Na Hrad! or 'To the Castle!' was the Czech battle cry during the Velvet Revolution and is still the most chest-thumping thing that a Praguer can call out. Winning hockey champs have earned the cheer, not just the Velvet president Václav Havel, which indicates the place that the Hradčany district holds in Czech hearts. It's suitably mythic, with as many fables about its history as documented facts.

With the spire of St Vitus's Cathedral, the city's signature skyline feature, forming the centre of the district, Hradčany invites and rewards exploration. It only took on its current shape in the 18th century under Empress Maria Theresa, and St Vitus's wasn't completed until 1929. As the president's office and the seat of the archbishopric, the complex remains the political, spiritual and national heart of the Czech Republic. It's also the top tourist attraction, even if

church-state struggles have resulted in neglect over the years.

The founders of **Prague Castle**, the Přemyslids, were the greatest of the Bohemian bloodlines and are somewhat steeped in mystery. They built the earliest part of the Hradčany fortress in the ninth century as a commanding stronghold, which overlooked miles of the surrounding area. Continuously occupied since then, the Castle has changed shape and form a dozen times, following the fortunes and successors of this family, which also ruled parts of Poland but died out in 1306.

Owing to the high walls that were added later, the best views of Prague are now to be had from the gardens and courtyards around the Castle – unless you feel fit enough to take a hike up the 96-metre-high Gothic St Vitus's Cathedral tower. It soars above the southern façade, which Charles IV

best chance of avoiding throngs of tourists is to visit during the evening, when it's most romantic. It's dark, but quite safe. However, the Castle grounds are well worth exploring at any time; you'll find a number of options for refuelling in the near vicinity and a handful of terrace restaurants visible below. Otherwise, there are richer pickings down the hill in Malá Strana.

Hradčany owes its grand scale and pristine condition to a fire in 1541 that destroyed the medieval district, and to the frenzied period of Counter-Reformation building that followed the Protestant defeat at the Battle of White Mountain in 1620. Little has changed here over the last two centuries.

The area's focal point is **Hradčanské náměstí**, one of the grandest squares in the city, lined with imposing palaces built by the Catholic aristocracy, anxious to be close to the Habsburg court.

The **Schwarzenberg Palace**, the National Gallery's newly launched collection of Baroque portraiture and sculpture masters, is the freshest attraction on the hill this year and well worth a visit, even after the sensory overload of touring the Castle itself.

entrusted to Peter Parler, whose work was later spiked by Nicolò Pacassi in 1770. The church's magnificent flying buttresses and Golden Gothic portals facing the city also show the 16th-century grace of Bonifác Wohlmut.

Czechs are understandably proud to show off the Castle, by day and by night, and have taken advantage of the reopening of its grounds to the public following the Velvet Revolution in 1989. The complex continues to undergo renovations, with a dozen rooms opened to the public beneath the **Old Royal Palace** two years ago, the first in a series of planned modern developments, which are balanced with archaeological surveys of its still emerging subterranean layers.

The rest of the district comprises the surrounding streets, which stretch north and west, across the hilltop. This is quiet and less touristy than the Castle itself, and the **Nový Svět** (or 'New World') pocket of streets is enchanting.

The Castle complex is open to the public until midnight and the

Sights & museums

Černín Palace

Černínský palác
Černínská 5 (224 181 111).
Metro Malostranská, then tram 22.
Map p58 A3 ❶
Now serving as the Czech Foreign Ministry, this imposing structure, with its grey façade articulated by a line of 30 pillars, was commissioned in 1669 by Humprecht Johann Černín, imperial ambassador to Venice; its construction expenses ruined the family. Gestapo interrogations were later conducted here during the Nazi occupation. Its curse surfaced in 1948, when Foreign Minister

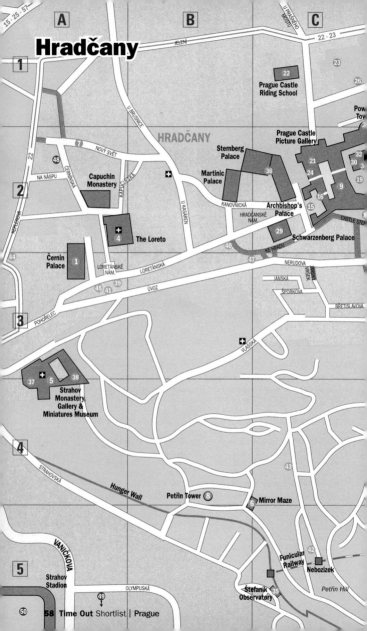

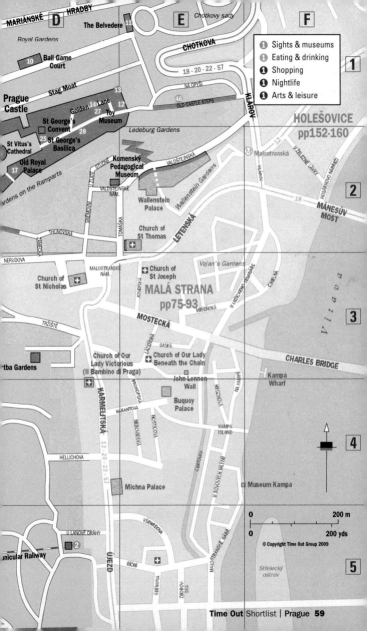

MARIÁNSKÉ HRADBY **D** Chotkovy sady **E** **F**

The Belvedere

Royal Gardens

CHOTKOVA **1**

10 Ball Game
Court

18 · 20 · 22 · 57

NA OPYŠI

Stag Moat

Prague Castle 13

Golden 14 Lane 12 46 OLD CASTLE STEPS KLÁROV

27 Toy Museum HOLEŠOVICE
pp152-160

28 12

St George's Convent

25 St George's Basilica *Ledebug Gardens*

St Vitus's Cathedral

Komenský Pedagogical Museum ⓂMalostranská U ZELENÉ LANKY

17 Old Royal Palace VALDŠTEJNSKÁ 18 WASHINGTONOVO NÁMĚSTÍ

Gardens on the Ramparts VALDŠTEJNSKÉ NÁM. Wallenstein Gardens **2** MÁNESŮV MOST

Wallenstein Palace

ZÁMECKÁ TOMÁŠSKÁ

THUNOVSKÁ Church of St Thomas ✚ LETENSKÁ

NERUDOVA

Church of St Nicholas ✚ MALOSTRANSKÉ NÁM. Church of St Joseph ✚ *Vojan's Gardens*

V l t a v a

MALÁ STRANA
pp75-93 MÍŠEŇSKÁ CIHELNÁ **3**

TRŽIŠTĚ MOSTECKÁ

BAŠTA CHARLES BRIDGE

Church of Our Lady Victorious (Il Bambino di Praga) ✚ Church of Our Lady Beneath the Chain ✚ Kampa Wharf

tba Gardens John Lennon Wall

KARMELITSKÁ HARANTOVA Buquoy Palace KAMPA ISLAND **4**

HELLICHOVA 12 · 20 · 22 · 57

Michna Palace Museum Kampa

U LANOVÉ DRÁHY 2 0 200 m

nicular Railway ÚJEZD 0 200 yds

© Copyright Time Out Group 2009

✚ *Střelecký ostrov* **5**

Legend:
1 Sights & museums
1 Eating & drinking
1 Shopping
1 Nightlife
1 Arts & leisure

Jan Masaryk, the last major political obstacle to Klement Gottwald's communist coup, had a fatal fall from an upstairs window a few days after the takeover.

Funicular

Petřín hill, Karmelitská 1 (no phone). Metro Malostranská. **Map** p59 D5 ➋

Recently restored and gliding again, this feat of engineering was 118 years old in 2008 and still offers a lazy (and fun) way to travel up to the top of the hill from Újezd, running roughly every ten minutes between March and October, from 9am until 11.20pm, and every 15 minutes in winter season, stopping halfway up the hill before continuing to the top. Your tram and metro tickets are all you need.

Karel Hynek Mácha

Petřín hill (no phone). Tram 12, 22, then funicular railway. **Map** p58 C5 ➌

This tragic romantic poet, who was the unofficial patron saint of lovers, has a statue in the park where every young couple in Prague (or so it seems) turns out on 1 May to smooch. Any lad who hesitates when his girl suggests this is not long for this world, or certainly not long the relationship.

Loreto

Loretánské náměstí 7 (220 516 740/ www.loreta.cz). Metro Malostranská, then tram 22. **Open** 9am-12.15pm, 1-4.30pm Tue-Sun. **Admission** 110 Kč; 90 Kč reductions. No credit cards. **Map** p58A2 ➍

The most famous of the world's copies of the church in Loreto, Italy, this Baroque building houses the bearded St Wilgefortis, the skeletons of another two female saints and the highest concentration of cherubs in Prague. The heart is a small chapel, the Santa Casa, spawned from the cult of Mary in Nazareth; it's said that the original was flown to Loreto by angels. Dating from 1626-31 and later completed by the Dientzenhofer team, it claims a brick from its Italian inspiration, as well as a

crevice left by a divine thunderbolt that struck an unfortunate blasphemer. The famous diamond monstrance, designed in 1699 by Fischer von Erlach and sporting 6,222 stones, is in the treasury.

Miniatures Museum
Muzeum miniatur

Strahovské nádvoří 11 (233 352 371/www.muzeumminiatur.com). Metro Malostranská, then tram 22. **Open** 9am-5pm daily. **Admission** 50 Kč; 30 Kč children. **Map** p58 A4 ➎

This obsessive collection on the grounds of Strahov Monastery lets you in on monkish work with the aid of magnifying glasses and microscopes. Portraiture on a poppy seed, a caravan of camels painted on a grain of millet, a prayer written out on a human hair and tiny copies of masterpieces by Rembrandt and Botticelli are on display.

Mirror Maze
Zrcadlové bludiště

Petřín hill (257 315 212). Tram 12,22, then funicular railway. **Open** *Jan-Mar, Nov, Dec* 10am-5pm Sat, Sun. *Apr* 10am-7pm daily. *May-Aug* 10am-10pm daily. *Sept* 10am-8pm daily. *Oct* 10am-6pm daily. **Admission** 70 Kč; 50 Kč children. **Map** p58 B4/B5 ➏

Housed in a cast-iron mock-Gothic castle, complete with a drawbridge and crenellations, is a hall of distorting mirrors that still causes remarkable hilarity among kids and their parents. Alongside stands a wax diorama of one of the proudest historical moments for the citizens of Prague: the defence of Charles Bridge during the Swedish attack of 1648 is brought to life in a fairground-style hall of wacky reflectors.

Nový Svět
New World

Černínská. Metro Malostranská, then tram 22. **Map** p58 A2 ➐

The enchanting backstreets north-west of the Castle, starting at Černínská, behind the Loreto, make up the small, storied parcel known as the New World.

The 16th-century quarter was built for Prague Castle retainers. Going down Kapucínská, you pass the Domeček, or 'Little House', at No.10, once home to the Fifth Department – the counter-intelligence unit of the Defence Ministry. Tycho Brahe, the Danish alchemist known for his missing nose and breakthroughs in accurate observations of orbits, lived at No.1, the Golden Griffin.

Petřín Tower
Rozhledna
Petřín hill (257 320 112/www. petrinska-rozhledna.cz). Tram 12, 22, then funicular railway. **Open** *Jan-Mar* 10am-5pm Sat, Sun. *Apr, Nov, Dec* 10am-7pm daily. *May-Sept* 10am-10pm daily. *Oct* 10am-8pm daily. Closed in poor weather. **Admission** 70 Kč; 50 Kč children. **Map** p58 B4 **⑧**

With the next-best view to the one afforded by St Vitus's Cathedral tower, this copy of the Eiffel Tower is a thrill to ascend. Built in 1891 for the Jubilee Exhibition, like the neighbouring mock-Gothic castle that houses the amusements below, it still stands strong (and sways on windy days).

Prague Castle
Hradčanské náměstí (224 372 423/ www.hrad.cz). Metro Malostranská, then tram 22. **Open** *Apr-Oct* 9am-5pm daily. *Nov-Mar* 9am-4pm daily. **Admission** 250-350 Kč; 125-175 Kč reductions; 300-500 Kč family, for two days. **Map** p58 C2 **⑨**
From the time of its founding by the Přemysl prince Bořivoj around AD 870, the citadel on the hill has served as the most impressive

Make the most of London life

manifestation of Prague's rulers – although its role as the seat of their power has been an on-again, off-again affair. The growing spurts of a complex as large as some Czech towns have been ushered in by each successive dynasty, with the Castle morphing completely over the centuries: in 973, the St Vitus chapter took form as a rotunda; a fire burnt through it in the tenth century; Count Břetislav I rebuilt it in 1041; the Přemyslids moved across the river to Vyšehrad and Charles IV ushered in the Golden Age in the 14th century. The final touches, including the present shape of St Vitus's Cathedral, came after 1918 in a furore of nation building.

Thus the castle's architectural styles, stretching from Romanesque to modernism, make for a rich tour. The imposing façade enclosing the castle is down to Empress Maria Theresa's desire for coherence but Nicolò Pacassi's work seems to lock away much of its beauty behind flat walls. Václav Havel did his best to enliven the palace, opening it up to the public and hiring the costume designer from the film *Amadeus* to remodel the castle guards' uniforms.

There is no charge to enter the grounds or chapel of St Vitus's Cathedral, but you will need a ticket (you can choose from short or long tours) to enter the Old Royal Palace (which features the excellent exhibit on Castle life), St George's Basilica, the Golden Lane and the Powder Tower (except from January to April and between October and December, when the tower is closed and the Golden Lane is free of charge). Entrance to the Toy Museum costs extra.

It's a stiff walk up to the castle from Malá Strana's Malostranská metro station. The least strenuous approach is to take the No.22 tram up the hill and get off at the Pražský hrad stop. There are a handful of adequate cafés within the castle complex, if you don't mind paying above the odds.

Ball Game Court
Míčovna

U Prašného mostu (224 373 579/ www.hrad.cz). Metro Malostranská, then tram 22. **Open** Events only. **Admission** varies. **Map** p59 D1 ⑩

On the southern side of the Royal Gardens, overlooking the Stag Moat, lies this Renaissance former hall. Built in 1563-69 by Bonifác Wohlmut, the court was originally conceived for Habsburg tennis matches, but hasn't seen sport for centuries. It's now periodically open for exhibitions and, despite awful acoustics, concerts. Look carefully at the elaborate black-and-white sgraffito above the figure of Justice (tenth from the right) and you'll spot some façade work modified under the old regime, which now contains a hammer and sickle.

Belvedere

U Prašného mostu (224 372 423/ www.hrad.cz). Metro Malostranská, then tram 22. **Open** Events only. **Admission** Varies. **Map** p59 E1 ⑪

With its signature copper roof resembling an overturned frigate, the Belvedere, also known as the Summer Palace, dominates the eastern end of the Royal Gardens. The stunning Renaissance structure was built by Paola della Stella between 1538 and 1564, creating what's hailed as the best example of Italianate style from the period in Central Europe (except for the roof, a compromise to the climate). It was commissioned by Ferdinand I as a gift for his wife, Anne, but she never got to enjoy it – she drew her last breath after producing the 15th heir to the throne. Occasional art shows are held here.

Black Tower
Černá věž

Na Opyši. Metro Malostranská, then tram 22. **Map** p59 E1 ⑫

Setting the stark, medieval tone of the Castle's east end, this tower tops the Old Castle Steps (Staré zámecké

Belvedere p63

schody), which lead up from the park just east of the Malostranská metro station. To the left of the entrance gate, where decorated palace guards stand all year, is a prime viewing spot over the red-tiled roofs, spires and domes of the Lesser Quarter.

Dalibor Tower
Daliborka
Zlatá ulička (224 372 423/ www.hrad.cz). Metro Malostranská, then tram 22. **Map** p59 D1/E1 ⑬
The former prison rooms, which housed an inmate who lent his name to the tower, isn't accessible to the public. But when standing beneath the tower, you can imagine Dalibor, who was later portrayed in Smetana's opera, amusing himself by playing the violin while awaiting his death sentence. Crowds of onlookers turned up at his execution to weep en masse.

Golden Lane
Prague Castle, Zlatá ulička (224 372 423/www.hrad.cz). Metro Malostranská, then tram 22. **Map** p59 D1 ⑭

This street is lined with tiny multi-coloured cottages that cling to Prague Castle's northern walls. They were thrown up by the poor in the 16th century out of whatever waste they could find. Some say its name alludes to a time when soldiers used the lane as a public urinal, but a more likely source is the 17th century goldsmiths who worked here. The house at No.22 was once owned by Kafka's sister Ottla, and the writer stayed here for a while in 1917, reputedly drawing the inspiration from the streets for his novel *The Castle*, a fact that's shamelessly milked today with souvenirs sold here.

Hradčanské náměstí gates
First courtyard. Metro Malostranská, then tram 22. **Map** p58 C2 ⑮
Linking the Castle's first courtyard with the outside world is this gateway that has been dominated since 1768 by Ignatz Platzer's monumental sculptures of battling Titans. They create an impressive, if not exactly welcoming, entrance. The changing of the guard takes place in this courtyard, a Havel-inspired attempt to add some ceremonial pzazz to the castle.

The change is carried out on the hour every day from 5am to 10pm, but the big crowd-pulling ceremony, complete with band, takes place at noon.

Matthias Gate

Matyášova brána

First courtyard (224 372 423/ www.hrad.cz). Metro Malostranská, then tram 22. **Map** p58 C2 ⑯

Built in 1614 by Rudolf II's rival and successor, Matthias, to imprint the Habsburg stamp on Prague Castle, this elaborate entryway provides access to the second courtyard. The admittedly impressive portal, topped by a double-headed German Imperial Eagle, remains a painful reminder to Czechs today. But, of course, it pleased Hitler when he came to stay in 1939.

Old Royal Palace

Starý královský palác

Third Courtyard (224 372 368/ www.hrad.cz). Metro Malostranská, then tram 22. **Map** p59 D2 ⑰

Part of the ticketed Castle tour, the palace offers three areas of royal chambers above ground level, all with badly photocopied engravings for displays, most with more Russian text than English, and, in the cellar, an exquisite permanent exhibition on palace life. The displays inhabit the 12th-century Romanesque remains of Prince Soběslav's residence. A worthwhile highlight at ground level is the Vladislav Hall, designed by Benedict Ried at the turn of the 16th century, which was where jousters once rode up the Riders' Staircase and where Václav Havel was sworn in in 1990. Its exquisitely vaulted ceiling represents the last flowering of Gothic art in Bohemia.

Paradise Gardens

Rajská zahrada

Below third courtyard (224 372 423/ www.hrad.cz). Metro Malostranská, then tram 22. **Open** *Apr, Oct* 10am-6pm daily. *May, Sept* 10am-7pm daily. *June-July* 10am-9pm daily. *Aug* 10am-8pm daily. **Admission** free. **Map** p58 C2 ⑬

From the Bull Staircase is the garden where the Catholic victims of the second and most famous defenestration by Protestants fell to earth, saved by a giant dung heap (an obelisk marks the spot). The gardens, initially laid out in 1562, were redesigned in the 1920s by Josip Plečnik. You can now make the descent to Malá Strana via the terraced slopes of five beautiful Renaissance gardens, which are open, like most gardens in Prague, from April to October only. The pride of the restoration is the lovely Ledebour Gardens (Ledeburská zahrada), featuring a series of fountains, ornate stone stair switchbacks and palace yards, and emptying you out on to the middle of Valdštejnská. Fit hikers might consider ascending to the castle this way as well, although there is an entrance fee of 60 Kč whichever way you decide to go.

Plečnik Obelisk

Third Courtyard (224 372 423/ www.hrad.cz). Metro Malostranská, then tram 22. **Map** p59 C2 ⑲

After the cathedral, the second most noticeable monument in the third courtyard is this fairly incongrous 17-metre-high granite obelisk, a memorial to the dead of World War I, erected by Josip Plečnik in 1928. The two tapering flagpoles nearby are also the Slovene's work; he was hired by President Tomáš Garrigue Masaryk to create a more uniform look for the seat of the First Republic.

Powder Tower

Prašná věž

Third courtyard (224 372 423/ www.hrad.cz). Metro Malostranská, then tram 22. **Open** *Apr-Oct* 9am-5pm daily. *Nov-Mar* 9am-4pm daily. **Admission** 50 Kč; 70 Kč family, or included in Prague Castle ticket. **Map** p59 C1-2 ⑳

One of the most atmospheric sections of the ticketed Prague Castle tour, the 15th-century Mihulka, as it's also known, was where Rudolf II, King of Bohemia

(1576-1612), employed his many alchemists, who were engaged in attempts to distil the Elixir of Life and transmute base metals into gold. Under renovation at press time, the tower is due to reopen soon, with exhibits on alchemy and Renaissance life at the Castle.

Prague Castle Picture Gallery
Obrazárna Pražského hradu
Second courtyard (224 373 531/ www.obrazarna-hradu.cz). Metro Malostranská, then tram 22. **Open** *Apr-Oct* 9am-6pm daily. *Nov-Mar* 9am-4pm daily; tours Mon-Fri. **Admission** 150 Kč; 80 Kč reductions; 150 Kč family. No credit cards. **Map** p59 C2 ㉑
On the north side of the courtyard near the Powder Bridge (U Prašného mostu) entrance to Prague Castle is this collection of Renaissance and Baroque works, which includes artworks by Rubens, Tintoretto, Titian and Veronese, as well as lesser-known masters. Though there's no hope of ever piecing together the Emperor Rudolf II's original collection, which has been scattered to the winds, the Castle has succeeded in recovering a few of the impressive works from the original cache.

Prague Castle Riding School
Jízdárna
U Prašného mostu (224 373 232/ www.hrad.cz). Metro Malostranská, then tram 22. **Open** exhibitions only. **Admission** varies. **Map** p58 C1 ㉒
On the north side of the Royal Gardens stands this impressive exhibition hall with soaring Baroque façade, which hosts the biggest-scale art shows in the Castle complex, often international in scope, with fascinating smaller-scale exhibits on Castle history and local artists. The king's troops indeed learned their horsemanship here but it was converted to an art hall around 50 years ago.

Royal Garden
U Prašného mostu
(224 372 423/www.hrad.cz). Metro Malostranská, then tram 22. **Open** *Apr, Oct* 10am-6pm daily. *May, Sept* 10am-7pm daily. *June-July* 10am-9pm daily. *Aug* 10am-8pm daily. **Admission** free. **Map** p59 C1 ㉓
When you cross over the Powder Bridge (U Prašného mostu) from the castle's second courtyard, you'll reach the Royal Garden (Královská zahrada), on the outer side of the Stag Moat (Jelení příkop). Laid out for Emperor Ferdinand I in the 1530s, it once included a maze and a menagerie, but was devastated by Swedish soldiers in the 17th century. In front of the Belvedere palace is the so-called Singing Fountain (Zpívající fontána), created in bronze by Bohemian craftsmen in the 1560s. It used to hum as water splashed into its basin but sings no longer, thanks to overzealous reconstruction.

Spanish Hall
Španělský sál
Second courtyard (224 372 423/ www.hrad.cz). Metro Malostranská, then tram 22. **Open** only during concerts. **Admission** varies. **Map** p58 C2 ㉔
Most Castle visitors don't get the chance to glimpse the inside of this hall, hidden atop a monumental stairway, just visible from inside the passage between the first and second courtyards. The magnificent gold-and-white Baroque hall is a 17th-century ceremonial chamber re-created in the 19th century, when the trompe l'oeil murals were covered with white stucco and huge mirrors and gilded chandeliers were brought in to transform the space into a glitzy venue for the coronation of Emperor Franz Josef I (who failed to show). In the 1950s, the Politburo met here, protected from assassins by a reinforced steel door.

St George's Basilica
Bazilika sv. Jiří
Jiřské náměstí (224 373 368/ www.hrad.cz). Metro Malostranská, then tram 22. **Open** *Apr-Oct* 9am-5pm daily. *Nov-Mar* 9am-4pm daily. **Admission** 250-350 Kč; 125-175 Kč reductions; 300-500 Kč family, for two days. **Map** p59 D2 ㉕

Dream gallery

Take a surreal turn at the home of great filmmakers.

Lunacy

The first tip-off that there's something strange about the enchanting cottage on a winding lane a few streets north-west of Prague Castle are the busts. A head with a strange, imperious face sprouts from the balcony, and others are visible around the garden wall. The tiny sign on the door of **Galerie Gambra** (p74) adds to the confusion. It informs passers-by that this micro-gallery on the ground floor of the home is dedicated to Surrealism, 'L'art brut' and Tactilism.

If you stick around, it's likely that a Japanese art student will wander up and approach the door with reverence. This is a place to which people make pilgrimages. Jan Švankmajer's status as a surrealist filmmaker and animator is hard to overestimate; the brothers Quay and, more recently, Neil Gaiman, the British writer of dark fantasies, including *Coraline*, have called the low-budget, stop-action Czech artist an inspiration. The fact that he lives in this house attached to the gallery

lends it a quality that no other art space in the city can claim.

The spirit of Švankmajer and his lifelong partner, the recently deceased Eva Švankmajerová, fill the little edifice, as does their art. The gallery showcases work by the Czech Surrealists, founded in the 1920s and still active today. Dreamy, disturbing paintings and sculptures fill Gambra, along with books an art maven would kill for.

Those familiar with Švankmajer's cult-generating films, from 1964's *The Last Trick* to 1970's *The Ossuary*, which got him banned from filmmaking for seven years, will be familiar with the role that Surrealism plays in his work. Much of that, seen in the couple's last joint venture, *Lunacy* (2005), was shaped by Švankmajerová, who art directed her husband's films. One reward awaiting pilgrims is the chance to see her playful imagery. With the 2010 release of *Surviving Life (Theory and Practice)*, the first film in decades in which they did not join up, you can expect to see more seekers at Černínova No.5.

St Vitus's Cathedral

Although not open to the public, the quaint, mustard-coloured Dientzenhofer Summer House, which stands to the right of the Royal Gardens entrance, was the presidential residence from 1948 to 1989. Paranoid old Gustav Husák had enormous slabs of concrete installed as defences against possible missile attacks, an addition so ugly that Václav Havel's wife, Olga, refused to let them move in. It has remained empty ever since.

Toy Museum
Jiřská 6 (224 372 294). Metro Malostranská, then tram 22.
Open 9.30am-5.30pm daily.
Admission 60 Kč; 120 Kč family; under-5s free. **Map** p59 D1 ㉗
Part of Czech émigré Ivan Steiger's large collection is displayed on the two floors of this museum in the Castle grounds. Brief texts accompany cases of toys, from teddy bears to an elaborate tin train set. Kitsch fans will love the robots and the enormous collection of Barbie dolls clad in vintage costumes that span the decades. Good for a rainy day but probably better for the young at heart than the actual young, most of whom greatly prefer playing with toys than looking at them from a historical perspective.

The Princely Collections
NEW *Jiřská 3 (602 595 998/ www.lobkowiczevents.cz). Metro Malostranská, then tram 22.*
Open 10.30am-6pm daily.
Admission 350 Kč; 690 Kč family.
Map p59 D2 ㉘
One of several palaces in Prague owned by the influential Lobkowicz family, this one has been recently updated to form a museum that is wholly independent from the Prague Castle tour. Aside from classical recitals, the pile, which dates to circa 1658, hosts an impressive collection of family armour, Mozart manuscripts and displays on the roots of the Czech lands' power players.

This basilica, a stop on the ticketed Prague Castle tour, was reconstructed by Italian craftsmen in 1142 after a fire, but was actually founded in 905, according to the oldest accounts. It burned again later and has been rebuilt several times, but the 16th-century image of St George slaying a dragon in the south tympanum is a highlight. In the original arcades are remnants of 13th-century frescoes and within are the bodies of a saint (Ludmila, who was strangled by assassins hired by Prince Wenceslas's mother Drahomíra) and a saint-maker (the notorious Boleslav the Cruel, who martyred his brother Wenceslas by having him stabbed to death). The basilica's restored simplicity and clean lines make a comforting contrast to the dizzying, Baroque flourishes that delineate most Prague churches.

Summer House
U Prašného mostu (224 372 423/ www.hrad.cz). Metro Malostranská, then tram 22. **Map** p58 C1 ㉖

Schwarzenberg Palace

NEW *Hradčanské náměstí 21 (233 081 713/www.ngprague.cz). Metro Malostranská, then tram 22.* **Open** 10am-6pm Tue-Sun. **Admission** 180 Kč; 200 Kč family. **Map** p59 C2 ㉙

The National Gallery relaunched its permanent display of Bohemian Baroque art in spring 2008 at the Renaissance-era Schwarzenberg Palace across from the Castle. The museum, which formerly housed the Military Museum, presents around 160 sculptures and 280 paintings from the late 16th to the late 18th century in the kingdom of Bohemia. The master of Baroque sculpture, Matthias Braun, who contributed some of the Charles Bridge's best ornaments, is in pride of place, along with Maximilian Brokof.

St Vitus's Cathedral

Prague Castle, third courtyard (724 933 441). Metro Malostranská, then tram 22. **Open** *Mar-Oct* 9am-5pm Mon-Sat, noon-5pm Sun. *Nov-Feb* 9am-4pm Mon-Sat, noon-4pm Sun. **Admission** free. **Map** p58 C2 ㉚

The geometric and formidable aspects of the city's greatest church are deceptive, if effective. For centuries, only St Vitus's Cathedral's western end and bell tower, looking incongruously dominant compared to the nave, stood here. The current form, in a convincing neo-Gothic rush of construction, was only added early in the 20th century in an effort to expand and unify while creating a new Czech icon that had little to do with its past as the shrine of Austrian Habsburg interlopers. It still forms the centrepiece of Prague Castle, but its pinnacles and buttresses are actually a patchwork. The cathedral was only completed in 1929, exactly 1,000 years after the murdered St Wenceslas was laid to rest on the site. In pagan times, Svatovít, the Slavic god of fertility, was worshipped here, which gives a clue as to why the cathedral was dedicated to his near namesake St Vitus (svatý Vit in Czech). Charles IV, who

won an archbishopric for Prague, hired Frenchman Matthew of Arras to construct the Gothic wonder, but it was completed by Swabian Peter Parler, hence the Sondergotik or German late Gothic design. The 19th-century nationalists who completed the work did so according to Parler's original plans, hence the difficulty in telling old from new. Inside, the vast nave is flooded with multicoloured light from the gallery of stained-glass windows. All 21 of them were sponsored by Bohemian finance institutions including (third on the right) an insurance company whose motto – 'those who sow in sorrow shall reap in joy' – is subtly incorporated into the biblical allegory. The most famous is the third window on the left, in the Archbishop's Chapel, created by Alfons Mucha. It depicts the struggle of Christian Slavonic tribes; appropriately enough, the work was paid for by Banka Slavia.

Chapel of St Wenceslas

Svatováclavská kaple
Open 8am-midnight daily.
Admission free. **Map** p59 D2 ㉛

On the right side of the nave is the site of the original tenth-century rotunda where 'Good King' Wenceslas was buried. Built in 1345, the chapel has 1,345 polished amethysts, agates and jaspers incorporated into its design and contains some of the saint's personal paraphernalia, including armour, chain shirt and helmet. The chapel itself is gated off, but you can catch a glint of its treasure trove over the railings. On state anniversaries, the skull of the saint is put on display, covered with a cobweb-fine veil. A door in the corner leads to the chamber that contains the crown jewels. A papal bull of 1346 officially protects the jewels, while legend has it that fate prescribes an early death for anyone who uses them improperly. The curse appeared to work on the Nazis' man in Prague, Reichsprotektor Reinhard Heydrich, who tried on the crown and was assassinated shortly afterwards by the resistance. The door to the chamber is locked with seven keys, symbolising the seven seals of Revelations, each looked after by a different Prague state or church official.

Crypt

Open *Apr-Oct* 9am-5pm daily. *Nov-Mar* 9am-4pm daily. **Admission** 50-350 Kč; 30-175 Kč reductions; 520 Kč family, for two days. **Map** p58 C2 ㉜

Temporarily closed for renovations at press time, the crypt is normally entered from the centre of the cathedral. Herein lie the remains of various Czech monarchs, including Rudolf II. Easily the most eye-catching tomb is Charles IV's modern, streamlined metal affair, designed by Kamil Roškot in the mid 1930s. However, the vault itself, hastily excavated between world wars, has a cramped look to it.

Gothic Golden Portal

Zlatá brána

Open 8am-midnight daily. **Admission** free. **Map** p58 C2 ㉝

This grandiose southern entrance to St Vitus's Cathedral, which is visible from the courtyard, sports a restored mosaic of multicoloured Venetian glass depicting the Last Judgement. A Getty-funded project returned the original lustre, taking years of work (outdoor mosaics don't do well this far north in Europe for climatic reasons). On either side of the central arch are sculptures of Charles IV and his wife, Elizabeth of Pomerania, whose talents allegedly included being able to bend a sword with her bare hands.

Great Tower

Open *Apr-Oct* 9am-5pm daily. *Nov-Mar* 9am-4pm daily. **Admission** 50-350 Kč; 30-175 Kč reductions; 520 Kč family, for two days. **Map** p58 C2 ㉞

Easily the most dominant feature of the cathedral, and accounting for Prague's signature spire, the Gothic and Renaissance tower (closed at press time as part of a larger renovation)

is topped with a Baroque dome. This houses Sigismund, the largest bell in Bohemia, which was made in the middle of the 16th century and weighs a hefty 15,120 kilograms. The clapper weighs slightly more than 400 kilograms. Getting Sigismund into the tower was no mean feat: according to legend, it took a rope woven from the hair of the city's noblest virgins to haul it into position.

Štefánik Observatory

Hvězdárna

Top of Petřín hill (257 320 540/ www.observatory.cz). Tram 12, 22, then funicular railway. **Open** *Jan, Feb, Nov-Dec* 6-8pm Tue-Fri; 10am-noon, 2-8pm Sat, Sun. *Mar, Oct* 7-9pm Tue-Fri; 10am-noon, 2-6pm, 7-9pm Sat, Sun. *Apr-Aug* 2-7pm, 9-11pm Tue-Fri; 10am-noon, 2-7pm, 9-11pm Sat, Sun. *Sept* 2-6pm, 8-10pm Tue-Fri; 10am-noon, 2-6pm, 8-10pm Sat, Sun. **Admission** 40 Kč, 30 Kč reductions; free under-3s. **Map** p58 C5 ㉟

If you can ever get the inconvenient hours right, Prague's observatory offers more rewards than the chance to try its double Zeiss astrograph lens. It's part of a proud tradition of historical astronomical connections. Both the haughty Dane Tycho Brahe and his protégé Johannes Kepler resided in the city. The duo features in the observatory's stellar displays (some in English). Equipped with a 40-centimetre Meade mirror scope since 1999, the facility offers glimpses of sunspots and solar flares during the day and panoramas of the planets, moon and nebulae on clear nights.

Sternberg Palace

Šternberský palác

Hradčanské náměstí 15 (233 090 570/www.ngprague.cz). Metro Malostranská, then tram 22. **Open** 10am-6pm Tue-Sun. **Admission** 150 Kč; 150 Kč family; free under-10s. No credit cards. **Map** p58 C2 ㊱

Strahov Library

Enlightened aristocrats trying to rouse Prague from provincial stupor founded the Sternberg Gallery here in the 1790s. The palace, which stands just outside the gates of Prague Castle, houses the National Gallery's European old masters. Although it is not a large or well-balanced collection, especially since some of its most famous works were returned to their pre-war owners, some outstanding paintings remain, including a brilliant Frans Hals portrait and Dürer's *Feast of the Rosary*. All in a setting that looks newly redone, although renovations were completed several years ago. There is now space for more paintings from the repositories, and improved ceiling frescoes that had long been covered up.

Strahov Library

Strahovské nádvoří 1 (233 107 749/ www.strahovskyklaster.cz). Metro Malostranská, then tram 22. **Open** 9am-noon, 1-5pm daily. **Admission** 80 Kč. No credit cards. **Map** p58 A3/A4 ⍟
The highlight of the monastery complex is its superb libraries, which appear on posters in universities all around the world. Within the frescoed Theological and Philosophical Halls alone are 130,000 volumes. There are a further 700,000 books in storage and together they form the most important collection in Bohemia. However, visitors are only allowed access during guided tours. When Joseph II effected a clampdown on religious institutions in 1782, the Premonstratensians managed to outwit him by masquerading as an educational foundation, and their collection was swelled by the libraries. The monks' taste ranged far beyond the standard ecclesiastical tracts, including such highlights as the oldest extant copy of *The Calendar of Minutae* or *Selected Times for Bloodletting*. Nor did they merely confine themselves to books: the 200-year-old curiosity cabinets house a collection of deep-sea monsters that any landlocked country would be proud to possess. Digital scans of rare, ancient books, which are in danger of disintegrating, can be found online at the website www.manuscriptorium.com.

Strahov Monastery

Strahovský klášter
Strahovské nádvoří 1 (233 107 705/
www.strahovskyklaster.cz).
Metro Malostranská, then tram 22.
Open 9am-noon, 1-5pm daily.
Admission 80 Kč. No credit cards.
Map p58 A3/A4 ⬤38

One of the world's oldest abbeys of Premonstratensian monks, founded in 1143. Since 1990, several have returned to reclaim the buildings nationalised by the communists after 1948. They can sometimes be seen from Úvoz street, walking laps around green fields and meditating, and services are once again being held in the Church of Our Lady, which is based on a 12th-century basilica ground plan. The Strahov gallery contains 1,500 artworks that have also been returned from the state. One interesting access route to the monastery is via the stairs at Pohořelec No.8, the westernmost square in the Hradčany district.

Eating & drinking

U Černého vola

Loretánské náměstí 1 (220 513 481).
Tram 22. **Open** 9am-10pm daily.
No credit cards. **Pub**. **Map** p58 A3 ⬤39

Likely the cosiest and least pretentious pub in the district, the 'Black Ox' is not quite as ancient as it appears. The murals make it look like it's been here forever, but in fact it was built after World War II. Its superb location, above the Castle, made it a prime target for redevelopment in the post-1989 building frenzy, but the rugged regulars bought it to ensure that local bearded artisans would have at least one place where they could afford to drink. The Kozel beer is brewed to perfection and although the snacks are pretty basic they do their job of lining the stomach.

U Císařů

Loretánská 5 (220 518 484/www.
ucisaru.cz). Metro Malostranská, then
tram 22. **Open** 9am-1am daily. **$$**.
Czech. **Map** p58 B2 ⬤40

A long-favoured spot for traditional Czech food within a short walk of Prague Castle, 'At the Emperor's' has platters of smoked meats, hearty roasts, decadent desserts, classy service and ye olde Bohemian interiors, along with a good wine cellar and street tables.

Malý Buddha

Úvoz 46 (220 513 894/ www.
malybuddha.cz). Tram 8, 22. **Open**
noon-10.30pm Tue-Sun. **$**. No credit
cards. **Asian**. **Map** p58 A3 ⬤41

The Little Buddha is a teahouse with a difference: great vegetarian spring rolls and noodle dishes accompany dozens of teas brewed by the laid-back owner. Sit in candlelight and inhale incense with your eggrolls.

Nebozízek

Petřín hill, Petřínské sady 411
(257 315 329/www.nebozizek.cz). Metro
Malostranská. **Open** 11am-11pm daily.
$$. **Czech**. **Map** p58 C5 ⬤42

Situated next to the middle stop of the funicular railway that runs up Petřín hill, this touristy restaurant can be worthwhile on a fine day for its patio view of Old Town across the river. Prices for traditional Czech grub are elevated with the view, but manageable.

Petřínské Terasy

Seminářská zahrada 13
(257 320 688/www.petrinsketerasy.cz).
Metro Malostranská. **Open** noon-11pm
Mon-Fri; 11am-11pm Sat, Sun. **$$**.
Czech. **Map** p58 C4 ⬤43

On days with clear visibility and when you're faint with hunger or thirst from a hike on the Petřín hill, the Petřín Terraces can make for a handy, if pricey option. Exquisite views of Prague Castle and the city go along with the Krušovice beer and indifferent service.

Restaurant Hradčany

Keplerova 6 (224 302 430/www.
hotel-savoy.cz). Tram 22. **Open** 6.30am-
10.30am, noon-3pm, 6-11pm daily. **$$$**.
Continental. **Map** p58 A3 ⬤44

One vine day

Enjoy a glorious idyll on the terrace of the Villa Richter.

Diners at the most ambitious new gourmet venture in the shadow of Prague Castle, **Villa Richter** (p74), are bound to notice the quality of wines. The local white vintages are the ideal complement to a lazy afternoon on the terrace, which lays claim to the finest view of Malá Strana in the city. Visitors may be less aware that they're drinking in history. Wine didn't fare well under the pre-1989 regime, having been viewed as the libation of the petit bourgeoisie, while beer was thought to be working-class and won heavy state subsidies.

So, vintners have had to rebuild traditions, a badly neglected infrastructure, professional practices at vineyards and an audience that can appreciate all of these. Villa Richter signifies the triumph of Czech wine. Built into a hill on the former St Wenceslas Vineyard, whose origins lie in the 10th century, the villa has revived what was, according to legend, one of the oldest wine growing terraces in Bohemia. The vines are believed to have been cultivated by St Wenceslas himself and the vineyard reopened to Prague Castle visitors in 2008 to celebrate the 1100th birthday of the great saint.

The site fosters 2,500 vines of Pinot Noir and Rhine Riesling, the former a tribute to Charles IV, who was the first to bring the variety to the Czech lands from France. The Riesling was a traditional variety for this spot. You can stroll among the vines, looking at displays on grape varieties undergoing their Bohemian renaissance, thanks to support from the Winery Fund of the Czech Republic. The villa itself is a restored 1836 summerhouse that rises harmoniously from the vineyard. Its crystal chandeliers, muted floral-brocade interiors and top-flight cuisine set the bar for this side of the Vltava. Chef Petr Hajný oversees the kitchens, which roll out Italian, Czech and Central European classics, paired with one of the thousands of vintages stored in the cellars. Somewhere up above, St Wenceslas is smiling.

The classy gourmet dining room at the Savoy has won several awards of late, with its mix of Czech classics and hip conceptions of Euro cuisine, from lamb shank with veal tarragon sauce to smoked trout with egg gnocchi. Service is of a high calibre and hotel guests get three courses for 38 euros.

U Ševce Matouše

Loretánské náměstí 4 (220 514 536/ www.usevcematouse.cz). Tram 22.
Open 11am-11pm daily. **$.**
Czech. Map p58 A3 ⑮

The classic steakhouse, Czech style, with done-to-order tenderloins in traditional sauces such as green peppercorn or mushroom. A short walk east of Prague Castle, it's housed in a cosy former shoemaker's workshop, where you could once get your boots repaired while lunching.

Villa Richter

NEW *Starých zámeckých schodech (257 219 079/www.villarichter.cz). Tram 22.*
Open 10am-11pm daily. **$$$.**
Continental. Map p59 E1 ⑯

This three-in-one shrine to Czech and Italian wine cellar, stocked with hundreds of select Mediterranean vintages and the best Moravian wines. Service is crisp, views astounding, the summer terrace is a fine idyll and the villa itself is a crystal-chandeliered shrine to old Prague living large. Surely the place to splurge. See box p73.

U Zavěšenýho kafe

Úvoz 6 (605 294 595/www.uzavesenyho kafe.com). Metro Malostranská.
Open 11am-midnight daily.
Pub. Map p58 B3 ⑰

With a strong local following, the 'Hanging Coffee Cup' is a kind of neighbourhood gathering point. It's an affordable, mellow place with plank flooring, trad grub (like onion soup and duck with sauerkraut) and a long association with local artists and intellectuals. The name derives from an old tradition of paying for a cup of coffee for someone who may arrive later without funds.

Arts & leisure

Galerie Gambra

Černínská 5 (220 514 527). Metro Malostranská, then tram 22.
Open *Mar-Oct* noon-5.30pm Wed-Sun. *Nov-Feb* noon-5.30pm Sat, Sun.
Map p58 A2 ⑱

A funky gallery that specialises in exhibiting surrealist art, Gambra happens to be owned by the world-renowned animator Jan Švankmajer, who lives in the attached house. The building forms part of the Nový Svět enclave, a collection of brightly coloured cottages restored during the 18th and 19th centuries – which is all that remains of Hradčany's medieval slums. The rest were destroyed in the great fire of 1541.

Klub 007

Vaníčkova 5, Koleje ČVUT dorm 7 (775 260 071/www.klub007strahov.cz). Metro Dejvická, then bus 143, 149, 217. **Open** 7pm-midnight Mon-Sat.
Map p58 A5 ⑲

This is student heaven – or, perhaps, hell. If you can find this place in the concrete basement of dorm 007, you'll never believe that it could be a must-see on any international ska tour of Central Europe. However it certainly is a big attraction, as you'll discover when the bands start up. This place has an authentic youth vibe.

Stadium Strahov

Diskařská 100, Břevnov (233 014 111). Metro Karlovo náměstí, then bus 176 or tram 22 to Újezd, then funicular.
Map p58 A5 ⑳

The biggest concert venue in town, Stadium Strahov is a concrete monstrosity that was constructed before World War II, without much to offer besides its ability to accommodate epic rock shows – which, these days, are booked more rarely than ever. To reach the venue you have to go on a bit of a trek; a special bus service is organised for larger gigs.

Wallenstein Palace p83

Malá Strana & Smíchov

Malá Strana

Blissfully lacking arterial roads, the city's left bank district remains permanently sleepy. In this district, you can stroll among fine, undeveloped streets and arcades, and visit crumbling palaces, formal gardens and classic pubs, while Prague Castle looms as you gaze up to the hilltop.

The enchanting backwater of Malá Strana has more than idylls to offer: the area's respected galleries, restaurants, music and clubbing options are as good as any in the city of Prague. An array of pretty Baroque churches complements this historic warren for artists, craftsmen working for the Castle and royal retainers, in which student-filled bars and cafés continue to exude a vibrant bohemian spirit.

Malá Strana (or the Lesser Quarter) lies between the Vltava river and Prague Castle, skirting the hill that makes up Hradčany. Its backstreets reward exploring, with old-world embassies, rustic old pubs (like Baráčnická rychta) and ornate doors and chapels (St Nicholas, Our Lady Victorious and Our Lady Beneath the Chain); one-time playgrounds of aristocrats, such as the formal **Wallenstein Gardens** and Vrtba Gardens, hold particular appeal. Founded by the Přemyslid Otakar II in 1287 – when he invited merchants from Germany to set up shop on the land beneath the Castle walls – the area was transformed into a sparkling Baroque district by the wealthy Catholic elite, who won huge parcels of land in the property redistribution that followed the Thirty Years' War.

Kitschy Mostecká Street leads from the **Charles Bridge** into the centre of the district, following the **Royal Route** – the path taken by the Bohemian kings to their coronation. **Malostranské náměstí** is a lively square edged by large Baroque palaces and Renaissance gabled townhouses perched on top of Gothic arcades, which inspired the stories of beloved Bohemian writer Jan Neruda, author of Prague Tales. The square has been quieter in recent years, but the venerated music club Malostranská Beseda, at No.21, is due to reopen after extensive renovations, which will quicken the pace. Local pubs too are as lively as ever, with **U Malého Glena** and **Popocafepetl** consistently packing 'em in; gourmands, meanwhile, gather at **U Malé Velryby** and increasingly swanky restaurants such as **Pálffy Palác** and **U Patrona**.

The Smíchov district, which lies upstream to the south, is where Prague shows its new face to the world; the place is full of trendy bars and shops and the style chasers that go with them.

Sights & museums

American Embassy

Tržiště 15. Metro Malostranská.
Map p77 A3 ❶
Located just off the district's main square, Malostranské náměstí, the US embassy resides in the 17th-century Schönborn Palace (Schönbornský palác), designed by one of Prague's many Baroque masters of Italian descent, Giovanni Santini-Aichel (who was actually born in Prague). Although most visitors never get to see them, its chambers have been lovingly restored and are open to the public for cultural events.

British Embassy

Thunovská 14. Metro Malostranská.
Map p77 A2 ❷

Once the target of communist surveillance teams from Prague Castle just above it, the British Embassy is situated at the end of an alleyway, just north of the main drag of Nerudova. It was known as 'Czechers' among the diplomatic set, but is now known mostly for its Baroque beauty. Leading up from here are the New Castle Steps (Nové zámecké schody), one of the most peaceful (and least strenuous) routes up to the Castle and a star location in the film Amadeus.

Chapel to St John of the Laundry

Kaple sv. Jana Na Prádle
South end of Kampa Park. Metro Malostranská. **Map** p77 B5 ❸
Washerwomen once rinsed shirts on the banks of the Čertovka. Today, it's taken up by snoozing office workers and bongo-beating hippies. The river and bridge views are as romantic as they come, while the chestnut trees make shady spots for reading and recharging. In spring, the park is filled with pink blossom. The restaurant Kampa Park (p86) stands at the north end of the island, where the Čertovka runs back into the river by Charles Bridge, offering the finest waterfront view of any dining establishment in town.

Church of Our Lady Beneath the Chain

Kostel Panny Marie pod Řetězem
Maltézské náměstí. Metro Malostranská. **Map** p77 B3 ❹
Seemingly a jumble of incongruous parts, this church features Gothic parts built by a military-religious order to guard the Judith Bridge, which spanned the Vltava before the Charles Bridge, close to where the Charles sits today. Its two heavy towers, standing at the entrance, contain some of the most prized apartments in Prague. The Hussite wars barred the construction of the church and it was never finished.

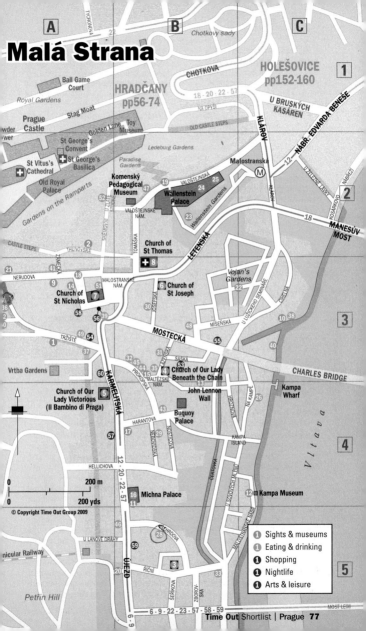

Malá Strana

A **B** **C**

Chotkovy sady

1

HOLEŠOVICE
pp152-160

CHOTKOVA

HRADČANY
pp56-74

Ball Game
Court

Royal Gardens

Stag Moat

U BRUSKÝCH
KASÁREN

NÁBŘ. EDVARDA BENEŠE

Prague
Castle

Golden Lane

Toy
Museum

St George's
Convent

St George's
Basilica

Ledeburg Gardens

Malostranska **M**

2

St Vitus's
Cathedral

Old Royal
Palace

Paradise
Gardens

Komenský
Pedagogical
Museum

19

VALDŠTEJNSKA

25

24

Wallenstein
Palace

18

MÁNESŮV
MOST

Gardens on the Ramparts

VALDŠTEJNSKÉ
NÁM.

23

Wallenstein Gardens

CASTLE STEPS

2

THUNOVSKA

Church of
St Thomas

Church of
St Thomas

8

LETENSKÁ

21

ZÁMECKÁ

41

9

14

18

51

Church of
St Nicholas

7

58

MALOSTRANSKÉ
NÁM.

6

Church of
St Joseph

Vojan's
Gardens

22

10 **38**

3

56

JOSEFSKÁ

30

48

MÍŠEŇSKÁ

40

TRŽIŠTĚ

1

49 **54**

37

MOSTECKÁ

55

31

SASKÁ

CHARLES BRIDGE

Vrtba Gardens

45

42

60

KARMELITSKÁ

44

15

35

PROKOPSKÁ

MALTÉZSKÉ
NÁM.

4

Church of Our Lady
Beneath the Chain

John Lennon
Wall

26

Kampa
Wharf

Church of Our
Lady Victorious
(Il Bambino di Praga)

5

43

17

HARANTOVA

29

NEBOVIDSKÁ

Buquoy
Palace

KAMPA
ISLAND

Vltava

HELLICHOVA

57

12 · 20 · 22 · 57

4

0   200 m

0   200 yds

© Copyright Time Out Group 2009

16

11

Michna Palace

12 Kampa Museum

46

U LANOVÉ DRÁHY

59

28

ŠEŘÍKOVA

ÚJEZD

nicular Railway

ŘÍČNÍ

3

5

Petřín Hill

6 · 9 · 22 · 23 · 57 · 58 · 59

6 · 9

MOST LEG

1 Sights & museums
1 Eating & drinking
1 Shopping
1 Nightlife
1 Arts & leisure

Church of Our Lady Victorious

Kostel Panny Marie Vítězné
Karmelitská 9 (257 533 646).
Tram 12, 22. **Open** 8.30am-7pm
Mon-Sat; 8.30am-8pm Sun. **Admission** free. **Map** p77 A4 ❺

The first Baroque church in Prague (built 1611 to 1613) belongs to the Barefooted Carmelites, an order that cares for the doll-like, miracle-working 400-year-old Bambino di Praga. The effigy, brought from Spain to Prague in the 17th century, is said to have protected nuns from the plague. A wardrobe of more than 60 outfits has been changed by the Order of English Virgins at sunrise on selected days for around 200 years.

Church of St Joseph

Kostel sv. Josefa
Josefská and Letenská streets.
Metro Malostranská. **Map** p77 B3 ❻
Though seldom visited by anyone but architecture lovers, this Baroque gem, set back from the road, features delicate lines created by Jean-Baptiste Mathey. Since 1989, it has been returned to the much-diminished Order of English Virgins, who were also one-time owners of the tranquil Vojan's Gardens (Vojanovy sady) nearby.

Church of St Nicholas

Kostel sv. Mikuláše
Malostranské náměstí (257 534 215).
Metro Malostranská. **Open** *Nov-Feb* 9am-4pm daily. *Mar-Oct* 9am-5pm daily. **Admission** 60 Kč; 30 Kč reductions. **Map** p77 A3 ❼
The star attraction for fans of Baroque architecture, this church dome and tower, visible from the Charles Bridge, form the signature image of Malá Strana. They were created to impress, part of the Catholic Church's campaign to fuel the Counter-Reformation. The rich façade by Christoph Dientzenhofer, completed about 1710, conceals an interior and dome by his son Kilián Ignaz, which is dedicated to High Baroque at

its most flamboyantly camp – bathroom-suite pinks and greens, swooping golden cherubs, swirling gowns and dramatic gestures; there's even a figure coyly proffering a pair of handcuffs.

Church of St Thomas

Kostel sv. Tomáše
Josefská 8 (257 532 675). Metro Malostranská. **Open** 11am-1pm Mon-Sat; 9am-noon, 4.30-5.30pm Sun. **Admission** free. **Map** p77 B3 ❽
On a backstreet east of Malostranské náměstí stands the Church of St Thomas. Its rich Baroque façade, tucked into a narrow lane, is easy to miss. Based on a Gothic ground plan, the church was rebuilt by Kilián Ignaz Dientzenhofer for the Augustinian monks. St Boniface, a fully dressed skeleton, occupies a glass case in the nave. Rubens painted the altarpiece (which is now a copy), named the *Martyrdom of St Thomas*.

Galerie Montanelli

Nerudova 13 (257 531 220/ www.galeriemontanelli.com).
Metro Malostranská. **Open** noon-6pm Mon-Fri. **Admission** free. **Map** p77 A3 ❾
At press time, this respected gallery was in the process of being converted and expanded into a museum, slated to open within the year. The work will continue fostering multiple generations of contemporary artists, a refreshing find on the main pedestrian route to the Castle. It represents some of the established firmament, such as Jiří and Běla Kolář, but bolsters the younger generation with group shows. Opened in 2003, it co-operates with institutions in Berlin and Frankfurt to reach wider audiences abroad.

Havel Library

NEW Knihova Václava Havla
Hergetova Cihelna, Cihelná 2b (222 220 112/www.vaclavhavel-knihovna.org). Metro Malostranská.
Open 10am-6pm Tue-Sun. **Admission** 60 Kč; 50 Kč reductions. **Map** p77 C3 ❿

The history man

The Havel Library showcases Václav's unique archive.

The Czech presidency of Václav Havel, from 1990 to 2003, signified a great deal more than the arrival of the first democratically elected holder of that office since 1948. For such a small country to have as its head of state a figure of global importance to freedom of expression is unusual. That this office should also be held by a witty, irascible chain smoker with a penchant for ironic stage plays and eloquent essays on human rights is truly remarkable.

Those prizes have not been lost on Czechs, even though many, as in emerging markets across the world, seem more focused on advancing their career than on debating ideals in coffeehouses as Havel and his friends did before 1989, at substantial personal risk.

Some of his best writings, such as *Living in Truth* and *Letters to Olga*, grew from his five years in prison, where communist officials tried to silence the man they deemed the country's chief troublemaker. But, as Havel discusses in his more recent and happier release, *To the Castle and Back*, even while president he kept up his writing, using the experience to develop his philosophy of good governance and citizenship.

His New Year's Day radio addresses, an old custom in the Czech lands, were part of a series of essays that Havel hoped would be published together. His letters, drafts of speeches and film footage, as in the documentary *Citizen Havel*, record the making of history as citizens of the former Eastern bloc learned to rebuild the democratic foundation of Bohemia.

The display of these records at the Havel Library on Malá Strana's river bank, assembled mainly from the ex-president's private collection to foster study about civil society, was designed by longtime Havel supporter Bořek Šípek. A replica of the Hradeček, the president's office in Prague Castle, helps to envision how the course of a dynamic democracy in was guided by a remarkable man.

Kampa Museum

In this archive (see box p79), the former playwright president's letters, dramas, effects and documentation go behind the scenes of his administration, from 1990 to 2003. It offers a glimpse into the life of one of the most inspiring leaders of the late 20th century. The collection, part of a long-term show run by Havel's library headquarters at Voršilská 10, is thoughtful and insightful. The ex-president's books are here in English as well.

Josef Sudek Atelier

Újezd 30 (251 510 760/www.sudek-atelier.cz). Metro Malostranská. **Open** noon-6pm Tue-Sun. **Admission** 10 Kč; 5 Kč students. **Map** p77 B4 ⑪

Still imbued with the creative spirit of its former resident, master of Czech photography Josef Sudek, this humble former studio is accessible through a residential building courtyard. Select shows of quality art photography are held in the intimate exhibition room, while Sudek memorabilia is on display in a separate small room.

Kampa Museum

U Sovových mlynů 2 (257 286 147/ www.museumkampa.cz). Metro Malostranská. **Open** 10am-6pm daily. **Admission** free. **Map** p77 C4 ⑫

One of the most respected and accessible art refuges in this district, the Kampa Museum has an enviable location on the waterfront of the city's loveliest island. Its impressive modern art collection was amassed over decades by Jan Mládek – an international financier and former Prague student – and his wife, art patron Meda Mládek, both of whom lived in exile before the Velvet Revolution. Sculpture by Otto Gutfreund and work by František Kupka sits alongside refreshing art from abroad. There is a gorgeous terrace café on the Vltava.

Lennon Wall

Maltézské náměstí. Metro Malostranská. **Map** p77 B4 ⑬

At the south end of the square, this graffiti-covered wall was a place of pilgrimage during the 1980s for the city's hippies, who dedicated it to their idol and scrawled messages of love, peace and rock 'n' roll across it. The secret police painted over the graffiti, only to have John's smiling face reappear a few days later. This continued until 1989 when the wall was returned to the Knights of Malta as part of a restitution package. The John Lennon Peace Club still encourages modest graffiti.

Lichtenstein Palace

Lichtenštejnský palác
Malostranské náměstí 13 (257 534 205). Metro Malostranská. **Open** 10am-6pm daily; 10am-7.30pm on concert days. *Concerts* 7.30pm. **Tickets** 60-150 Kč. **Map** p77 A3 ⑭

The elegant, well-situated Lichtenstein Palace is the home of the Czech Academy of Music. Regular concerts are given in the Gallery and in the Martinů Hall, although the real star is the summer open-air series of popular operas that take place in the courtyard.

Maltese Square

Maltézské náměstí. Metro Malostranská. **Map** p77 B3 ⑮

The Knights of Malta lived in this quiet square, now lined with mellow cafés and pubs, for centuries until the communists dissolved the order. However, the order regained great swathes of property under the restitution laws. Around the corner, on Saska ulička, are several pretty flower shops and boutiques for clubbing gear.

Michna Palace

Michnův palác
Újezd 40. Metro Malostranská. **Map** p77 B4 ⑯

Built in 1640-50, this fine Baroque pile was intended to rival the Wallenstein Palace (p83), itself built to compete with Prague Castle (p61). With these gargantuan ambitions, Francesco Caratti took Versailles as his model in designing the Michna gardens. Today, they contain little but tennis courts.

PRAGUE BY AREA

Museum of Music

Karmelitská 2 (257 257 777/
www.nm.cz). Metro Malostranská.
Open 10am-6pm Mon, Wed-Sun.
Admission 100 Kč; 50 Kč reductions.
Map p77 B4 ⑰

With proud displays of some of the 250,000 artefacts it holds, many having been lovingly restored after the damages of the 2002 Vltava floods, this museum forms a genuine treasury in a music-infused city. It offers the creds of the National Museum, plus an impressive palace space in which to encounter an incredible collection of instruments, along with exhibits on the greats, from 1920s jazz star Jaroslav Ježek to the *dudy*, or medieval bagpipes.

Nerudova street

Nerudova. Metro Malostranská.
Map p77 A3 ⑱

The prime walking lane heading up to Prague Castle is a fine place to begin deciphering the ornate signs that decorate many of the city's houses: the Three Fiddles at No.12, for example, or the Devil at No.4. This practice of distinguishing houses continued up until 1770, when that relentless modernist Joseph II spoiled all the fun by introducing numbered addresses. The street is crowded with restaurants, cafés and shops, which are aimed at the ceaseless flow of tourists to and from the Castle.

Paradise Gardens

Rajská zahrada
Valdštejnské náměstí. Metro
Malostranská. **Open** *Apr-Oct*
10am-6pm daily. **Admission** 60 Kč;
50 Kč reductions. **Map** p77 B2 ⑲

An impressive collection of greenery, terraces and Baroque arches, which make for one of the most unusual ways to access Prague Castle above. Some will surely find it easier to start from Prague Castle (descend the Bull stairs from the third courtyard) and descend to Malá Strana.

Petřín hill

Petřínské sady
Karmelitska 1. Metro Malostranská.
Map p77 B5 ⑳

The highest, greenest and most peaceful of Prague's seven hills, this area is the largest expanse of sylvan in the centre – a favourite spot for tobogganing children in the winter and canoodling couples in the summer. The hill also features many of the city's Gothic and Romanesque buildings. The southern edge of the hill is traversed by the so-called Hunger Wall (Hladová zeď), an eight-metre-high stone fortification, commissioned by Charles IV in 1362 in order to provide work for the city's poor.

Thun-Hohenstein Palace

Thun-Hohenštejnský palác
Nerudova 20. Metro Malostranská.
Map p77 A3 ㉑

Now the Italian embassy, this precious pile, built by Giovanni Santini-Aichel in 1726, is distinguished by the contorted eagles holding up the portal, the heraldic emblem of the Kolowrats for whom the palace was built. The Italians were trumped for a while by the Romanians, who used to inhabit the even more glorious Morzin Palace (Morzinský palác) at No.5, also the work of Santini-Aichel.

Vojanovy sady

U Lužického semináře (no phone).
Metro Malostranská. **Open** *Oct-Apr*
8am-5pm daily. *Mar-Sept* 8am-7pm
daily. **Map** p77 B3/C3 ㉒

Not as trafficked nor as carefully groomed and ordered as the district's nearby Wallenstein Gardens, this walled sanctuary of greenery and peacocks is a local secret love and great for a relaxing stroll.

Wallenstein Gardens

Letenská, towards Malostranská
metro station. Metro Malostranská.
Map p77 B2 ㉓

A door in a wall leads to the best-kept formal gardens in the city. In the early

Wallenstein Gardens

17th century they belonged, along with the adjoining Wallenstein Palace, to General Albrecht von Wallenstein, who was commander of the Catholic armies in the Thirty Years' War and known to be a formidable property speculator. Free concerts are often held here in summer.

Wallenstein Palace

Valdštejnský palác
Valdštejnská 3 (257 071 111/www. senat.cz). Metro Malostranská. **Open** 10am-6pm Tue-Sun. **Admission** 100 Kč; 50 Kč reductions. **Map** p77 B2 ㉔
The palace (which contains the Czech Parliament) is a suitably enormous, opulent pile, designed by Milanese architect Andrea Spezza in the latter half of the 1620s. It once housed a permanent staff of 700 servants, along with 1,000 horses. A little-noticed entrance to the palace gardens, which lies just to the right of the Malostranská metro station exit, provides a wonderful way of cutting

through the district and leaving the droves of tourists behind.

Wallenstein Riding School

Valdštejnská jízdárna
Valdštejnská 3 (257 073 136/ www.ngprague.cz). Metro Malostranská. **Open** 10am-6pm Tue-Sun. **Admission** 100 Kč; 50 Kč reductions. **Map** p77 B2 ㉕
Part of the Wallenstein Palace complex and run by the National Gallery, this space holds popular shows, with topics ranging from the Czech National Revival (symbolist Max Švabinský is beloved) to 20th-century Chinese masters.

Eating & drinking

At the Charles Bridge

Na Kampě 15 (257 531 430). Metro Malostranská. **Open** 11am-midnight daily. **Pub**. **Map** p77 C4 ㉖
An unpretentious pub-restaurant serving potato thyme soup and topinka (fried toast with raw garlic) close to the

Paradise Gardens p82

Charles Bridge. Swing around the corner to the pub with the mustard walls or hit the scattering of outdoor tables on the edge of Kampa Park.

Baráčnická rychta

Tržiště 23 (257 532 461/www. baracnickarychta.cz). Metro Malostranská. **Open** 11am-11pm Mon-Sat; 11am-9pm Sun. **$**. **Czech**. **Map** p77 A3 ㉗
Incredibly enough, this old-time pub still stands, just downhill from Prague Castle. This former hall of barons and landlords has made only grudging nods to the present, with designer lamps illuminating its heavy, communal tables and dark wood interiors. Like something out of Jan Neruda's *Prague Tales*.

Bar Bar

Všehrdova 17 (257 312 246/www. bar-bar.cz). Tram 12, 22. **Open** noon-midnight Mon-Thur, Sun; noon-2am Fri, Sat. **$**. **French**. **Map** p77 B5 ㉘

On a curving backstreet near Kampa Island, Bar Bar has been a local secret for years. The open sandwiches, salads and grill dishes will pass muster, whereas the savoury crêpes are real highlights. It also serves dessert-style pancakes with lemon and sugar, priced very reasonably. It is run by a group of artists and animators, and the waiters are cool and flexible should you have any special requests.

Barego

Nebovidská 19 (233 088 777/ www.mandarinoriental.com/prague). Metro Malostranská. **Open** 10am-3am daily. **Bar**. **Map** p77 B4 ㉙
The epitome of the smart cocktail scene in Malá Strana, the Mandarin Oriental's gorgeous little design bar is a great place in which to witness the city's new chic ethic. The Monastery Smoky Martini, the house special, goes well with the atmosphere, as the international elite meet to trade notes.

Blue Light

Josefská 1 (257 533 126/
www.bluelightbar.cz). Metro
Malostranská. **Open** 6pm-3am daily.
Bar. Map p77 B3 ⑳

A pleasant, dark, jumble of a bar that attracts local cognoscenti, who gather here for cocktails under the jazz posters that cover the dilapidated walls. By day, Blue Light is a good spot to sit with a friend, especially when there's room at the bar. At night it becomes more rowdy and conversation gets wellnigh impossible, but the vibe is certainly infectious. Good selection of malt whiskies.

Bohemia Bagel

Lázeňská 19 (257 218 192/
www.bohemiabagel.cz). Metro
Malostranská. **Open** 7.30am-7pm
daily. **Café. Map** p77 B3 ㉛

With an expanded menu, this American-owned chain continues to grow. After bringing the first true bagel café to post-1989 Prague, it moved on to free coffee refills, fresh muffins, breakfast bagels and bagel sandwiches. For innovative, good-value dinner specials, sample the Holešovice branch (p153).

Café El Centro

Maltézské náměstí 9 (257 533 343/
www.elcentro.cz). Metro Malostranská.
Open noon-midnight daily. **$$.**
Spanish. Map p77 B3 ㉜

This easily overlooked Malá Strana bar, just a block off the main square, specialises in mambo soundtracks and tropical cocktails. Although paella is a highlight of the menu, it's primarily a bar for daiquiri-lovers. The postage-stamp patio at the rear is a boon.

C'est la Vie

Říční 1 (721 158 403/www.cestlavie.cz).
Tram 12, 22. **Open** *Apr-Dec* 11.30am-
1am daily. *Jan-Mar* 6pm-1am Mon-Fri;
11.30am-1am Sat, Sun. **$$. Central**
European/Italian. Map p77 B5 ㉝

Self-advertised as a 'trendy restaurant for those who want to be in', this improbably upmarket place is geared towards Czuppies, but it may be worth cutting through the cool attitude for a river embankment table, baked butterfish with mushroom risotto or filet mignon with a good cabernet. Service doesn't keep up with the ambitious menu.

Cowboys

Nerudova 40 (296 826 107/www.
kampagroup.com). Metro Malostranská.
Open noon-11pm daily. **$$.**
Americas. Map p77 A3 ㉞

Despite Stetsons, kinky leather vests and hottie servers, Cowboys is a lot classier than the restaurant that previously inhabited this labyrinth of brick cellars. For the location, service and T-bones, not to mention occasional live rock and folk, it offers incredible value, along with a terrace and great views of the city.

Cukrkávalimonáda

Lázeňská 7 (257 530 628). Metro
Malostranská. **Open** 9am-7pm
Mon-Sat; 9.30am-7pm Sun. **Café.**
Map p77 B3 ㉟

Best for salads, cakes and coffees, this calming, characterful caff just off the main drag from the Charles Bridge is situated on a lovely, quiet corner of Maltézské náměstí. The short list of wines and daily light lunch specials make for handy open-air refreshment in the summertime.

David

Tržiště 21 (257 533 109/
www.restaurant-david.cz). Metro
Malostranská. **Open** 11.30am-11pm
daily. **$$. Czech/Central European.**
Map p77 A3 ㊱

Another backstreet Malá Strana gem, David has a long history of serving quiet, excellent meals for patrons who eschew publicity. Definitive Bohemian classics like roast duck with red and white sauerkraut or rabbit fillet with spinach leaves and herb sauce. Booking is essential.

Gitanes

*Tržiště 7 (257 530 163). Metro
Malostranská.* **Open** noon-midnight
daily. **$**. **Balkan**. Map p77 A3 ③⑦

Offering a bracing taste of spice in a
traditional, safe, central European setting, this two-room place just off the
district's main square serves Balkan
favourites, such as sweetcorn *proja*
with cheese, stuffed peppers and
home-made bread with paprika milk-
fat spread, all accompanied by hearty
red wine. Warm service, gingham furnishings and doilies combine to give
you the feeling that you're visiting
your Balkan granny's house, only
with much cooler music.

Hergetova Cihelna

*Cihelná 2b (296 826 103/reservations
800 152 692/ www.kampagroup.com).
Metro Malostranská.* **Open** 11.30am-
1am daily. **$$**. **Americas/
International**. Map p77 C3 ③⑧

Impressive value and creative culinary
efforts, two signature qualities of
owner Nils Jebens, make this a hot
reservation, even in winter. Great
Belgian beers, killer casual chow and
knock-out riverside tables (complete
with blankets for when the weather
is chilly). Celebrities gather in the
upstairs bar. Also, try Jebens' A-list,
if less affordable, restaurant Kampa
Park next door.

Jo's Bar

*Malostranské náměstí 7 (257 530 162/
www.josbar.cz).* Metro Malostranská.
Open 11am-2am daily. **Bar**. Map
p77 A3 ③⑨

This street-level bar is an adjunct to
the rollicking downstairs Jo's Bar &
Garáž (p88). It was once renowned for
being every backpacker's first stop
in Prague and the source of nachos in
the Czech Republic, but founder Glen
Emery has since moved on, so now
Jo's Bar is under new ownership. It's
still a good place to meet fellow trav-
ellers, but lacks the sense of being in
the centre of things.

Kampa Park

*Na Kampě 8B (296 826 112/
www.kampagroup.com). Metro
Malostranská.* **Open** 11.30am-1am
daily; kitchen closes at 11pm. **$$**.
Central European/Seafood.
Map p77 C3 ④⓪

Gourmet seafood and the best tableside
views of the Charles Bridge have been
winning this place rave reviews from
heavy-hitter foreign critics for more than
a decade. Lobster tail or seared scallops
and capers make great starters, followed
by mains, from turbot and pumpkin
purée to wild mushroom risotto with garlic foam. A slick bar-room scene happens
inside, which draws presidents and
Hollywood heartthrobs. Its gorgeous
riverside terrace is open all year.

U Kocoura

*Nerudova 2 (257 530 107). Metro
Malostranská.* **Open** 11am-midnight
daily. **Pub**. Map p77 A3 ④①

With iconic status in the Prague pubbing world, this smoky, well-worn
place was briefly owned by the Friends
of Beer (a former political party that
has morphed into a civic association).
Although its manifesto is a bit vague,
the staff's ability to pull a good, cheap
pint is beyond question.

Latin Art Café

NEW *Jánský vršek 2 (774 343 441/
www.latinartcafe.com). Metro
Malostranská.* **Open** noon-midnight
daily. **Bar**. Map p77 A3 ④②

This backstreet hideout is a spicy
respite of salsa, bossa lounge and
Roma music, with live sets heating
things up on weekend nights, while
revellers enjoy the sangria, beer and
bar snacks. This café is genial, disor-
ganised and offers a complete break
from traditional Czech pubbing.

U Malé Velryby

*Maltézské náměstí 15 (257 214 703).
Metro Malostranská.* **Open** 11am-
midnight daily. **$$**. **Fusion**.
Map p77 B4 ④③

Owner Jason Le Gear oversees this exciting culinary addition to this district. The veteran chef of several hit Prague restaurants has launched his own operation, with delicate seafood and perfectly wrought steaks, lamb shanks and duck. Hearty home-made breads and tapas, and a great wine list is available in the open-kitchen dining room.

U Malířů

Maltézské náměstí 11 (257 530 000/ www.umaliru.cz). Tram 12, 22.
Open 11.30am-11pm daily. **$$$$.**
Central European. Map p77 B3 ㊹
No longer one of Prague's most expensive restaurants, a status it held for years among the business crowd, this quaint 16th-century house with original painted ceilings has shifted to Central European food but still ladles on the decadence in its conceptions of venison, duck and pork. A bottle will, of course, double the cost of a meal.

U Maltézských rytířů

Prokopská 10 (257 530 075/www. umaltezskychrytiru.cz). Tram 12, 22.
Open 1-11pm daily. **$$. Czech/
Central European**. Map p77 B3 ㊺
The Knights of Malta once offered this as an inn for the crusader monks. Now a restaurant has been set up in the candlelit, Gothic cellar with a noteworthy venison chateaubriand. Mrs Černíková does a nightly narration on the house's history, then harasses you to eat the incredible strudel. Booking essential.

Noi

NEW *Újezd 19 (257 311 411/ www.noirestaurant.cz). Metro Malostranská.* **Open** 9am-midnight daily. **Thai**. Map p77 b5 ㊻
A new star of Prague's growing Thai food scene, Noi presents a Zen-like space with a calming back patio. For the weight-conscious, there is a range of 600-calorie lunch specials. Combined with great service, authentically burning curries and Phad Khee Mao Kai, Noi adds up to a culinary signal fire.

Pálffy Palác

Valdštejnská 14 (257 530 522/ www.palffy.cz). Metro Malostranská.
Open 11am-11pm daily. **$$$.**
Continental. Map p77 B2 ㊼
Set in an atmospheric Baroque palace owned by the Ministry of Culture, Palác was founded by Prague clubbing mogul Roman Řezníček. This gem built its reputation in the '90s with expertly cooked rabbit in wine sauce and roebuck marinated in honey and juniper.

U Patrona

Dražického náměstí 4 (257 530 725/ www.upatrona.cz). Metro Malostranská.
Open 10am-1am daily. **$$. Czech**.
Map p77 B3 ㊽
An oasis of quality in an area that's dominated by naff souvenir shops, U Patrona serves delicate conceptions of Czech game classics at just a few tables. The country's first glass-walled kitchen lets the clientele know just what's going into the soup.

St Nicholas Café

Tržiště 10 (257 530 204). Metro Malostranská. **Open** noon-2am Mon-Thur, Sun; noon-3am Fri, Sat.
Café. Map p77 A3 ㊾
An atmospheric vaulted cellar decked with steamer trunk tables and painted arches, St Nick's has a mellow but lively crowd that gathers in the nooks for late evening conversation, keeping the pizza oven busy. Or give the brew a rest and take up a glass of Havana Club rum.

U Sedmi Švábů

Jánský vršek 14 (257 531 455/www. svabove.cz). Metro Malostranská.
Open 11am-11pm daily; kitchen closes at 10pm. **$$. Czech**. Map p77 A3 ㊿
Another cellar maze of vaulted, torch-lit rooms, this *krčma*, or Czech medieval tavern, has a name which translates as the Seven Swabians. It's a trippy if borderline-tacky experience, with occasional troubadours, traditional sweet honey liqueur and salty platters of pork knuckle.

Starbucks

Malostranské náměstí 28 (257 214 725/www.starbuckscoffee.cz). Metro Malostranská. **Open** 7am-9pm Mon-Fri; 8am-9pm Sat, Sun. **Café**. **Map** p77 A3 (51)

The first Czech beachhead of the global chain has proven a hit with tourists and locals seeking a branded coffee experience. Most others are staying well clear. Prime location for convenience, it must be said, and the success has resulted in several new branches around town.

U Zlaté studně

U Zlaté studně 166 (257 533 322/www.zlatastudna.cz). Metro Malostranská. **Open** 7am-11pm daily. **$$$**. **Continental**. **Map** p77 A2 (52)

In mild weather, a stop here is the perfect reward for tramping about the Prague Castle complex – you can walk right in from the castle gardens. Run by the management of the standard-setting Aria hotel, At the Golden Well offers spectacular views of the Malá Strana district below, sharp service and a menu that starts with duck livers marinated in armagnac.

PRAGUE BY AREA

Shopping

Květinařství U Červeného Lva

Saská ulička (604 855 286). Metro Malostranská. **Open** 9am-7pm Mon-Sat; 11am-7pm Sun. **Map** p77 B3 (53)

This crowded shop is fairly bursting with colour and variety. Bundles of dried flowers hang from the ceiling and plants, cut flowers and wreaths cover every available space.

Phase 2

Tržiště 8. (257 532 998). Metro Malostranská. **Open** 10am-6pm Mon-Fri; noon-6pm Sat. **Map** p77 A3 (54)

British expat Eki Ekanem's enchanting vintage clothes store shows a practiced hand at gold mining. Treasures from First Republic jewellery to fabulous clutches, wraps and dresses fill out the boutique. A good source for a wearable, one-of-a-kind Prague memento.

Truhlář Marionety

NEW *U Lužického semináře 5 (602 689 918). Metro Malostranská.* **Open** 10am-7pm Mon-Fri. **Map** p77 B3. (55)

There are no cheesy souvenir marionettes here: the puppets are works of art. More than 40 Czech designers contribute to the stock, and the shop could almost be a museum, given the level of craftsmanship on display. Choose from a range of small plaster replicas or pick up an original.

Nightlife

Jo's Bar & Garáž

Malostranské náměstí 7 (257 530 162). Metro Malostranská. **Open** 9pm-2am daily. **Map** p77 A3 (56)

Once a key venue on the expat clubbing scene, Jo's is pretty sleepy these days, but occasionally rouses itself for amusing parties for backpackers and students. It's another stone cellar club, two levels down from the once legendary bar that served the Czech Republic's first nachos.

Popocafepetl

Újezd 19 (602 277 226/www.popocafepetl.cz). Metro Malostranská. **Open** 4pm-2am daily. **Map** p77 A4 (57)

Student parties linked to Prague's Radio 1 pack the kids into this small, underground venue, but Popo (see box p89) also puts on hot live Latin and world music acts during the week and Sunday evenings, which keeps the overall mix interesting. Its compact size and highly eclectic line-up makes for a buzzy and bohemian atmosphere. It's all very informal, loud and tipsy. The entrance fee for an evening of authentic music is the cost of a couple of beers at many venues in the district. Not to be confused with the same company's bar/restaurant in Vinohrady.

Pop into Popo

For the hottest music, visit this buzzy student club.

It could be a sign of student commuting patterns, but on a website survey for Malá Strana's hottest rock and world music club, **Popocafepetl** (p88), some 1,846 patrons said they prefer to pile into the small, underground venue on Tuesdays, Wednesdays or Thursdays. A mere 1,576 viewed Friday as the big night at Popo, as it's known to the cognoscenti.

However, the thousands of students who pour out of Prague on weekends to visit their home towns and bring their mothers their dirty laundry are probably not the answer to this curious anomaly. More likely, the kids (and not just kids) are pouring into the bar that's named after a Mexican volcano to see great live acts, such as rockers Agáve 9, Insane Projekt, Snoo or Zrní.

There's also the Brit pop group Pure, which is usually a laugh, or Duende, which performs tuneful pop jazz. There's even Irish dance music, courtesy of Rí Rá.

All for an entrance fee of only 50-100 Kč, which would scarcely get you two beers at many other places in the district. All booked on weeknights at Popo.

So it's affordable, centrally located, small enough to feel buzzy and highly eclectic. This last feature perhaps doesn't strike regulars as anything odd – indeed most Prague clubs, whether they book live bands or opt for the DJ route, tend to mix up music rather than specialise in a certain genre. But few of the city's venues can boast this level of diversity, with real musicians for real people, and the regulars seem to know it.

On Sundays, when the student set rolls back into town, there are more hot live acts awaiting at this club under the moniker Gypsy Nights. Balkan, Roma or Latin music usually set the right tone for starting another week of work. Hot groups to look out for are Gitans; the entrance fee is 50 Kč, and girls get in free. No dummies, these Popo programmers!

Rubín

NEW *Malostranské náměstí 9 (776 483 912/www.astudiorubin.cz). Metro Malostranská.* **Open** 7pm-4am daily. **Map** p77 A3 ⑤⑧

Also known at A Studio Rubín, this funky theatre bar is open all night long and attracts a low-budget but high-living clientele of students and backstage types. Noisy, rollicking and dark, it's ever approachable – and if you arrive at theatre time, there's often an avant-garde drama or an indie rock band blasting in the back room theatre space.

Újezd

Újezd 18 (no phone). Metro Malostranská. **Open** *Bar* 11am-4am daily. *Café* 6pm-4am daily. **Map** p77 B5 ⑤⑨

In the form of its earlier incarnation as Borát, this three-storey madhouse attracted crowds of alternative music fans. These days, with a young Czech crowd in dreadlocks and a thick, smoky atmosphere, Újezd is home to some loud, badly amplified local rock music. The well-worn café upstairs is complete with battered wooden chairs and shouted conversation rises up from the bar below.

Arts & leisure

U Malého Glena

Karmelitská 23 (257 531 717/www. malyglen.cz). Metro Malostranská. **Open** 10am-2am daily. **Map** p77 A3 ⑥⓪

From looking at the rowdy pub at street level, you would never guess that the downstairs bar is one of Prague's top jazz holes. Tall mugs of Bernard beer are swung with gusto by expats and Czechs alike, the servers are certainly sexy and there are large tables and benches, which make the venue perfect for groups. Downstairs at U Malého Glena, you can listen to hot live jazz music and blues every night, until well after the clock has struck midnight.

Sights & museums

Futura

Holečkova 49 (251 511 804/ www.futuraprojekt.cz). Metro Anděl. **Open** 11am-6pm Wed-Sun. **Admission** free. **Map** p91 A2 ⑥①

Curating at this industrial space sets the standard for innovative work this side of the Vltava. The renovated building houses well-designed exhibition halls: white-cubes, cellar spaces, a labyrinthine series of nooks devoted to video works and a Projekt Room presenting experimental shows of work by up-and-coming artists. Recent exhibitions have included Chinese videographers and 'generational confrontational' avatars Ivan Kafka and Tomáš Svoboda.

Staropramen Brewery

Nádražní 84 (257 191 402/www. staropramen.cz). Metro Anděl. **Admission** 100 Kč (tours by appointment only). **Map** p91 B5 ⑥②

The biggest and baddest of Prague's breweries hasn't changed much in over a century and still fills tankers and tankards with the city's signature suds (though many insist they prefer Pilsner). The 60-minute tours (English available) are well worth booking and include a good history of Bohemian brewing. There's a restaurant on site too, with nicely done Bohemian classics – well beyond the usual pub grub.

Eating & drinking

El Barrio de Angel

Lidická 42 (725 535 555/www. elbarrio.cz). Metro Anděl. **Open** 11.30am-midnight Mon-Wed; 11.30am-1am Thu-Sat; noon-midnight Sun. **$$**. **Americas**. **Map** p91 B4 ⑥③

Descend into this hip, dark, wood-planked shrine to Argentine beef. Start with a chimichanga de pollo or a light rocket salad, but don't leave without

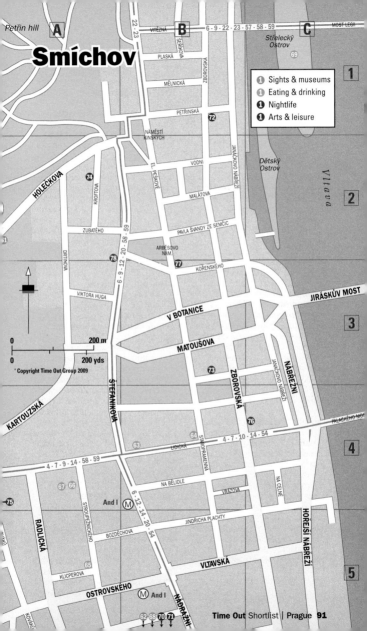

Smíchov

Petřín hill

Legend
- 1 Sights & museums
- 1 Eating & drinking
- 1 Nightlife
- 1 Arts & leisure

Copyright Time Out Group 2009

trying a burger or steak: finely scorched, tender as the night, and complemented by reasonably priced, full-bodied wines. Save room for the dulce de leche.

U Buldoka

Presslova 1 (257 329 154/www.u buldoka.cz). Metro Anděl. **Open** 8pm-4am daily. **Pub. Map** p91 B4 ㉔
At once old-world and modern, 'At the Bulldog' is one of the last classic pubs in the district. Well-poured Staropramen beer and excellent traditional grub go with an international sensibility, quick service and a cool dance club below deck; all-day specials of *halušky* (Slovak gnocchi with bacon) and *guláš* soup.

La Cambusa

Klicperova 2 (257 317 949/www.la cambusa.cz). Metro Anděl. **Open** 7pm-midnight Mon-Fri. **$$.** **Seafood. Map** p91 A5 ㉕
Prague's original premier seafood establishment, much-loved by ex-President Havel, has probably been surpassed for delicate sauces, decor and service but it's a proud neighbourhood institution that's still pretty good.

Jet Set

Radlická 1c (257 327 251/www. jetset.cz). Metro Anděl. **Open** 11am-2am daily. **Café. Map** p91 A4 ㉖
Dark, sleek and with a DJ booth as the tell-tale sign, this HQ of hipness for the neighbourhood features a decent, light Mediterranean bar food menu and good coffee. Cocktails are more iffy, as is conversation, unless you're happy to shout it out among your after-party cohorts.

Nagoya

Stroupežnického 23 (251 511 724/ www.nagoya.cz). Metro Anděl. **Open** 6-11pm Mon-Sat. **$$.** **Sushi. Map** p91 A4 ㉗
Part of the city's growing Japanese craze, Nagoya is a worthwhile addition

to the cuisine, though you'll still pay as much or more for such fare in Prague than in London or New York.

Potrefená Husa

Nádražní 84 (257 191 111/ www.potrefenahusaandel.cz). Metro Anděl. **Open** 11.30am-1am Mon-Thur, Sun; 11.30am-2am Fri, Sat. **$.** **Czech. Map** p91 B5 ㉘
This Staropramen-licensed restaurant chain, the Czech Republic's first, has built up a reputation for renewed classics such as hearty Bohemian soups, smoked meat dishes and a complement of modern salads and sides. Young, fast servers hustle your orders while the fashionable hang out at the bar, going in for newer Staropramen variations such as the foamy Velvet or the ruby-red Granát.

Střelecký ostrov

Střelecký ostrov 336 (224 934 028/ www.streleckyostrov.cz). Metro Národní třída, then tram 18. **Open** 11am-11pm daily. **$.** **Czech/Mediterranean. Map** p91 C1 ㉙
Sitting on a lovely, tranquil Vltava river island in the centre of town, this terraced spot caters to the casual with decent pizzas, but also manages to serve up crispy steaks, Czech traditional food and a decent wine list. Previous endeavours here were ruined by floods, but the current management is banking on better luck.

Nightlife

Big Sister

Nádražní 46 (257 310 043/ www.bigsister.net). Metro Anděl. **Open** 6pm-3am daily. **Map** p91 B5 ㉚
The most astounding recent wave in Prague's booming sex business, Big Sister nakedly cashes in on the Big Brother phenomenon, but puts its live internet cameras inside a free brothel (excluding admission) at which all the punters agree to appear on the web in exchange for gratis action.

Bluesrock Club

Nádražní 39 (774 338 310/
www.bluesrockclub.cz). Metro Anděl.
Open 5pm-5am daily. **Map** p91 C5 ⓲
Founded by the management of the
long-closed Bunkr club, this magnet for
local and touring rock and blues bands
is a bunker of a sort. Its underground
arched brick chambers are unpretentious and affordable, although they display a little inconsistency.

Drake's

Zborovská 50 (257 326 828/
www.drakes.cz). Metro Anděl.
Open 24hrs daily. **Map** p91 B1 ⓲
Drake's is popular with an older and
beefier gay crowd. Pay the high admission price and enjoy the many services
and entertainments 24 hours a day.
This popular after-hours place is, after
all, the grande dame of the Prague
scene. Video booths, daily strip shows
at 9pm and 11pm, glory holes and an
S&M dungeon.

Futurum

Zborovská 7 (257 328 571/
www.musicbar.cz). Metro Anděl.
Open 8pm-1am daily. **Map** p91 B3 ⓲
A clubbing beacon for the Smíchov
district, this remade community centre has a formal exterior that belies
the hip and groovy space within. Pop
DJs on Fridays and Saturdays but
concerts with fun local rockers, such
as Traband or odd American and
Brit punk bands, ska and electronica
acts, among other genres.

Punto Azul

Kroftova 1 (www.shadowazyl.cz).
Metro Anděl. **Open** 6pm-2am Mon-Sat;
7pm-midnight Sun. **Map** p91 A2 ⓲
Punto Azul is so far underground that
you might need canaries to test the
quality of the air. Also known as
Shadow Azyl, this student dive is on
every wirehead's map, with a dance
space that isn't much bigger than a
circuit board. Still, it plays host to
avant-garde wired DJs.

Arts & leisure

Bertramka

Mozartova 169 (257 317 465/www.
bertramka.com). Metro Anděl. **Open**
Apr-Oct 9am-6pm daily. *Nov-Mar*
9.30am-4pm daily. **Map** p91 A4 ⓲
The house where Mozart stayed when
in Prague is now a museum devoted
to him that puts on regular concerts,
nearly all of which feature his timeless
music. It's also host to the new String
Quartets festival that takes place in the
late summer, which has won critical
praise for its top performers.

Delroy's Gym

Zborovská 4 (257 327 042/
www.delroys-gym.cz). Metro Anděl.
Open 7am-10pm Mon-Fri;
9am-9pm Sat, Sun. **Map** p91 C4 ⓲
Delroy's is spatially challenged but has
a strong following nevertheless. It specialises in martial arts and boxing,
although it has courses ranging from
aerobics to self-defence. The service and
quality, along with the English-speaking staff, set it apart.

Squash & Fitness Centrum Arbes

Arbesovo náměstí 15 (257 326 041).
Metro Anděl, then tram 6, 9, 12, 20.
Open 7am-11pm daily. **Map** p91 B3 ⓲
A smart fitness club with well-managed
courts to accommodate Prague's latest
sport obsession, and a central location.

Švandovo divadlo

Štefánikova 57 (234 651 111/
www.svandovodivadlo.cz).
Metro Anděl, then tram 6, 9, 12, 20.
Map p91 A2 ⓲
There is no more accessible theatre
in Prague for anglophones than Švando-
vo, which offers surtitles in English for
all its productions. A boon for anyone
wanting to explore otherwise untrans-
lated Czech work, particularly classics
by František Langer and Gabriela
Preissová (whose play *Její pastorkyňe*
served as the basis for Janáček's *Jenůfa*).

PRAGUE BY AREA

Old Town Square

Staré Město

PRAGUE BY AREA

This district comprises everything that Prague once felt was worth walling in with palisades and still constitutes its real treasure. It's clear after a stroll through the former market square at the heart of Staré Město, or 'Old Town', why so many Czech kings preferred living here to the cold and lonely Prague Castle. With its dark, Gothic arches and spires, and a medieval streetplan guaranteed to pleasantly disorientate you, the city's old centre is just a kilometre square but appears to be an infinite source of mystic energy.

Featuring a vast sweep of architectural styles and, incredibly, many pockets that seem unchanged by post-Velvet Revolution development, this quarter has not yet given in to the beseiging crystal shops and stag parties. Celetná and Karlova, the main walking streets, emanate from the Old Town Square, overseen by a statue of a

gaunt Jan Hus, the great Czech martyr. Because Czechoslovakia fell to the Nazis without resistance, the old centre remained virtually untouched until 1989, apart from the creeping damage that resulted from four decades of communist neglect after 1948. Nowadays, Staré Město is decidedly on the rise, with a thriving bar scene along Dlouhá and V Kolkovně streets, and a surprising number of clubbing options, often hidden down dark staircases (watch out for throngs of Czech youth kitted out from head to toe in designer club togs, or young Americans in tattered jeans, as a hint).

Bounded on the north and west by the Vltava river, the Staré Město district is haunted by the former walled Jewish ghetto of Josefov, marked by the teetering tombstones of the **Old Jewish Cemetery**. Two of the country's best symphony halls, the **Rudolfinum** and **Municipal House**, home to the Prague Spring festival, are here. It also hosts some of Prague's best restaurants, serving definitive Czech, Italian, French, Asian and seafood options. The gallery scene features more international cross-breeding than ever, as seen at the renovated **House at the Golden Ring**, while Czech art that hasn't been exhibited since the censored 1970s is resurging at Prague City Gallery's various venues. The district still draws regular hordes of obnoxious stag parties, but they're easy to avoid by moving off onto the more interesting smaller lanes.

Sights & museums

Astronomical Clock
Orloj
Staroměstské náměstí (724 508 584).
Metro Staroměstská. **Open** *Nov-Mar*
11am-5pm Mon; 9am-5pm Tue-Sun. *Apr-Oct* 11am-6pm Mon; 9am-6pm Tue-Sun.
Admission 70 Kč. **Map** p96 C3 **❶**
Engineers are still impressed by the ingenious horological parts, some of which date back to 1410, that make up the clock face on this icon of the city. The *Orloj* tells the time in four different ways – including Babylonian, which divides each day into 12 parts – and the innermost ring accurately marks the current zodiac sign with a sun orb. Every hour on the hour, from 8am to 8pm, wooden statuettes of saints appear here, with Greed, Vanity, Death and the Turk below. Luckily, the Astronomical Clock was spared when the Nazis blew up the adjoining Old Town Hall in 1945.

Bethlehem Chapel
Betlémská kaple
Betlémské náměstí 4 (224 248 595).
Metro Národní třída or Staroměstská.
Open *Nov-Mar* 10am-5.30pm Tue-Sun.
Apr-Oct 10am-6.30pm Tue-Sun.
Admission 50 Kč. **Map** p96 B4 **❷**

The original incarnation of this huge church was erected in 1391. It served as the base for the proto-Protestant Jan Hus, the Czechs' greatest martyr, who was burnt at the stake for excoriating the papacy in 1415. Having fallen to pieces by the 20th century, it was ironically reconstructed by the communists following World War II; the party saw Hus as a useful working-class revolutionary – but forbade sermons here.

Charles Bridge
Karlův most
East end of Karlova street. **Open** 24hrs daily. **Admission** free. **Map** p96 A3 **❸**
The stone bridge built by Charles IV in consultation with his numerologists, who declared that 5.31am, 9 July 1357 was an auspicious time to start, is still the city's finest single visual (and the most popular spot for pickpockets and buskers). The statues arrived in the 17th century, when Josef Brokof and Matthias Braun, among other masters of the time, were commissioned to inspire the mass conversions of Bohemian Protestants to the Catholicism of the ruling Habsburgs. Water damage repairs had narrowed the walkways at the time of going to press, but the city has pledged to keep the bridge open.

Church of Our Lady before Týn
Kostel Matky Boží před Týnem
Staroměstské náměstí (222 318 186).
Metro Náměstí Republiky or Staroměstská. **Open** *Services* 6pm Wed-Fri; 8am Sat; 9.30am, 9pm Sun.
Admission free. **Map** p96 C3 **❹**
A landmark of Staré Město, this improbably spiky church, where the heads of Protestant Czech nobles were buried after they lost the Battle of White Mountain in 1620, dates from the late 14th century. The lovingly lit spires (a must by night) top what became a centre of the reforming Hussites' movement in the 15th century, before

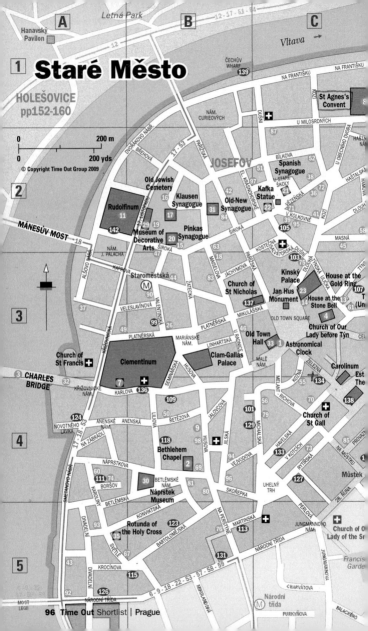

Staré Město

A1 · Hanavský Pavilon
Letná Park

A1 · B1 · C1

HOLEŠOVICE
pp152-160

Vltava →

ČECHÚV WHARF **139**

NA FRANTIŠKU

NA FRANTIŠKU

St Agnes's Convent **8**

NÁM. CURIEOVÝCH

DUŠNÍ

U MILOSRDNÝCH

JOSEFOV

0 — 200 m
0 — 200 yds
© Copyright Time Out Group 2009

BÍLKOVA

Spanish Synagogue

Old Jewish Cemetery **16**

Klausen Synagogue **17**

Rudolfinum **11**

142

29 **19**

Museum of Decorative Arts **20**

Pinkas Synagogue **15**

Old-New Synagogue **31**

Kafka Statue **22**

ŠIROKÁ

MÁNESÚV MOST —18

NÁM. J. PALACHA

ALŠOVO NÁBŘ.

KAPROVA

Staroměstská **44**

ŽATECKÁ

VELESLAVÍNOVA

VALENTINSKÁ

90

99

PLATNÉŘSKÁ

MARIÁNSKÉ NÁM.

Church of St Nicholas **137**

Jan Hus Monument **14**

Kinský Palace **23**

House at the Gold Ring **107**

House at the Stone Bell **4**

OLD TOWN SQUARE

Church of Our Lady before Týn

Church of St Francis

CHARLES BRIDGE **32**

136

Clementinum **7**

Clam-Gallas Palace

Old Town Hall **33**

Astronomical Clock

MALÉ NÁM.

Carolinum **134**

Est The

138

Church of St Gall

124

NOVOTNÉHO LÁVKA

ANENSKÉ ANENSKÁ

109

RETÉZOVÁ **50**

9

HUSOVA

101

129

MICHALSKÁ

79

133

V KOTCÍCH

127

118

Bethlehem Chapel **2** **69**

60 **111** **74** BORŠOV

NÁPRSTKOVA

KAROLÍNY

BETLÉMSKÁ

30

Náprstek Museum

BETLÉMSKÉ NÁM.

81

80

SKOŘEPKA

UHELNÝ TRH

Můstek

Church of Our Lady of the Sr

Rotunda of the Holy Cross **35**

KONVIKTSKÁ

123

BARTOLOMĚJSKÁ

76

113

NA PERŠTÝNĚ

MARTINSKÁ

131

NÁRODNÍ TŘÍDA

Francis Garde

43

DIVADELNÍ

KROCÍNOVA

115

92

126

MOST LEGII

NÁRODNÍ TŘÍDA

MIKULANDSKÁ

Národní třída

PURKYŇOVA

CHARVÁTOVA

BALACKÉHO

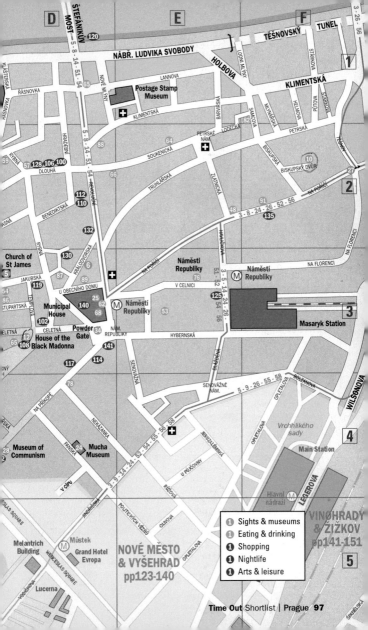

Map labels and text:

D | **E** | **F**

ŠTEFÁNIKŮV MOST

TĚSNOVSKÝ TUNEL

1

NÁBŘ. LUDVÍKA SVOBODY

HOLBOVA

LODNÍ MLÝNY

STÁROVA

KLIMENTSKÁ

120

NOVÉ MLÝNY

LANNOVA

Postage Stamp Museum

ŘÁSNOVKA

KLIMENTSKÁ

BARVÍŘSKÁ

MLYNÁŘSKÁ

HELMOVA

VOJTAJ

STŘECHOV

PETRSKÉ NÁM.

LODECKÁ

SAMCOVA

PETRSKÁ

VLASTĚŘSLAVA

NOVOMĚSTSKÁ

MÍKOVCOVA

65

88

64

SOUKENICKÁ

82

BISKUPSKÁ

BISKUPSKÝ DVŮR

10

NA POŘÍČÍ

2

57 128 106 100

DLOUHÁ

HRADEBNÍ

66

TRUHLÁŘSKÁ

ZLATNICKÁ

91

135

48 3 · 8 · 24 · 26 · 52 · 56

NA FLORENCI

BENEDIKTSKÁ

112 110

132

HAVLÍČKOVA

Church of St James

130

KRÁLODVORSKÁ

6

Náměstí Republiky

76

Náměstí Republiky

NA FLORENCI

NA PORIČÍ

3

JAKUBSKÁ

119

87

89

RYBNÁ

ŠTUPARTSKÁ

86

Municipal House

102

140

25

62

68

Náměstí Republiky

V CELNICI

53

51 · 12

125 3 · 14 · 24 · 26 · 54 · 56

Masaryk Station

CELETNÁ

Powder Gate

34

HYBERNSKÁ

12

65

House of the Black Madonna

108

141

117

114

SENOVÁŽNÁ

HYBERNSKÁ

BOLZANOVA

WILSONOVA

78

NA PŘÍKOPĚ

SENOVÁŽNÉ NÁM.

5 · 9 · 26 · 55 · 58

OPLETALOVA

Vrchlického sady

4

28

Museum of Communism

PANSKÁ

NEKÁZANKA

24

Mucha Museum

5 · 54 · 55 · 56 · 58

JERUZALÉMSKÁ

OPLETALOVA

Main Station

V CÍPU

3 · 9 · 26 · 24 · 55 · 56

U PŮŠOVNY

RŮŽOVÁ

LEGEROVA

POLITICKÝCH VĚZŇŮ

OLIVOVÁ

Hlavní nádraží

VINOHRADY & ŽIŽKOV pp141-151

Melantrich Building

Můstek

Grand Hotel Evropa

NOVÉ MĚSTO & VYŠEHRAD pp123-140

OPLETALOVA

Hlavní nádraží

5

Lucerna

❶ Sights & museums
❶ Eating & drinking
❶ Shopping
❶ Nightlife
❶ Arts & leisure

Charles Bridge p95

being commandeered by the Jesuits in the 17th. The southern aisle houses astronomer Tycho Brahe's tomb.

Church of St James
Kostel sv. Jakuba
Malá Štupartská & Jakubská streets (224 828 816). Metro Náměstí Republiky. **Open** 9.30am-noon, 2-4pm Mon-Sat; 2-3.45pm Sun. **Admission** free. **Map** p97 D3 ⑤
Acoustically speaking, St James is the finest church in the city for organ recitals, the entire structure reverberating magnificently. With 21 altars, fine frescoes and a dessicated human forearm next to the door, St James stands out. The latter item belonged to a 15th-century jewel thief who tried to steal gems from the statue of the Virgin. The Madonna grabbed him, according to popular accounts, and the limb had to be cut off.

City Bike
Králodvorská 5 (776 180 284/ www.citybike-prague.com). Metro Náměstí Republiky. **Open** 9am-7pm Mon-Fri. **Map** p97 D3 ⑥

With Mongoose Pro mountain bikes on offer, Prague's leading cycle tour operator's thrice daily two-hour rides around Old Town are more popular than ever, although the guys at City Bike also run their two-hour rides (with helmet and guide) along the river and citywide. Tours depart at 10.30am, 1.30pm and 4.30pm; call to book in advance.

Clementinum
Klementinum
Mariánské náměstí 4 (221 663 111). Metro Staroměstská. **Open** *Library* Jan-Mar 10am-4pm daily. Apr-Oct 10am-8pm daily. Nov, Dec 10am-6pm daily. **Admission** 220 Kč. **Map** p96 A4 ⑦
During the 12th and 13th centuries this was the Prague headquarters of the Inquisition. The Jesuits moved in during the 16th century, creating the Church of St Saviour (Kostel sv. Salvátora) to reawaken Catholicism in the Protestant populace. At the centre stands the Astronomical Tower, where Johannes Kepler once stargazed. Czech students still use the library and the Chapel of Mirrors is a fabulous Baroque setting for chamber concerts.

Convent of St Agnes of Bohemia

Klášter sv. Anežky České
*U milosrdných 17 (224 810 628/
www.ngprague.cz). Metro Náměstí
Republiky.* **Open** 10am-6pm Tue-Sun.
Admission 150 Kč; 200 Kč family.
Map p96 C1 ❽

The oldest surviving Gothic building
in Prague, with foundations dating to
1231, houses a collection of Bohemian
and Central European medieval art
from 1200 to 1550. This intimate and
manageable part of the National
Gallery is a fitting home to the 14th-
century Master of Třeboň, who defined
the distorted 'Beautiful Style' that held
sway here till the 16th century. Master
Theodoric's soft style works are treasures, as are his religious sculptures.

Czech Museum of Fine Arts

*Husova 19-21 (222 220 218/
www.cmvu.cz). Metro Staroměstská.*
Open 10am-6pm Tue-Sun. **Admission**
50 Kč; 20 Kč reductions. **Map** p96 B4 ❾

Housed within a block of renovated
Renaissance townhouses, the Czech
Museum of Fine Arts exhibits mainly
20th-century Czech art, with shows by
foreign artists such as Karen LaMonte
and surveys of contemporary art from
lands including Slovakia and Northern
Ireland. The museum also hosts big
exhibitions with overarching themes,
such as people, nature and technology,
and special shows aimed at children
around Christmas.

Galerie Jiří Švestka

*Biskupský dvůr 6 (222 311 092/
www.jirisvestka.com). Metro Náměstí
Republiky.* **Open** noon-6pm Tue-Fri;
11am-6pm Sat. **Admission** free.
Map p97 F2 ❿

Returned émigré Jiří Švestka has been
specialising since 1995 in bold, interna-
tionally recognised Czech artists
(Milena Dopitová, Krištof Kintera and
Jiří Černický, for instance) and also
exhibits international names, such as

Tony Cragg, in this former photography studio. Great art bookshop too.

Galerie Rudolfinum

*Alšovo nábřeží 12 (227 059 309/
www.galerierudolfinum.cz). Metro
Staroměstská.* **Open** 10am-6pm
Tue-Sun. **Admission** 120 Kč; 60 Kč
reductions. **Map** p96 A2/B2 ⓫

Following a European Kunsthalle
model, this gallery in the 19th-century
Rudolfinum concert building remains
one of the best venues for Czech and
international contemporary and modern art. Retrospectives of enigmatic
modernists such as Alén Diviš and
Mikuláš Medek, major shows by
artists of the middle generation including Petr Nikl and František Skála –
and, because the director is an expert,
shows of Chinese art.

House of the Black Madonna

Dům U Černé Matky Boží
*Ovocný trh 19 (224 211 746).
Metro Náměstí Republiky.*
Open 10am-6pm Tue-Sun. **Admission**
100 Kč; 150 Kč family. **Map** p97 D3 ⓬

This fantastic Cubist building and
gallery strives to present a totally
plane-defying vibe. Worth a visit for
the Josef Gočár-designed building
alone, it's about the finest example of
Cubist architecture in Prague, but with
meagre English-language info. Still,
one of the most stylish cafés in town is
attached, as is a shop (Kubista; p117)
that recreates pieces from this seminal
design movement.

House at the Golden Ring

Dům U Zlatého prstenu
*Týnská 6 (224 827 022). Metro Náměstí
Republiky.* **Open** 10am-6pm Tue-Sun.
Admission 90 Kč; 160 Kč family.
No credit cards. **Map** p96 C3 ⓭

Following its reconstruction (which
was completed in 2008), this beloved,
unpredictable former Renaissance
manor features a three- to five-year
exhibition of Jiří Příhoda's intriguing

Wanted. Jumpers, coats and people with their knickers in a twist.

From the people who feel moved to bring us their old books and CDs, to the people fed up to the back teeth with our politicians' track record on climate change, Oxfam supporters have one thing in common. They're passionate. If you've got a little fire in your belly, we'd love to hear from you. Visit us at **oxfam.org.uk**

Be Humankind **Oxfam**

Registered charity No. 202918

architectural art, plus new statuary and gallery space. A broad spectrum of 20th-century Czech works is shown here, organised intriguingly by theme rather than by artist or period, and consistently well-curated and fresh. International shows, often exploring digital media, provide balance.

House at the Stone Bell

Dům U Kamenného zvonu
Staroměstské Náměstí 13 (224 827 526/www.citygallery prague.cz). Metro Staroměstská. **Open** 10am-6pm Tue-Sun. **Admission** varies. **Map** p96 C3 ⑭
This Gothic sandstone building on the east side of Old Town Square, with a gorgeous Baroque courtyard and three floors of exhibition rooms, some of which have their original vaulting, favours retrospectives of Czech artists such as Toyen and Adolf Hoffmeister, and also hosts the Zvon Biennale.

Jewish Museum

Židovské Muzeum
U Staré Školy 1 (221 711 511/ www.jewishmuseum.cz). Metro Staroměstská. **Open** *Apr-Oct* 9am-6pm Mon-Fri, Sun. *Nov-Mar* 9am-4.30pm Mon-Fri, Sun. Closed Jewish holidays. **Admission** 300 Kč; 200 Kč reductions; under-6s free. *Old-New Synagogue* 200 Kč. No credit cards. **Map** p96 B2 ⑮
The six sites that make up the Jewish Museum (all listed separately below) have recently been expanded and share exhibits with other galleries in the city. Opening hours are the same for all of the venues, but vary according to the season, as noted above. Together, they form a bitter tribute to the third pillar of Czech society that all but disappeared during the Holocaust after centuries in Bohemia. Many of the contents, now overseen by the thriving Jewish Community organisation, were seized from Jews by the Nazis, who had hoped for a museum dedicated to an extinct race.

Former Ceremonial Hall

Obřadní síň
U starého hřbitova 3A, Josefov (222 317 191). **Map** p96 B2 ⑯
The Romanesque turrets and arches of this building at the exit of the cemetery appear as old as the gravestones but date to just 1906. It hosts fascinating exhibitions on topics such as Jewish customs and traditions focusing on illness and death.

Klausen Synagogue

Klausova synagoga
U starého hřbitova 3A, Josefov (222 310 302). **Map** p96 B2 ⑰
The great ghetto fire of 1689 destroyed the original Klausen Synagogue, along with 318 houses and ten other synagogues. Hastily reconstructed in 1694, its permanent exhibition investigates the enduring power of religion during the lives of the ghetto's former inhabitants. It's crowned by two tablets of the Decalogue, along with a golden inscription, which is clearly visible from the Jewish Cemetery.

Maisel Synagogue

Maiselova synagoga
Maiselova 10, Josefov (224 819 456). **Map** p96 B3 ⑱
Mordecai Maisel, mayor of the Jewish ghetto under Rudolf II, was one of the richest men in 16th-century Europe. He heralded from a lucrative trading monopoly and paid for the construction of the splendid original synagogue. This burned down in 1689 and the architecture was then rebuilt in a Baroque style. The building was then reconstructed again during the late 19th century, and now houses exhibitions about the Jewish history of Bohemia and Moravia.

Old Jewish Cemetery

Starý Židovský hřbitov
Široká 3, Josefov (no phone). **Map** p96 B2 ⑲
All of Prague's Jewish population was buried here until the late 1600s, and

Edifying

To feast your eyes, visit the National Gallery's collection.

The Czech National Gallery, as you might expect in a city with so many centuries of fiefdom and religious wars and so many palaces to fill, has a vast art collection that can scarcely be contained by buildings all over Prague and beyond.

Organising it would be no simple task, even if the art did not constitute a political hot potato. As it is, large parts were sequestered away from public view before 1989 and other great collections have been plundered over the years.

What now forms the National Gallery's holdings dates back to a cataloguing in 1796 of hundreds of artworks, ranging at the time from patriotically charged portraits of Hussite leaders to medieval icons and triptychs.

With the desire to 'elevate the deteriorated taste of the local public', the gentry of the dawning Industrial Age set out to enshrine the Czech arts, a mission taken up anew with the founding of modern Czechoslovakia in 1918 and again

after World War II – that is, until Marxist-Leninist edification of the working classes became a priority.

With an absurdist playwright president in charge for the first 13 years after the Velvet Revolution, the National Gallery has made a high priority of reviving avant-garde art from the last century, along with bringing magnificent pieces of religious art back from obscurity. Controversial gallery director Milan Knížák, a former émigré and Fluxus artist, who lived abroad after 1968, has overseen a massive reshuffle of the organisation's eight venues during the last year.

Staré Město now hosts three richly stocked ones, the Convent of St Agnes of Bohemia (p99), the House of the Black Madonna (p99) and Kinský Palace (p103), the last of which has restored its Gothic façade and interiors to better host a range of work that spans Dutch old masters and 20th-century photography, to say nothing of the annual Zvon show of fresh young artists.

With the newly opened Schwarzenberg Palace collection of Baroque art taking some of the pressure off in Malá Strana, Old Town's St Agnes can properly focus on productive collaborations, such as the 2009 exhibition of medieval art about the life of the Czech patron saint, St Wenceslas, which showed off some fine church-owned artworks.

Cubist art now gets proper props at the Black Madonna as well. Could it finally be that deteriorated taste is being properly retired? Bravo.

12,000 tombstones are crammed into this tiny, tree-shaded patch of ground – a forceful reminder of the cramped ghetto, which remained walled until the late 1700s. Forced to bury the dead on top of one another, an estimated 100,000 bodies lay 12 levels deep. Headstone reliefs indicate the name or occupation of the deceased: scissors, for a tailor, a lion for Rabbi Leow.

Pinkas Synagogue

Pinkasova synagoga
Široká 3, Josefov (222 326 660).
Map p96 B2 ⑳
Founded in 1479, this temple's walls were inscribed in the 1950s with the names of more than 80,000 Czech Holocaust victims. After the Six Day War, the Czechoslovak government blotted them out during a period of 'restoration', but they're all back, a job completed in 1994. Don't miss the exhibition of drawings by children who were interned at Terezín.

Spanish Synagogue

Španělská synagoga
Vězeňská 1, Josefov (224 819 464).
Map p96 C2 ㉑
Reopened after long neglect in 1998, this temple's domed interior glows with green, red and faux gold leaf, and houses varied and inspired new exhibitions on Jewish history, and a stunning exhibition of synagogue silver. Its predecessor predated the Altneu Synagogue but it was rebuilt in 1868 in the then-fashionable Moorish style.

Kafka statue

Dušní street. Metro Staroměstská.
Map p96 C2 ㉒
Jaroslav Rona's appropriately surreal bronze sculpture of Franz Kafka is, incredibly, the only monument to whom most of the world considers to be Prague's greatest writer. Small plaques have been tacked onto his former residences, but it took 80 years following the brooding writer's death for a proper tribute to be constructed, which indicates just how uncomfortable Kafka's literary legacy made the authorities feel.

Kinský Palace

Staroměstské Náměstí 12.
(224 810 758/www.ngprague.cz).
Metro Staroměstská. **Open** 10am-6pm Tue-Sun. **Admission** 100 Kč; 150 Kč family. **Map** p96 C3 ㉓
The National Gallery's newly restored Kinský Palace focuses on calming and redolent Czech landscape painting from the 17th to the 20th centuries, which was influenced by Dutch masters, such as Roelandt Savery and Pieter Stevens, who were brought into the country by mad Rudolph II. Still lifes and photographs from the 19th century to the present – a Czech forte – round out the offerings.

Mucha Museum

Kaunický palác, Panská 7
(221 451 333/www.mucha.cz).
Metro Můstek. **Open** 10am-6pm daily.
Admission 120 Kč. **Map** p97 D4 ㉔
The most famous of all Czech visual artists, Alfons Mucha (1860-1939) created mass-produced decorative panels and posters for the stage actress Sarah Bernhardt in Paris, and did much to spread the art nouveau movement throughout Europe. His paintings, lithographs, drawings, sketches and notebooks from his Paris days are here, along with photographs and an engaging video about his life.

Municipal House

Obecní dům
Náměstí Republiky 5 (222 002 101/
www.obecni-dum.cz). Metro Náměstí
Republiky. **Open** 10am-6pm daily.
Admission 100-150 Kč for exhibitions.
Map p97 D3 ㉕
This whole building, circa 1910, is a work of art, a shrine to Czech national aspirations, containing murals, mosaics and sculptures by everyone from Mucha to Myslbek. However, the exhibition rooms on the top floor of this art

PRAGUE BY AREA

Old Jewish Cemetery p101

Open 9am-6pm Tue-Sun.
Admission 100 Kč; 180 Kč family;
under-6s free; 1 Kč first Thur of the
month reductions. Map p97 F2 ㉗

Antonín Langweil spent 11 years
of the early 1800s building an incredibly precise room-sized paper model of
Prague. This prize exhibit is the only
complete depiction of what the city
actually looked like before the Jewish
ghetto was ripped down. Other displays trace the city's development
from pre-historic times through to the
17th century.

Museum of Communism

Na Příkopě 10 (224 212 966/
www.muzeumkomunismu.com).
Metro Můstek. Open 9am-9pm daily.
Admission 180 Kč. Map p97 D4 ㉘
The first of its kind in the country,
the Museum of Communism puts the
communist era into historical perspective with archive photographs, files
of hundreds of relics and displays of
exhibits curated by respected histori-
ans. Mock-ups of a school-room and
interrogation room from the period
are eerie indeed, and part of the the-
matic organisation of communism as
dream, reality and nightmare.

Museum of Decorative Arts

Uměleckoprůmyslové muzeum
Ulice 17 listopadu 2 (251 093 111/
www.upm.cz). Metro Staroměstská.
Open 10am-7pm Tue; 10am-6pm
Wed-Sun. Admission 80-120 Kč.
Map p96 B2 ㉙
Constructed between 1897 and 1900,
this neo-Renaissance museum is a
work of art in itself, boasting richly
decorated halls, stained- and etched-
glass windows, and intricately painted
plaster mouldings. Its clever exhibits
are grouped according to material:
there is an excellent 20th-century collection and older, lavishly crafted furniture, tapestries, pottery, clocks and
books, along with a fine display of
ceramics and glass.

nouveau masterpiece are the most
accessible – and feature well-curated
shows with an emphasis on historically
important Central European artists and
decorative work.

Municipal Library

Mariánské Náměstí 1 (entrance
on Valentinská) (222 310 489/
www.citygalleryprague.cz). Metro
Staroměstská. Open 10am-8pm
Tue-Sun. Admission 120 Kč; 60 Kč
reductions. Map p96 B3 ㉖
This travertine-covered 1925-28 building is home to a great deal more than
books. The second floor halls, run by the
Prague City Gallery, showcase large-
scale shows of modern art that's had a
major impact. Such shows have covered
Czech 20th-century photography or the
medium's development in Germany.

Museum of the City of Prague

Muzeum Hlavního města Prahy
Na Poříčí 52 (224 816 773/
www.muzeumprahy.cz).

PRAGUE BY AREA

Náprstek Museum

Náprstkovo muzeum
Betlémské náměstí 1 (224 497 500/
www.aconet.cz/npm). Metro Národní
třída. **Open** 10am-6pm Tue-Sun.
Admission 80 Kč. **Map** p96 B4 ③⓪
The 19th-century nationalist Vojta
Náprstek was fascinated by primitive
cultures and gathered ethnographic
curiosities from Czech travellers in
this extension to his house. Native
loot, derived from the Americas,
Australasia and the Pacific Islands
are beautifully arranged.

Old-New Synagogue

Červná 2, Josefov (no phone).
Metro Staroměstská.
Open *Apr-Oct* 9.30am-6pm
Mon-Thur, Sun; 9.30am-5pm Fri.
Nov-Mar 9.30am-5pm Mon-Thur,
Sun; 9am-2pm Fri. **Admission**
200 Kč; 140 Kč reductions;
free under-6s. **Map** p96 B2 ③①
Still used for services after 700 years of
existence, this simple, stark brick
building is a fine example of Gothic
style, with interiors that harmonise
around the number 12, after the tribes
of Israel – windows, bunches of grapes
and vines are all part of the magic
quantity. The tall seat marked by the
gold leaf belonged to Rabbi Low.

Old Town Bridge Tower

Staroměstská mostecká věž
Křižovnické náměstí (224 220 569).
Metro Staroměstská. **Open** *Jan, Feb*
10am-5pm daily. *Mar* 10am-6pm daily.
Apr, Nov, Dec 10am-7pm daily. *May-*
Oct 10am-10pm daily. **Admission** 70
Kč; 50 Kč reductions. **Map** p96 A4 ③②
The tower of the 14th-century Gothic
gate to Charles Bridge, with Peter
Parler's frill visible on the east side,
offers a wonderful close-up view of
Prague's domes and spires, the way-
ward profile of Charles Bridge, the naff
Klub Lávka and the most gigantic
addition to the Prague clubbing scene,
Karlovy Lázně, all below on the river
and beyond.

Old Town Hall & Astronomical Clock Tower

Staroměstská radnice
Staroměstské náměstí (724 508 584).
Metro Staroměstská. **Open** *Town Hall*
11am-6pm Mon; 9am-6pm Tue-Sun.
Tower May-Sept 10am-10pm daily.
Oct-Apr 10am-7pm daily. **Admission**
60 Kč. **Map** p96 C3 ③③
Only half the original Old Town Hall,
built around 1338, remains standing
today. The Nazis blew it up at the
end of World War II but the clock
tower survived and has a viewing platform definitely worth the climb (see
also p91). Exhibitions such as the
World Press Photo show enliven the
town hall itself, as do tours of its ornate
chambers, which take in the dungeon,
former headquarters of the Resistance
during the Prague Uprising in 1945.
Enemy supplies and arms were stolen
through underground passages. A
plaque on the side of the clock tower
thanks the Soviet soldiers who liberated the city afterwards.

Astronomical Clock

Powder Gate

Prašná brána

U Prašné brány (no phone). Metro Náměstí Republiky. **Open** *Apr-Oct* 10am-6pm daily. **Admission** 70 Kč; 50 Kč under-10s. **Map** p97 D3 ❸❹

This 15th-century relic of the fortifications that used to ring the town mouldered until it finally gained a new purpose, and a name, when it was used to store gunpowder in 1575. Severely damaged by the Prussians in 1757, it's now a neo-Gothic star again.

Rotunda of the Holy Cross

Rotunda sv. Kříže

Konviktská and Karoliny Světlé streets. Metro Náměstí Republiky. **Open** *Apr-Oct* 10am-6pm daily. **Admission** 50 Kč; 40 Kč under-10s. **Map** p97 D3

This humble 11th century stone tower, with rounded nave and a simple apse, is one of three such structures in Prague, which constitute the oldest standing architecture in the city. It's origins are hazy but the Old Town charmer is believed to be a former private chapel for medievalburghers. Alas, it's not open for services.

Eating & drinking

Aldente

Věženská 4 (222 313 185/ www.aldentetradstoria.cz). Metro Staroměstská. **Open** noon-3.30pm, 6pm-midnight daily. **$$. Italian.** **Map** p96 C2 ❸❻

One pearl on a string of trattorias owned by Toni Ciullo that links Turin and Prague, this relaxed, inviting place serves up the real thing, from veal tongue in a Piemont sauce to appealing tasting menus that may feature Tuscan salamis and cheese, boar ragout and mascarpone in sweet wine. Flying the flag on a street that forms the city's culinary Little Italy, Aldente offers street tables on a decorous lane, expert staff and, of course, a well-stocked but reasonably priced wine cellar.

Allegro

Veleslavínova 2A (221 427 000/ www.fourseasons.com/prague/dining/ dining.html). Metro Staroměstská. **Open** *Restaurant* 7am-11pm daily. **$$$$. Czech/Italian.** **Map** p96 A3 ❸❼

The winner of the Czech Republic's first Michelin star, the Four Seasons' flagship was brought up to world-class speed by chef Vito Mollica, who has since passed the mantle on to others. The menu, an inspired Tuscan-meets-Czech list, features delights like veal fillet, pan-fried foie gras and truffles or monkfish saltimbocca. The wine list is great and the terrace looks out on Prague Castle across the Vltava.

Amici Miei

Věženská 5 (224 816 688/www. amicimiei.cz). Metro Můstek. **Open** 11am-11pm daily. **$$$. Italian.** **Map** p96 C2 ❸❽

Amici Miei offers outstanding cuisine in a slightly overlit hall, discreetly curtained off from the street. Highlights include veal scallops, simple, comforting tagliata with parmesan and rocket, and unusually warm and attentive service, plus an excellent Italian wine list.

Angel

V kolkovně 7 (773 222 422/ www.angelrestaurant.cz). Metro Staroměstská. **Open** 11.30am-midnight Mon-Sat; 11am-4pm Sun. **$$. Asian fusion.** **Map** p96 C2 ❸❾

This fresh new entry into the Old Town dining scene is already a buzzword, thanks no doubt to its engaging menu of South-east Asian delights. Javanese slow-cooked lamb shank, prawns in coconut chutney and scallops with laksa and pineapple are all conceived by veteran Prague chef Sofia Smith in a simple, Zen-like space.

Ariana

Rámová 6 (222 323 438/ www.ariana.dreamworx.cz). Metro Náměstí Republiky. **Open** 11am-11pm daily. **$. Afghan.** **Map** p96 C2 ❹❶

Angel

A gleaming zinc bar, floor-to-ceiling windows and a credible sushi platter with suitably aesthetic *nigiri* are some of the highlights here. The reasonably priced breakfast menu and powerhouse lattes are further draws at this elegant café. Posing is actively encouraged.

Bellevue
Smetanovo nábřeží 18 (222 221 443/ www.bellevuerestaurant.cz).
Metro Národní třída. **Open** noon-3pm, 5.30-11pm daily. **$$$$. Central European.** Map p96 A5 ㊸
An early leader on the Prague dining scene, the traditional Bellevue still delivers, although service can be inconsistent and the menu hasn't evolved in years. However, veal loin in black truffle sauce and fallow venison in juniper reduction still go mighty well with Sunday jazz brunch. The restaurant offers wonderful views of Prague Castle; booking is essential.

A comfy Afghan restaurant with tender, spiced lamb and sumptuous vegetarian chalous. Familial service goes with the straightback chairs, rugs and brass lamps. You'll find yourself lingering longer than expected and needing a walk in Old Town after the feast.

Bakeshop Praha
Kozí 1 (222 316 823). Metro Staroměstská. **Open** 7am-7pm daily. **Bakery.** Map p96 C2 ㊶
Steadily growing in floor space and menu length, this comfort-food emporium launched by San Franciscan Anne Feeley has been buzzing since it first opened its doors. Zesty quiches, traditional nut breads, muffins and peanut butter cookies, plus a Northern California vibe. Grab a copy of *The Guardian* and hang out on a bench to savour your java and croissants.

Barock
Pařížská 24, Josefov (222 329 221).
Metro Staroměstská. **Open** 10am-1am daily. **Café.** Map p96 B2 ㊷

La Bodeguita del Medio
Kaprova 5(224 813 922/ www.labdelm.cz). Metro Staroměstská. **Open** 10am-2am daily. **Bar.** Map p96 B3 ㊹
Pretty much packed with revellers since its opening in 2002, the Czech branch of the 60-year-old Havana institution that claims credit for inventing the mojito (and hooking Hemingway on it, of course) is a jumping joint. Live salsa bands, Cuban and creole seafood, and oceans of good rum.

Bohemia Bagel
Masná 2 (224 812 603/www. bohemiabagel.cz). Metro Staroměstská. **Open** 7am-11pm Mon-Fri; 8am-11pm Sat, Sun. **Café.** Map p96 C2 ㊺
One of the republic's first true bagel cafés has expanded its offerings to go well beyond the free coffee refills, fresh muffins, breakfast bagels and bagel sandwiches. Grill foods, soups, breakfast fry-ups, burgers and made-to-order salads now go along with the Jewish wonder bread. For purists, there are still

poppyseed, cinnamon raison, tomato basil and chocolate chip bagels. There's also internet access and a play corner for the kiddies. What's not to like?

Brasileiro

U Radnice 8 (224 234 474/ www.ambi.cz). Metro Staroměstská. **Open** 11am-midnight daily. **$$.** **Steakhouse**. **Map** p96 B3 ㊻

In the authentic tradition of Brazilian butchery, this hit locale in the Old Town Hall building serves all the fine cuts of meat you can eat for the fixed price of 495 Kč until 6pm, upping the ante to 625 Kč thereafter. Czech meat lovers can't seem to get enough.

Le Café Colonial

Široká 6, Josefov (224 818 322/ www.lecafecolonial.cz). Metro Staroměstská. **Open** 10am-midnight daily. **$$.** **French**. Map p97 B3 ㊼

Airy, with teak accents, miniature quiches, delicate pork and delightful salads. More formal dining's on the other side where there's a veranda and designer furniture in Matisse-inspired tones. Resolutely French.

Café Imperial

Na Poříčí 15 (246 011 600/www. cafeimperial.cz). Metro Náměstí Republiky. **Open** 7am-11pm daily. **Café**. **Map** p97 E2 ㊽

A lot like stepping into a Stanley Kubrick film, this ornate art nouveau shrine, walls and ceiling covered with sculpted porcelain, has been restored to the opulence it had when it opened in 1914. Now attached to the nearly as posh Hotel Imperial, the old-world dining room serves elegant renditions of trad schnitzels and rump steak, but seems more suited to lighter fare, conversation and crisp white wine.

Café Indigo

Platnéřská 11 (no phone). Metro Staroměstská. **Open** 9am-midnight daily. **Café**. **Map** p96 A3 ㊾

Student heaven, and – despite its industrial art theme and front room like a fish tank – a comfortable café. With a limited menu and cheap wine, the Indigo has an upbeat and easygoing vibe and serves as a community centre for scholars from nearby Charles University. Service is above average for this genre, though it's smoky.

Café Montmartre

Řetězová 7 (222 221 244). Metro Staroměstská. **Open** 9am-11pm Mon-Fri; noon-11pm Sat, Sun. **Café**. **Map** p96 B4 ㊿

One of the last great holdouts in the category of old- style coffeehouse bar, this buzzy spot is where Czech literati like Gustav Meyrink and Franz Werfel tippled before it became a Jazz Age hotspot. Creative miscreants still gather around the threadbare settees and battered tables.

Casa Andina

NEW *Dušni 15, Prague 1 (224 815 996/www.casaandina.cz). Metro Staroměstska.* **Open** 11am-11pm Mon-Wed, Sun; 11am-2pm Thur, Fri; 2pm-2am Sat. **$$.** **Americas**. **Map** p97 C2 (51)

Casa Andina offers Latin American fare done with flair in a warm setting, which makes for an altogether surprising discovery in Old Town. Try the escabeche or chicken skewer in Ají Panca sauce for a taste of the house speciality: savoury Peruvian cuisine. An excellent Chilean wine list goes with the culinary concept.

La Casa Blů

Kozí 15 (224 818 270/www.lacasablu. cz). Metro Staroměstská. **Open** 9am-11pm Mon-Fri; 11am-11pm Sat; 2-11pm Sun. **$.** **Mexican**. **Map** p96 C2 (52)

With the atmosphere of an island of warm Latin American flavours, this rustic room has folk rugs draped over the chairs, street signs in Spanish, tequila specials and an authentic Mexican menu. Try the buzzer even if the door's locked; you can often get in after closing time. Free Wi-Fi.

Celnice

V Celnici 4 (224 212 240/www.celnice. com). Metro Náměstí Republiky. **Open** 11am-2am Mon-Wed, Sun; 11am-1am Thur-Sat. **$$$. Czech**. Map p97 E3 ⑬
One of several Pilsner-licensed restaurants in the city, Celnice is a mix of classic Czech, with updated fare like *kyselo*, or sauerkraut soup, pickled Prague ham and pastas and a sleek, modern sushi bar with DJ dance fare emanating from the basement on weekend nights.

Chateau

Jakubská 2 (222 316 328/www. chateaurouge.cz). Metro Náměstí Republiky. **Open** 4pm-4am daily. **Bar**. Map p97 D3 ㉞
Chateau is still the prime meat market and locus for collegiate overdoing it in Old Town, although somehow it can still be a laugh. While certainly not suitable for the claustrophobic, this venue does attract hordes of partying young Americans and travelling twentysomethings of all stripes and nationalities, especially the newly expanded downstairs club.

Čili

Kožná 8 (777 945 848). Metro Můstek. **Open** 11am-midnight daily. **Bar**. Map p96 C4 ㉟
A quiet but decisive hit on the competitive Prague bar scene, this narrow room is a hit for its hidden location on a narrow backstreet off Old Town Square, and for its outsize mojitos, G&Ts and comfortably broken-in, living room vibe. The overstuffed leather armchairs are the prize spots.

Country Life

Melantrichova 15 (224 213 366). Metro Národní třída. **Open** 9am-7pm Mon-Thur; 8.30am-5pm Fri; 11am-6pm Sun. **$. Vegetarian**. Map p96 C4 ㊱
This Czech neohippie cafeteria specialises in cheap, organically grown vegetarian fare. Among the menu highlights are massive DIY salads, fresh carrot juices, delectable lentil soups and crunchy wholegrain breads. It's best to avoid the lunchtime crush.

Dahab

Dlouhá 33 (224 827 375/ www.dahab.cz). Metro Náměstí Republiky. **Open** 2pm-1am daily. **$.** **Middle Eastern**. Map p97 D2 ㊲
With a newly developed menu of Middle Eastern treats served in the dimly lit back tea room (the greasy spoon on the Dlouhá street end is only for the adventurous), Dahab is more appealing than ever. Try a tagine or couscous with mint tea and settle into pillow seating in what resembles a candlelit harem. Turkish coffees too.

DeBrug

Masná 5 (724 122 994). Metro Náměstí Republiky. **Open** 10am-1am daily. **$$. Belgian**. Map p96 C2 ㊳
The Prague passion for Belgian-style mussels, frites and beer continues to blossom. First it was Stella Artois in Czech beer heaven (once unimaginable); now the seafood bistro trend is spreading throughout the city. This elegant bar/restaurant, with fleet-footed service, illustrates why.

La Degustation

Haštalská 18 (222 311 234/ www.ladegustation.cz). **Open** 6pm-midnight Mon-Sat. **$$$$.** **Czech/ Central European**. Map p97 D2 ㊴
The seven-course menu will take up most of an afternoon or evening, promising 'the flavours and tastes of molecular cuisine'. That the restaurant usually pulls it off is no mean feat – and makes the pretension forgivable. Choose from three fixed-price meals: Bohemian Bourgeoise, Earth & Sea or Traditional Bohemian with Wagju beef, organic Argentine ribs, sweetbreads, tongue, truffles, and Valrhona Jivara chocolate.

Lehká Hlava p112

Duende

Karoliny Světlé 30 (775 186 077/ www.barduende.cz). Metro Národní třída. **Open** 1pm-midnight Mon-Fri; 3pm-midnight Sat; 4pm-midnight Sun. **Café. Map** p96 A4 ⑥⓪

Attracting low-budget Prague intellectuals from the publishing and film scenes, and other affable regulars, Duende is second home to many. The Latin-flavoured café-bar is more than the sum of its parts: eclectic events pop up, ranging from live folk music to bizarre video projections. The tattered sofas and fringed lampshades add character.

Ebel Coffee House

Týn 2 (224 895 788/www.ebelcoffee.cz). Metro Náměstí Republiky. **Open** 9am-10pm daily. **Café. Map** p96 C3 ⑥①

Serious coffees, courtesy of journalist and designer Malgorzata Ebel, who was one of Prague's first suppliers of good beans (more than 30 prime arabica varieties are stocked), plus passable quiches, bagels and brownies, served in a lovely cobbled courtyard or in the cosy wood-trimmed room. In short, a caffeine-junkie's heaven.

Francouzská Restaurace

Náměstí Republiky 5 (222 002 770/ www.francouzskarestaurace.cz). Metro Náměstí Republiky. **Open** 11am-11pm daily. **$$. French/Central European. Map** p97 D3 ⑥②

With the city's finest art nouveau pile as a backdrop, this absurdly ornate dining room, recently featured in the film *I Served the King of England* and is also a consistent award-winner for its excellent cuisine. Try a classic roast duck or allow the chefs to go wild with a prawn saffron risotto.

Franz Kafka Café

Široká 12, Josefov (222 318 945). Metro Staroměstská. **Open** 10am-10pm daily. **Café. Map** p96 B2 ⑥③

Dim, old-world and almost austere, this little coffeehouse takes you on a journey back in time: frosted glass, dark, deep wooden booths, old engravings of the Jewish Quarter (it lies just around the corner from the Jewish Cemetery) and, naturally, lots of portraits of Franz Kafka perfectly set the scene. Decent coffee and convivial street tables make it a fine place for a break.

Góvinda Vegetarian Club

*Soukenická 27 (224 816 631). Metro
Náměstí Republiky.* **Open** 11am-6pm
Mon-Fri. **$**. **Vegetarian**. Map p97 E2 ⓺⓸
Cheap but not so cheerful, this Krishna
restaurant offers a simple and self-ser-
vice vegetarian Indian meal for a mere
85 Kč. Although basic, it's a clean spot
in which to share a table while seated
on floor cushions (there are also chairs).

Grand Café Orient

NEW *Ovocný trh 19 (224 224 240/
www.grandcafeorient.cz). Metro
Náměstí Republiky.* **Open** 9am-10pm
Mon-Fri; 10am-10pm Sat, Sun.
Café. Map p97 D3 ⓺⓹
This is probably the most stylish caff
in the Old Town district, which is saying something, providing an unmiss-
able opportunity to sip a cappuccino in
a cubist building. The café, which is
attached to the House of the Black
Madonna, lies on the tourist track, but
makes a worthwhile stop. Decent service and breakfast.

Himalaya

*Soukenická 2 (233 353 594/www.
himilayarestaurant.cz). Metro Náměstí
Republiky.* **Open** 11am-11pm Mon-Fri;
noon-11pm Sat, Sun. **$**. **Indian**.
Map p97 D2/E2 ⓺⓺
Easily the most affordable, credible
Indian option for a relaxed dinner in
the Old Town area, this cosy split-level
spot is good for the soul of many an
expat who feels starved of spice.
Samosas, vindaloo, rogan and korma
feature on the well-thumbed menu.

Kabul

*Karolíny Světle 14 (224 235 452/
www.aa.cz/kabulrestaurant). Metro
Národní třída.* **Open** 10am-11pm daily.
$. **Afghan**. Map p96 A5 ⓺⓻
Done up in Persian rugs and hanging
lanterns, Hasib Saleh's little restaurant
is a local fave, serving fine specialities
such as ashak pastry and okra fingers,
all with fresh flatbread. The place fills
up at lunchtime.

Kavárna Obecní dům

*Náměstí Republiky 5 (222 002 763/
www.vysehrad2000.cz). Metro Náměstí
Republiky.* **Open** 7.30am-11pm daily.
Café. Map p97 D3 ⓺⓼
Easily the most epic café space in town,
this balconied, art nouveau sipping
space with grand piano is located
at street level in the magnificently
restored Municipal House. Replete with
secessionist brass chandeliers, odd
characters and a few grande dames,
there's no more memorable venue.

Klub Architektů

*Betlémské náměstí 5A (224 401 214).
Metro Národní třída.* **Open** 11.30am-
midnight daily. **$**. **Central European**.
Map p96 B4 ⓺⓽
Great-value down in the cellar of an
architecture and design gallery next
door to the Bethlehem Chapel. The cuisine is credible and creative European
and the waiters are gracious and
friendly. Just don't trip on the steep
stairs. Patio tables in mild weather.

Kogo Pizzeria & Caffeteria

*Havelská 27 (224 214 543/www.
kogo.cz). Metro Můstek.* **Open** 8am-
11pm Mon-Fri; 9am-11pm Sat, Sun.
$$. **Mediterranean**. Map p96 C4 ⓻⓪
Prices have risen at this popular local
chain of fashionable Mediterranean
restaurants, but a visit is still a treat.
Heaps of salads, soups and starters
offer cheaper, lighter options. Scampi,
bruschetta, bean soup, focaccia and
pizzas are served fast and stylishly.

Kolkovna

*V kolkovně 8 (224 819 701/www.
kolkovna.cz). Metro Staroměstská.*
Open 11am-midnight daily. **$**.
Czech. Map p96 C2 ⓻⓵
An art nouveau interior and trad pub
grub (potato pancakes, beer-basted
goulash) attracts local patrons to a re-
creation of old Prague. Licensed by the
brewery Pilsner Urquell, so you know
the beer will be good. Often packed, alas.

Kozička

Kozí 1 (224 818 308/www.kozicka.cz).
Metro Náměstí Republiky. **Open** noon-
4am Mon-Fri; 6pm-4am Sat; 7pm-3am
Sun. **Bar/steakhouse**. **Map** p96 C2 ⑫
Looking a bit threadbare these days,
the 'Little Goat' is still a popular, unpretentious local scene that dwells in a
subterranean labyrinth. Homely nooks
and crannies, mighty steaks served till
11pm and Krušovice available on tap.

KU Bar Café

Rytířská 13 (221 181 081/www.
kubar.cz). *Metro Můstek.* **Open** 7pm-
4am daily. **Bar**. **Map** p96 C4 ⑬
Natalie Portman shook it up here all
night in 2006, but anyone more inter-
ested in good DJ tracks, drink-mixing
and atmosphere will find this place
heavy on pretence, if possibly fun for
one (pricey) shot.

Lehká Hlava

Boršov 2 (222 220 665/www.
lehkahlava.cz). *Metro Můstek.*
Open 11.30am-11.30pm Mon-Fri;
noon-11.30pm Sat, Sun. **$$**.
Vegetarian. **Map** p96 A4 ⑭
Now with brunch offerings, this
appealingly spaced-out holistic eaterie
offers affordable meals in a setting that
could be an art gallery. In fact, it's a
soothing New Age veggie venue with
a good track record. New brunch offer-
ings beef up the other options: whole-
wheat ragoût, goat's cheese dishes and
an amazing range of teas and juices.
The entrance is in the courtyard.

Mama Lucy

Dlouhá 1 (222 327 207). *Metro*
Staroměstská. **Open** 11am-midnight
daily. **$$**. **Mexican**. **Map** p96 C3 ⑮
There's rarely a wait here and it's
handily located, a block off Old Town
Square. This definitive Czech-Mex
establishment serves fajitas, burritos,
enchiladas and quesadillas, which are
passable, if hardly inspired. All are
served with a smile, but at rates that
reflect its location.

U Medvídků

Na Perštýně 7 (224 211 916/
www.umedvidku.cz). *Metro Národní*
třída. **Open** 11.30am-11pm daily. **$$**.
Czech. **Map** p96 B5 ⑯
Five centuries of cred as a beerhall
have made the Little Bears a mecca for
Budvar drinkers. The menu exceeds
your expectations for traditional pub
grub, with pork in plum sauce and fil-
lets in dark beer reduction, among
other treats. Hardcore diners might
care for tlačenka, or head cheese.
Invariably packed with locals.

Metamorphis

Malá Štupartská 5 (221 771 068/
www.metamorphis.cz). *Metro Náměstí*
Republiky. **Open** 9am-1am daily. **$$**.
Mediterranean. **Map** p96 D3 ⑰
Sedate and capable, this family-run
pasta café and pension is, alas, directly
on a main tourist route to Old Town
Square, and thus is often filled with
bustling crowds. The cellar restaurant
within is enhanced by live jazz at night.
Metamorphis is the only place within a
few blocks of Old Town Square to eat
alfresco after 10pm.

Millhouse Sushi

Na Příkopě 22 (221 451 771/
www.millhouse-sushi.cz). *Metro Náměstí*
Republiky. **Open** 11am-11pm daily. **$$**.
Sushi. **Map** p97 D3 ⑱
For a break from heavy Bohemian trad,
this modernist nagiri and maki bar,
complete with conveyer belt, does the
trick . Located as it is in the Slovanský
dům shopping mall, it's handy if you're
on a movie date and the California rolls
are as fine as any in town. Service
almost justifies the menu prices.

U modré kachničky

Michalská 16 (224 213 418/www.
umodrekachnicky.cz). *Metro*
Staroměstská. **Open** 11.30am-11.30pm
daily. **$$**. **Czech**. **Map** p96 C4 ⑲
One of the thriving little dining rooms
that have appeared since the Velvet
Revolution, U modré kachničky is set

in a granny's house on a narrow side street. The kitchen offers modernised classics, such as roast duck with pears and boar steak with mushrooms.

Monarch

Na Perštýně 15 (224 239 602/www. monarch.cz). Metro Národní třída.
Open noon-midnight Mon-Sat.
Wine bar. Map p96 B4 ㉚
With a touch of sophistication, great lighting, discreet back corners and racks of great wines, this is the place for connoisseurs. You'll find South American or Californian imports, the best local bottles and knowledgeable, friendly service. Good selection of regional sausage and over 25 varieties of cheese available.

Papas

Betlémské náměstí 8 (222 222 229/ www. papasbar.cz). Metro Vltavská.
Open 11am-midnight daily. **Bar.**
Map p96 B4 ㉛
A cocktail specialist with deep maroon red interiors, Papas is no shrinking violet, and a fave of expat students and 'Czuppies' alike. Caipirinha's are mixed with gusto by the energetic staff and the bar food is colourful and varied enough to do well for lunch.

Perpetuum

Lodecká 4 (224 810 401/www. cervenatabulka.cz). Metro Náměstí Republiky. **Open** 11.30am-11pm daily.
$$. Central European.
Map p97 F1 ㉜
Whimsical playschool decor, lava-grilled lamb, comforting poultry dishes and other robust favourites: baked duck leg with bacon dumplings, apple and sauerkraut is a stand-out on the menu, cheerily served alongside skewered rabbit with cream and lime sauce. Service is above par and prices are fair.

Pivnice u Pivrnce

Maiselova 3, Josefov (222 329 404). Metro Náměstí Republiky.
Open 11am- midnight daily. **$.**
Czech. Map p96 B3 ㉝

Rough, ready and looking set to stare down the next century unchanged, this pub prides itself on serving traditional Czech pork and dumplings with above-average presentation. Svíčková (beef in lemon cream sauce), duck with sauerkraut and walls covered with crude cartoons are guaranteed to offend.

Pravda

Pařížská 17, Josefov (222 326 203/ www.pravdarestaurant.cz). Metro Staroměstská.
Open noon-midnight daily. **$$$.**
International. Map p96 B2 ㉞
Owner Tommy Sjoo, who helped bring fine dining to post-1989 Prague, now runs a nicely airy and elegant restaurant. Chicken in Senegal peanut sauce vies with Vietnamese nem spring rolls and borscht, all done credibly. High ceilings, an Old Europe atmosphere, aproned waiters and graceful service.

U Provaznice

Provaznická 3, Nové Město (224 232 528). Metro Můstek.
Open 11am-midnight daily.
Pub. Map p96 C4 ㉟
Incredibly, this classic pub, with all the Bohemian trad fare (duck, smoked meat and dumplings) is buzzy, reasonably priced and within spitting distance from the Můstek metro.

La Provence

Štupartská 9 (296 826 155/ reservations 800 152 672/ www.kampagroup.com). Metro Náměstí Republiky. **Open** noon-11pm daily.
$$$. French. Map p97 D3 ㊱
Under the management of Nils Jebens, the Czech Republic's answer to Terence Conran, La Provence is a comfy rural French restaurant that does foie gras, tiger prawns, roast duck and monkfish.

Red Hot & Blues

Jakubská 12 (222 323 364). Metro Náměstí Republiky.
Open 9am-11pm daily. **$.**
Mexican. Map p97 D3 ㊲

Perhaps best on Sunday mornings for eating brunch on the patio, this requisite expat institution first introduced Cajun and Mexican platters to Bohemia. Now conveniently heated and enclosed for winter, it's a reliable and relaxed place to visit. You're best off avoiding the overpriced drinks specials.

U Sádlů
Klimentská 2 (224 813 874/ www.usadlu.cz). Metro Náměstí Republiky/tram 5, 14, 26. **Open** 11am-1am Mon-Sat; noon-midnight Sun. **$**. **Czech**. Map p97 D2 ⏰

OK, it's medieval kitsch – but efficient, tasty and affordable. A good quantity of mead with pepper steak or boar can make for a great Friday night out here. But reading the illuminated menu by torchlight can be a challenge.

Sarah Bernhardt
U Obecního domu 1 (222 195 195). Metro Náměstí Republiky. **Open** 6.30am-11pm daily. **$$$**. **Central European**. Map p97 D3 ⏰

The favourite model for Alfons Mucha has lent more than her name to this fabulously gilded lobby restaurant of the Hotel Paříž. The award-winning chef has revived the place of late and a series of tasting menus overseen by celeb guest chefs and a vinotheque with take-out foie gras have built up further buzz.

Siam-I-San
Valentinská 11 (224 814 099). Metro Staroměstská. **Open** 10am-midnight daily. **$$**. **Thai**. Map p96 B3 ⏰

This chic Thai restaurant sits above a designer glassware shop, and has the biggest selection of fiery South-east Asian appetisers in town. Eating here like being in a fishbowl, but it's handy for Old Town, and fairly priced.

Siam Orchid
Na Poříčí 21 (222 319 410/ www.siamorchid.cz). Metro Náměstí Republiky. **Open** 10am-10pm daily. **$$**. **Thai**. Map p97 F2 ⏰

An easy-to-miss family joint, up the stairs in a shopping passage, Siam Orchid has the most authentic, unpretentious Thai food in town. Try chicken satay and delicious mains of fried tofu with mung beans, fiery chicken and cod curries, plus Thai beer.

Slavia
Smetanovo nábřeží 2 (224 218 493/ www.cafeslavia.cz). Metro Národní třída. **Open** 8am-11pm daily. **Café**. Map p96 A5 ⏰

A struggling Václav Havel and pals once tippled and plotted the overthrow of communism at the Slavia. But they would not recognise it these days. The new, art deco-style fixtures and crisp service were overdue, but they are not the stuff of Jaroslav Seifert's classic poem *Café Slavia*. Castle views, free Wi-Fi and a decent salmon toast contribute to the charm. But watch out for the pickpockets.

Století
Karolíny Světlé 21 (222 220 008/ www.stoleti.cz). Metro Národní třída. **Open** noon-midnight daily. **$**. **Continental**. Map p96 A5 ⏰

Comfortable and imaginative, Století doesn't waste any effort on empty flourishes. Encompassing a good choice of food for vegetarians, including a delicate spinach soufflé, the list of affordable mains otherwise favours roast beef, chicken and pork, served with interesting sauces such as cold orange curry and cayenne.

Le Terroir
Vejvodova 1 (602 889 118). Metro Můstek. **Open** 11am-11pm daily. **Wine bar**. Map p96 B4 ⏰

With its massive wine list, strong on Spanish and French labels, this stone-walled cellar doubles as an upscale resto, with delicate, nouvelle treatments of rabbit, venison and lamb. It's evolved since opening as a smart wine bar a few years ago, but can still be a bit stiff, like many such places here.

Tretter's

V kolkovně 3 (224 811 165/www.
tretters.cz). Metro Staroměstská.
Open 7pm-3am Mon-Sat; 11am-2am
Sun. **Bar**. **Map** p96 C2 ⑨⑤

With bar staff who've all graduated
from Miloš Tretter's academy, you
won't find any slouching. The shakers
are always flying, the maroon scheme
and retro decor provide a classy vibe
and there are occasional blues singers
– that and 50 cocktails created by the
owners. Try the Moncheri, a coffee,
cherry liqueur and cream confection.

U Vejvodů

Jilská 4 (224 219 999/www.restaurace
uvejvodu.cz). Metro Můstek.
Open 10am-3am Mon-Thur; 10am-4am
Fri-Sat; 10am-2pm Sun. **$$**. **Czech**.
Map p96 B4 ⑨⑥

Another brewery-licensed mega beer-
hall (Pilsner Urquell), this multilevel
pub caters to big tour groups; stick to
the smaller front room to avoid them.
It has quick service and old-style wood
interiors, accented by huge copper beer
vat lids. For an olde pub feel, fine brews
and trad fare, it's hard to beat.

La Veranda

Elišky Krásnohorské 2 (224 814 733/
www.laveranda.cz). Metro
Staroměstská/tram 17, 18. **Open** noon-
midnight Mon-Sat; noon-10pm Sun.
$$$. **Fusion**. **Map** p96 C2 ⑨⑦

This top-rated dining room and cellar
has morphed into an affordable gem
with great value lunch specials. Taking
pride in using only local beef, rabbit
and lamb derived from South Bohemia,
La Veranda serves up approachable
modern conceptions of the Czech classics, along with al dente pastas and
specialities, such as quail and coffee
crème brûlée.

U Zlatého tygra

Husova 17 (222 221 111/www.
uzlatehotygra.cz). Metro Staroměstská.
Open 11am-11pm daily. **Pub**.
Map p96 B4 ⑨⑧

Small, full of cranky old locals and an
equally testy staff, At the Golden Tiger
was once the second home of Prague's
favourite writer, the crotchety Bohumil
Hrabal. But it has lost virtually all its
appeal since its famous patron fell to his
death from a hospital window in 1997.

Shopping

Alma Mahler

Valentinská 1 (222 325 865/
www.almamahler.cz). Metro
Staroměstská. **Open** 10am-7pm
Mon-Fri. **Map** p96 B3 ⑨⑨

This quaint, family-run shop collects
items from homes all over the country,
specialising in Bohemian glass, porcelain, textiles and jewellery. It has good
variety and makes for an excellent
place in which to browse.

Antik v Dlouhé

Dlouhá 37 (224 826 347). Metro
Staroměstská. **Open** 10am-7pm
Mon-Fri; noon-6pm Sat, Sun.
Map p97 D2 ⑩⓪

A gold mine of Bohemian goodies from
yesteryear, ranging from handmade
toys to lovely art deco table lamps. Tin
advertising signs and lovely pins,
brooches and rings, some quite affordable and all unique, are stocked. The
friendly staff speak English too.

Art Deco

Michalská 21 (224 223 076). Metro
Staroměstská or Národní třída. **Open**
2-7pm Mon-Fri. **Map** p96 B4 ⑩①

Dress-up fun galore: vintage clothing
and lots of jewellery, as well as an inter-
estingly varied mix of other goodies.
The prices are fair as well.

Artěl

Celetná 29 (entrance on Rybná)
(224 815 085/www.artelglass.com).
Metro Náměstí Republiky. **Open**
10am-8pm daily. **Map** p97 D3 ⑩②

Something different in the classic art of
Czech crystal – that's been designer
Karen Feldman's conception since

Roxy p120

opening this speciality business in the 1990s, now with a downtown retail location. A variety of designs are etched into glassware by local artisans, which have proven to be hot sellers.

Atelier Tatiana
Dušní 1 (224 813 723/www.tatiana.cz).
Metro Staroměstská. **Open** 10am-7pm
Mon-Fri; 11am-4pm Sat. **Map** p96 C3 **103**
Tatiana Kováříková's clothing is a mixture of high-fashion elegance and practicality. Garments are perfectly cut and beautifully styled, complete with lovely details.

Big Ben Bookshop
Malá Štupartská 5 (224 826 565/
www.bigbenbookshop.com).
Metro Náměstí Republiky.
Open 9am-7pm Mon-Fri; 10am-5pm
Sat; noon-5pm Sun. **Map** p97 D3 **104**
Big Ben probably has the widest selection in town, with fiction, non-fiction, an excellent children's section and a good pick of English newspapers and magazines. If your title isn't in stock, staff will order it. Booksellers are friendly and knowledgeable; the place sells gift certificates too.

Boheme
Dušní 8 (224 813 840/
www.boheme.cz). Metro Náměstí
Republiky. **Open** 11am-7pm Mon-Fri;
11am-5pm Sat. **Map** p96 C2 **105**
Jan and Hana Stocklassa set up the label behind this shop in 1991 and the latter's designs for wearable but distinctive knits and leather have been a hit ever since. With an understated sense of style and monochrome classic tones, it's not hard to see why.

La Casa del Habano
Dlouhá 35 (222 312 305/
www. lacasadelhabano.cz).
Metro Staroměstská. **Open** 9am-9pm
daily. **Map** p97 D2 **106**
A franchise of the Cancun-based chain of luxe cigar emporiums-cum-bars, this darkwood, clubby room is bound to attract the Czech nouveaux riches with its 40-year-old single malts, humidors and fine selection of Cuban stogies.

Dr Stuart's Botanicus
Týnský Dvůr 3 (224 895 446/
www. botanicus.cz). Metro Náměstí
Republiky. **Open** 10am-8pm daily.
Map p96 C3 **107**

PRAGUE BY AREA

As well as a wide range of soap, lotions and bathing salts and gels, Botanicus also has herb-infused oils, teas, honey and other food stuffs. Products are entirely Czech, with all the ingredients grown on a farm just outside Prague.

Kubista

Dům u Černý Matky Boží, Celetná 34 (224 236 378/www.kubista.cz). Metro Náměstí Republiky. **Open** 10am-6pm Tue-Sun. **Map** p97 D3 **108**

Cubism proved quintessential to the development of modern art and architecture in Prague and here you can find it on a variety of finely crafted objects. For an authentic piece of Boho culture, check out the original cubist porcelain and furniture, as well as the excellent replicas and art books.

Manufaktura

Karlova 26 (221 110 079). Metro Staroměstská. **Open** 10am-6pm daily. **Map** p96 B4 **109**

For a truly Czech gift, and one that's natural to boot, try the chainstore whose motto is 'inspired by nature'. There are blue print items, which incorporate a fabric dyeing technique used in Bohemia in the 18th century, tablecloths, handkerchiefs and more.

Modes Robes

Benediktská 5 (224 826 016/www. cabbage.cz/modes-robes). Metro Náměstí Republiky. **Open** 10am-7pm Mon-Fri; 10am-4pm Sat. **Map** p97 D2 **110**

The interior of this tiny shop is as much a reason to visit as the stock. Designed by a Czech artist, Modes Robes has been selling unique clothing, accessories and art for over ten years. Dresses for every age are flattering.

Pavla & Olga

Karoliny Světle 30 (no phone). Metro Národní třída. **Open** 10am-7pm daily. **Map** p96 A4 **111**

This boutique, run by two hip Czech sisters, is made up of just one small room, yet manages to get itself featured in all the glossy magazines with its wonderful creations for local celebrities. These include fresh, sophisticated designs and quality materials – alas, nothing for guys, though.

Pohodlí

Benediktská 7 (224 827 026/ www.etno.cz). Metro Náměstí Republiky. **Open** 11am-7pm Mon-Fri; 10am-4pm Sat. **Map** p97 D2 **112**

'We are the world, and we have the music from all corners to prove it' seems to be the motto here. Indian and African music is stocked, plus some local Czech and Moravian folk, along with world as well.

Rock Point

NEW *Martinská 2 (224 228 060/ www.rockpoint.cz). Metro Můstek.* **Open** 10am-8pm Mon-Fri, 10am-6pm Sat-Sun. **Map** p96 B5 **113**

This hip and friendly Czech-owned chain stocks an extensive range of equipment for skiing, hiking, rock climbing and just about every other kind of outdoor sport. Sales offer deals on nifty accessories.

Slovanský Dům

Na Příkopě 22, (221 451 400/ www.slovanskydum.cz). Metro Můstek. **Open** 10am-8pm daily. **Map** p97 D3 **114**

Prague's slickest downtown mall on Na Příkopě contains the city's most popular multiplex cinema, a decent Italian café, and a nice sushi restaurant. Jewellery and fashion shops fills out the rest. Once you're shopped out, revive with a Thai massage.

Toalette

Karoliny Světle 9 (777 128 729). Metro Národní třída. **Open** 10am-7pm Mon-Fri. **Map** p96 B5 **115**

Monika Burdová's vintage clothesshop-cum-boutique is a great find on one of Old Town's most appealing little lanes. Quirky streetwear meets affordable fashion by local artists.

Trafika Můstek

Václavské náměstí (no phone). Metro Můstek. **Open** 8am-10pm daily.
Map p96 C4 **116**

If you are looking for an English-language periodical, this kiosk at the base of Wenceslas Square should have exactly what you need.

Nightlife

Banco Casino

Na Příkopě 27 (221 967 380/www. bancocasino.cz). Metro Náměstí Republiky. **Open** 24hrs daily.
Map p97 D3 **117**

Classy enough to serve as a set in Prague-shot Bond flick *Casino Royale*, the Banco is a reputable, plush establishment with private salons and high-tech slots for those not into green felt.

Blues Sklep

Liliová 10 (774 277 060/www.blues sklep.cz). Metro Můstek. **Open** 7pm-2.30am daily. **Map** p96 B4 **118**

Local artists and the occasional touring band draw regular crowds to the Blues Cellar's intimate, relaxed space. Top-flight performances are not always guaranteed, but with shows running 9pm to midnight, it won't take up the whole night.

Buddha-Bar

NEW *Jakubská 8 (221 776 300/ www.buddha-bar-hotel.cz). Metro Náměstí Republiky.* **$$$**.
Map p96 D3 **119**

The splashiest opening of 2009 was the launch of a branch of this global phenomenon in Prague's Old Town. The characteristically decadent hotel above is a satellite of the Paris-based Buddha Bar group (see p169). Here, you'll find a trademark exotic and oppulent atmosphere of lantern-lit Asian accents and an epic bar, with a cool DJ programming policy. This high-end venue provides enlightened partying for those who still have portfolios.

U Bukanýra

NEW *Nábřeží Ludvika Svobody, under Štěfánik Bridge (777 221 705/ www.bukanyr.cz).Metro Náměstí Republiky.* **Open** 4pm-midnight Tue-Thur; 4pm- 6am Fri; 9pm-6am Sat.
Map p97 D1 **120**

The programme at this floating barge party can be a little iffy. House DJs hold sway when 'At the Buccaneer' is operating, but it's not unheard of for the club to go dark for several weeks at a time. Still, the barge is good fun when it's open. There are no worries about getting pirated away; this buccaneer doesn't cruise.

Cabaret Captain Nemo

Ovocný trh 13 (224 211 868/ www.escort.cz). Metro Můstek. **Open** 8pm-5am daily. **Map** p97 D3 **121**

Captain Nemo is a handy Staré Město strip club that employs mainly Czech talent and goes for a nautical theme, although it's not clear whether anyone has noticed yet.

Casino Palais Savarin

Na Příkopě 10 (224 221 636/ www.czechcasinos.cz). Metro Náměstí Republiky. **Open** 4pm-3am daily.
Map p97 D4 **122**

Old-school Mitteleuropa gambling with hushed, well-groomed croupiers, and an old, grand palace stairway to sweep you inside. The vibe at the Casino Palais Savarin is professional and assured, so dress up for the evening and expect to be served complimentary drinks.

Friends

Bartolomějská 11 (226 211 920/ www.friends-prague.cz). Metro Národní třída. **Open** 4pm-3am daily.
Map p96 B5 **123**

Friends is a relaxed, comfortable, grown-up sort of place to party, and a great spot in which to become acclimatised to Prague's gay scene. Originally located around the corner, this new incarnation revives one of the longest

Round-up rhapsodies

Why are Prague's ensembles music to filmmakers' ears?

For classical music fans in Prague, there's often a familiar ring to that soundtrack they hear during a Western, when the band of hardy cowpokes is riding herds across a magnificent vista. The Czech Philharmonic, like a handful of other orchestras in Eastern Europe facing funding crises, is the go-to group for a rising number of filmmakers, who want to achieve the epic effect on an indie budget.

No doubt having heard David Lynch rave about the Czech Phil's chamber ensemble – they feature on many of the surrealist filmmaker's creepy soundtracks – scores of producers have joined up with Prague's lean and hungry orchestras. Ranging from the Czech National Orchestra to a group of filmscore specialists called the FILMharmonic Orchestra Prague, they have discovered serious bang for the buck.

Some films, like *Open Range*, have even been guilty of using Czech musicians to try to shore up weak storylines or a lack of dramatic tension, possibly in the hope that 'sweep' alone might carry the picture. (This one, despite a starring role for Robert Duvall, disappeared from screens quickly.)

As is the case for the Czech film sector in general, competition from the east for foreign production dollars is heating up. The recent David Fincher and Tarsem Singh fantasy *The Fall* enlisted the Bulgarian Symphony Orchestra's services to great effect in creating its exotic dreamworld. The opening sequence, a black-and-white ode to silent filmmaking overlaid with a stirring recording of Beethoven's 7th Symphony, sets the grandiose tone. But spending a few weeks in the company of world-class musicians is a prospect that is obviously still appealing to many.

So Michael Kamen can attest: the sci-fi composer, best known for his work on *Event Horizon* and *What Dreams May Come*, used tracks by the Czech Phil on the robot movie *The Iron Giant*, produced by Pete Townshend.

established and best-known gay bars in the city. There is a sizeable dance floor, which provides space for proper dancing to amusingly kitsch tunes, which roll out over a good sound system all through the night (DJ parties take place Wed-Sat). Other attractions include Wi-Fi.

Karlovy Lázně
Smetanovo nábřeží 19 (222 220 502/www.karlovylazne.cz). Metro Národní třída. **Open** 11am-5am daily. **Map** p96 A4 ❹
If you are drawn to the kind of club where teens line up for an hour to get in, this place will be right up your street. The city's megaclub, which was set up in a former public baths building with five floors of action (a different genre on each), is situated next to the Charles Bridge. Which makes navigation easier when you're, like, totally wasted, dude.

Millennium Casino
V Celnici 10 (221 033 401/www. millenniumcasino.cz). Metro Náměstí Republiky. **Open** 3pm-4am daily. **Map** p97 E3 ❺
Plush, classy and palatial, the Millennium looks like an appropriate playground for any passing super-spies. It's part of a spick and span hotel and retail complex just east of Staré Město; free drinks for players add to the fun.

N11
Národní třída 11, Nové Město (222 075 705/www.n11.cz). Metro Národní třída. **Open** 8pm-4am Tue-Thur; 7pm-5am Fri, Sat. Call for Sun opening hrs. **Map** p96 A5 ❻
Lining up a fairly tame programme of pop music, rock and reggae tracks, laid down by skilled DJs, N11 doesn't set out to challenge its patrons. However, this smoke- and drug-free party place (which serves decent food at reasonable prices) features a great sound system and light racks, along with occasional live acts.

Petrovič
Rytířská 8 (224 210 635). Metro Můstek. **Open** 6pm-midnight daily. **Map** p96 C4 ❼
Not just a handy downtown Russian restaurant with authentic cuisine and staff, but also an occasional venue for jazz or folk recitals in a deep club cellar.

Roxy
Dlouhá 33 (224 826 296/ www.roxy.cz). Metro Náměstí Republiky. **Open** 7pm-2am Mon-Thur; 7pm-4am Fri, Sat. **Map** p97 D2 ❽
The run-down Roxy is Prague's top destination for house, R&B and jungle music, thanks largely to plugged-in party organisers. Star acts, which no other club could afford, get talked into doing shows here, as do local kings of the decks. Free Mondays pack the place with students.

U Staré Paní
Michalská 9 (224 228 090/ www.ustarepani.cz). Metro Můstek/ Národní třída. **Open** 7pm-2am daily. **Map** p96 B4 ❾
Located in the cellar of the hotel of the same name, U Staré Paní is one of Old Town's top venues for local talents. The dark space, with modern decor and a few decent wines at the back bar, forms a club in more ways than one, with players and audiences who are well known to each other. This can be good and bad.

Tropison cocktail bar
Náměstí Republiky 8 (224 801 276/ www.tropison.com). Metro Náměstí Republiky. **Open** 8pm-5am Mon-Fri; 7pm-5am Sat; 6pm-5am Sun. **Map** p97 D3 ❿
The service and uninspiring menus aren't likely to tempt you, but the view from Tropison's cocktail bar terrace will. Your chance to boogie down on the grave of communism (which was once a state run department store) at the silly Latin dance parties. Put it down as a 'maybe'.

Rudolfinum p122

Vagon

Národní třída 25 (221 085 599/
www.vagon.cz). Metro Národní třída.
Open 6pm-5am Mon-Sat; 6pm-1am
Sun. **Map** p96 B5 ⓭

This smoky little cellar hosts bands
playing fresh, unrecorded rock, jam
nights and reggae, live and on the
sound system. A student bar with a
love for chilled-out, dreadlocked hang-
ing-out. The entrance is hidden in a
shopping passage.

Velmý Jemný Klub Limonádový Joe

Revoluční 1 (221 803 304/
www.velmijemnyklub.cz). Metro
Náměstí Republiky. **Open** 10am-3am
daily. **Map** p97 D2 ⓲

Limonádový Joe was a beloved Czech
singing cowboy from the movies and
this eclectic, local club, situated next to
the Kotva department store, has a bit
of a western theme. But mostly it's
known for a retractable roof, late hours,
cheap drinks and playing host to amusing local rock bands.

Vertigo

Havelská 4 (774 744 256/www.vertigo-
club.cz). Metro Můstek. **Open** 9pm-4am
daily. **Map** p96 C4 ⓳

Vertigo offers three levels of café and
clubbing space, with decent DJs, decor,
lights and sound, along with the obligatory LCD displays. It can range from
being on the quiet side to attracting
lively crowds these days.

Arts & leisure

AghaRTA

Železná 16 (222 211 275/www.
agharta.cz). Metro Můstek/
Staroměstská. **Open** *Club* 7pm-1am
daily. *Concerts* 9pm. *Jazz shop*
5pm-midnight Mon-Fri; 7pm-midnight
Sat, Sun. **Map** p96 C4 ⓭

Named after one of Miles Davis's most
controversial LPs, this jazz mecca has
moved to Old Town from its old digs
off Wenceslas Square, but has kept its
lively following intact. The owners run
the AghaRTA fest, which has brought
the likes of Chic Corea and John
McLaughlin to town, but regular local
acts are well worth catching. Look out
for the club's own ARTA label.

Archa Theatre

Divadlo Archa
Na Poříčí 26 (221 716 333/www.
archatheatre.cz). Metro Náměstí
Republiky or Florenc. **Map** p97 F2 ⓭

Arguably the most important centre for new and experimental work in the Czech Republic, Archa covers a wide variety of art forms: dance, music, theatre, film and puppetry. Czech artists such as Iva Bittová and Petr Nikl grace the stage and Václav Havel's new play, *Odcházení (Leaving)*, premièred here, rather than the National Theatre.

Chapel of Mirrors

Zrcadlová kaple
Klementinum, Mariánské náměstí (221 663 111/212). Metro Staroměstská. **Open** Concerts usually start at 5pm or 8pm. **Map** p96 B4 ⓲⓳⓴
This pink marble chapel in the vast Clementinum complex hosts all manner of Romantic, Baroque and original chamber and organ recitals – oddly enough, along with regular Gershwin.

Church of St Nicholas

Chrám sv. Mikuláše
Staroměstské náměstí (224 190 994). Metro Staroměstská. **Open** Concerts usually start at 5pm or 8pm. **Map** p96 B3/C3 ⓲⓳⓴
The church can't compete with its namesake across the river in Malá Strana, but still hosts regular organ, instrumental and vocal recitals in a plainer yet still pretty setting. Most focus on popular Baroque art.

Estates Theatre

Stavovské divadlo
Ovocný trh 1 (224 901 448/ www.nd.cz). Metro Můstek/ Staroměstská. **Map** p96 C4 ⓲⓳⓴
This shrine for Mozart lovers – where *Don Giovanni* and *La Clemenza di Tito* received their premieres – still features his works. The theatre, built by Count Nostitz in 1784 and now restored to its former glory, also offers interesting lesser-known work. Gaetano Donizetti's *Don Pasquale* and Theodor Veidl's *Die Kleinstädter* are among the pieces that have been staged here. It hosts much theatre but still regular opera. Some dance performances use taped music!

Jazz Boat

Čechův most (731 183 180/www.jazz boat.cz). Metro Staroměstská. **Open** 8.30pm-11pm daily. **Map** p96 B1 ⓲⓳⓴
Find the EVD pier No.5 just downstream from the Čechův bridge and board the *Kotva* for the most tuneful cruise in town, where top jazz players serenade your dinner of schnitzel and beer (not included in the 590 Kč entry).

Municipal House

Obecni dům
Náměstí Republiky 5 (222 002 336/ 101/www.obecni-dum.cz). Metro Náměstí Republiky. **Map** p97 D3 ⓲⓳⓴
The highest form of Czech art nouveau, built around the Smetana Hall, home to the Prague Symphony Orchestra. The Prague Spring Festival kicks off here every year, in a setting of ceiling mosaics of old Czech myths.

Palace Cinemas Slovanský dům

Na Příkopě 22 (840 200 240/www. palacecinemas.cz). Metro Náměstí Republiky. **Map** p97 D3 ⓲⓳⓴
Prague's most central multiplex shows recent Czech films with English subtitles and international ones in their original language. The cinema boasts a high-tech digital projector that can simulcast live concerts or screen digital films. There is a 30% ticket discount on Wednesdays.

Rudolfinum

Alšovo nábřeží 12 (227 059 352/ www.ceskafilharmonie.cz). Metro Staroměstská. **Map** p96 A2 ⓲⓳⓴
Stately and commanding, this former parliament building is one of Europe's finest concert venues. The neoclassical 19th-century pile has two halls: the Dvořák Hall, for orchestral works, and the Suk Hall, for chamber, instrumental and solo vocal music. Opinion is divided about the acoustics of the former, but the grandeur and musicianship make a visit to the Rudolfinum eminently worthwhile.

Wenceslas Square p131

Nové Město & Vyšehrad

Nové Město

Ever the business-like counterpoint to the mysticism of Staré Město ('Old Town') to the north, this district of rational, broad avenues, intelligently laid out by Charles IV a mere six centuries ago to facilitate trade, is indeed a modern conception. Nové Město, or 'New Town', mixes offices with Baroque burghers' homes, its tram lines and traffic lanes invariably in motion.

It can't compete with the charms of the old quarter, but this former collection of horse markets oriented around Wenceslas Square still has appeal. The vast rectangular 'square' has taken heat for having put profits ahead of aesthetics – prominent neon signs advertising adult clubs are more prevalent than ever – but its art nouveau façades are stunning by day and places like the Lucerna shopping arcade and

the restored rondo-cubist Myšák sweet shop reveal an enduring pride in reviving Prague history.

The area offers a growing array of worthy dining and gallery options with a buzz surrounding restaurants such as **Oliva**, **Bredovský dvůr**, **Modrý zub** and **Pivovarský dům**. Classic clubbing goes on at the **Radost FX Café**, **Nebe** and the **Lucerna Music Bar**.

Aside from being the hub of Prague's burgeoning consumer culture, central Nové Město is where modern art competes for billing with traditional and local streams. Progressive galleries such as the **Leica Gallery** and the **Prague House of Photography** show off this Czech forte, while the **Gallery Art Factory** takes art to the street.

The area is bounded roughly to the north by Národní, which forms the border with Staré Město, and to the east by Legerova, marking

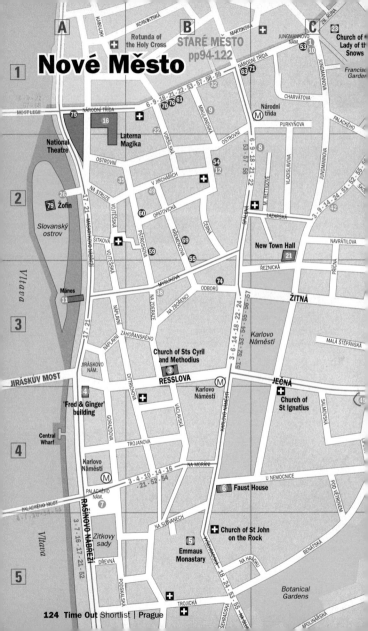

Nové Město

A KAROLINY · KONVIKTSKÁ

Rotunda of the Holy Cross

B STARÉ MĚSTO pp94-122 · MARTINSKÁ

C 28. ŘÍJNA · 29 · Church of Lady of the Snows · JUNGMANNOVO NÁM. · 53 · 1 · 10 · Francisc Garden

1

Národní třída · 63 · 71 · JUNGMANNOVA · CHARVÁTOVA

MOST LEGII · NÁRODNÍ TŘÍDA · 75 · 6 · 9 · 18 · 21 · 53 · 57 · 59 · 70 · 76 · 61 · 32 · 9 · Národní třída Ⓜ · Národní třída · PURKYŇOVA · PALACKÉHO

16 · Laterna Magika · 22 · VORŠILSKÁ · MIKULANDSKÁ · OSTROVNÍ · 8 · 6 · 9 · 18 · 21 · 53 · 57 · 59 · VLADISLAVOVA · JUNGMANNOVA · 3 · 9 · 14 · 24 · 51 · 52 · 55 · SKÉ

National Theatre · OSTROVNÍ · NA STRUZE · 35 · V JIRCHÁŘÍCH · 54 · 12 · M. RETTIGOVÉ · LAZARSKÁ · 42 · NAVRÁTILOVA

2 · 26 · 79 Žofin · MASARYKOVO NÁBŘEŽÍ · 17 · 21 · VOTEŠSKÁ · ŠITKOVA · 48 · OPATOVICKÁ · 60 · KŘEMENCOVA · ČERNÁ · SPÁLENÁ · LAZARSKÁ

Slovanský ostrov · VOJTĚŠSKÁ · PŠTROSSOVA · 59 · 69 · 55 · New Town Hall · **21** · ŘEZNICKÁ · PŘÍČNÁ

Vltava

Mánes · **11** · NÁPLAVNÍ · MYSLÍKOVA · 38 · NA ZDERAZE · 74 · ODBORŮ · ŽITNÁ · MALÁ ŠTĚPÁNSKÁ

3 · 17 · 21 · ZÁHOŘANSKÉHO · NA ZBOŘENCI · 3 · 6 · 14 · 18 · 22 · 24 · Karlovo Náměstí · 3 · 52 · 55 · 56 · 57

JIRÁSKŮV MOST · JIRÁSKOVO NÁM. · DITTRICHOVA · Church of Sts Cyril and Methodius · **3** · RESLOVA · Karlovo Náměstí · JEČNÁ · Church of St Ignatius · 45 · SALMOVSKÁ

4 · 'Fred & Ginger' building · GORAZDOVA · VÁCLAVSKÁ · Karlovo Náměstí Ⓜ · Church of St Ignatius

Central Wharf · TROJANOVA · NA MORÁNI · U NEMOCNICE · POD VĚTROVEM

Karlovo Náměstí Ⓜ · PALACKÉHO NÁM. · **7** · 3 · 4 · 10 · 14 · 16 · 21 · 52 · 54 · **6** Faust House

PALACKÉHO MOST · RAŠÍNOVO NÁBŘEŽÍ · Church of St John on the Rock · NA HRÁDKU

5 · **Vltava** · 3 · 7 · 16 · 17 · 21 · 52 · Žitkovy sady · DŘEVNÁ · **5** Emmaus Monastery · VYŠEHRADSKÁ · 18 · 24 · 53 · 55 · Botanical Gardens

PODSKALSKÁ · TROJICKÁ · SVOBODOVA · NA HRÁDKU · BENÁTSKÁ · APOLINÁŘSKÁ

Bar lit 101

Go behind the scenes of Brendan McNally's novel.

Writer and former military and security journalist **Brendan McNally** found much of his inspiration for *Germania* (Simon and Schuster) in the characters, streets and cafés of Prague that he encountered while living in the city during the 1990s.

Today, he is still an on and off resident of the city. He confesses that, while the historical novel is set in the last days of the Third Reich (it charts the unlikely true story of a band of Jewish acrobats who were drawn into dangerous German intrigues), many of its scenes arose with the help of Prague muses. Some of his most generous resided at two Nové Město drinking holes.

'Coming back to Prague after ten years, the hardest lesson was to stop trying to relive the old days,' he explains. 'Most of the old grungy spots of the 1990s are long gone or, worse, cleaned up. However I still try to pay a visit to

one old *kavárna*, Velryba (The Whale; Opatovická 24, www.kavarnavelryba.cz). It hasn't changed at all, except that the waiters all speak English now.'

Only blocks away is a different redoubt that has squarely rejected the advances of time and Western ideas of customer service, he says.

'Another great dive place that hasn't changed one little bit since Jaroslav Hašek hung out there a hundred years ago is U Kotvy (Spálená 11, 224 930 129).

'The inside is still only for hardcore winter-time beer drinkers, but once the beer garden opens, you would swear that you were back in old Bohemia, drinking with all the great ghosts. An old Czech rock star buddy was awarded an apartment over it because of his dissident acts.'

However, another old favourite of McNally's in nearby Staré Město had quite a different appeal.

'My happiest discovery was the Café Imperial (p106). It's pricey but worth it, because it provides you with the perfect Habsburg café experience – the cheapest time travel experience,' he recalls. 'The fun extra is, they'll let you hurl doughnuts at other customers.'

Sadly, the custom of selling *koblihy*, or jam-filled Czech doughnuts, for bombing other diners, has actually now been dropped at the Café Imperial. These days, it features expensive upholstery and attracts finely dressed patrons, who would be much put out by the sudden necessity for dry cleaning. But no one need tell Brendan that.

the border with Vinohrady. The arterial Wilsonova, with its heavy traffic, forms an ugly gash down the middle and along the eastern edge of the district. On the west lies the Vltava river, whose embankment makes for lovely walks as afternoon light illuminates ornate architecture.

Sights & museums

Adria Palace

Jungmannovo náměstí 28. Metro Můstek. **Map** p124 C1 ❶
A living monument to the heady pre-war movement called Rondocubism, this arcade and collection of galleries and offices features a fine terrace from which to take in the rest of the architecture all around the busy commercial stretch of Národní street below. Built from 1923 to 1925, it's only now that it's really beginning to be revived.

Antonín Dvořák Museum

Muzeum Antonína Dvořáka
Villa Amerika, Ke Karlovu 20 (224 918 013/www.nm.cz/ceske-muzeum-hudby/antonin-dvorak.php). Metro IP Pavlova. **Open** *Apr-Sept* 10am-1.30pm, 2-5.30pm Tue-Sun. *Oct-Mar* 9.30am-1.30pm, 2-5pm Tue-Sun. **Admission** 50 Kč. **Map** p125 D4 ❷
A fair way off the beaten path, but a calming place for classical music lovers to breathe in the atmosphere that inspired one of the great Czech composers. Catching a chamber recital of Dvořák's music in this villa by Kilian Ignaz Dientzenhofer is a special thrill.

Church of Sts Cyril & Methodius

Kostel sv. Cyrila a Metoděje
Resslova 9 (224 920 686). Metro Karlovo náměstí. **Open** *Mar-Oct* 10am-5pm Tue-Sun. *Nov-Feb* 10am-4pm Tue-Sun. **Admission** 60 Kč. **Map** p124 B3 ❸
The scene of a pivotal event in the Czech resistance movement during World War II, this Baroque, 1730s church is scarred by shelling. That

occurred when two Czech paratroopers, trained in England, Josef Gabčík and Jan Kubiš, were found hiding here by the Nazis. Dropped into Bohemia in late 1941 to assassinate Reinhard Heydrich, Reichsprotektor of Bohemia and Moravia, they succeeded but met their end when the SS and Gestapo bombarded the church all night until the assassins took their own lives.

Dancing Building

Tančící dům
Masarykovo nábřeží & Resslova streets. Metro Karlovo náměstí. **Map** p124 A4 ❹
One of the most controversial of Prague's famous buildings, this collaboration between the Croatian architect Vlado Milunič and the US-based Frank Gehry, completed in 1996, is no shrinking violet. Its whimsical glass tower is known locally as 'Fred and Ginger' for the pinch in the centre that makes it resemble the famous hoofers in action.

Emmaus Monastery

Emauzy
Vyšehradská 49 (221 979 211/ www.emauzy.cz). Metro Karlovo náměstí. **Open** *June-Sept* 11am-5pm Mon-Fri; *Oct-May* 11am-4pm Mon-Fri. **Admission** 30 Kč. **Map** p124 B5 ❺
One of the few places where the devastation of World War II is visible in Prague (most of it was in its human toll), this 14th-century church lost its roof to an Allied bombing crew that was off course and mistook the city for Dresden. Its two modern replacement spires look incongruous but are said to be reaching up in an appeal for mercy.

Faust House

Faustův dům
Karlovo náměstí 40. Metro Karlovo náměstí. **Map** p124 B4 ❻
The locus of a persistent legend despite the total lack of any real evidence, this highly ornate 17th-century villa is where Edward Kelly, the earless English alchemist, once lived. The story is that a

poor student was lured into a pact with the Prince of Darkness, accepting riches in exchange for his soul, which Satan then snatched through a hole in the roof.

František Palacký statue

Palackého náměstí. Metro Karlovo náměstí. **Map** p124 A4 ⑦
This huge bronze tribute to the 19th-century historian who took 46 years to write the first history of the Czech people in Czech was created by Stanislav Sucharda. The solemn Palacký sits on a giant pedestal, oblivious to the beauties and demons flying around him.

Galerie České pojišťovny

Spálená 14 (224 054 368/www. galeriecpoj.cz). Metro Národní Třída. **Open** 10am-6pm daily. **Admission** 10Kč. **Map** p124 C2 ⑧
This innovative venue departs from the tradition of local art galleries. Follow one of three passages (from Spálená, Purkyňova or Vladislavova streets) through a courtyard to this exhibition space in an art nouveau building by Osvald Polivka. Contemporary Czech photography and painting by artists of the middle generation, such as Tomáš Cisařovský, Jaroslav Rona and Richard Konvička are exhibited here.

Galerie Gambit

Mikulandská 6 (602 277 210/ www.gambit.cz). Metro Národní třída. **Open** noon-6pm Tue-Fri. **Admission** free. **Map** p124 B1 ⑨
This pocket-sized art gallery focuses on small exhibitions of new works by leading Czech postmodernists – the likes of Michael Rittstein, Petr Nikl and Barbora Lungová – while also presenting fresh young artists, contemporary design and themes such as Eros in art.

Galerie Kritiků

Jungmannova 31 (224 494 205/ www.galeriekritiku.cz). Metro Národní Třída. **Open** 11am-6pm Tue-Sun. **Admission** 40 Kč; 20 Kč reductions. **Map** p124 C1 ⑩

This elegant space in the Adria Palace, with its grand pyramid skylight, has proved itself to be a class act. It is particularly strong on group shows. Its offerings of international art often come from Japan.

Galerie Mánes

Masarykovo nábřeží 250 (224 930 754/www.nadace-cfu.cz). Metro Karlovo náměstí. **Open** 10am-6pm Tue-Sun. **Admission** varies; free children. **Map** p124 A3 ⑪
A fine functionalist art work in its own right, this building straddling a lock of the Vltava river is the largest of the Czech Fund for Art Foundation's network of galleries. The beautiful, if run-down, piece of 1930s culture by Otakar Novotný hosts anything from international travelling shows to exhibitions of contemporary Czech artists and sometimes filmmakers.

Galerie Velryba

Opatovická 24 (224 931 444/ www.kavarnavelryba.cz). Metro Národní třída. **Open** noon-10pm Mon-Sat. **Admission** free. **Map** p124 B2 ⑫
If you can find this space, down the back stairs of a popular local student/art bar – the trendy Velryba café – you win bragging rights. The gallery nurtures students in the photography department of the Czech film academy FAMU and, increasingly, photography departments of other schools.

Gallery Art Factory

Václavské náměstí 15 (224 217 585/ www.galleryartfactory.cz). Metro Můstek. **Open** 10am-6pm Mon-Fri. **Admission** varies. **Map** p125 D1 ⑬
A welcome break from the commercialism of Wenceslas Square, this innovative space is lodged in the interior of the former printing house of the main communist-era newspaper. The painted concrete floors and old industrial hardware serve as a backdrop to shows by Slovak artists, and the gallery also

National Museum p130

organises the annual Sculpture Grande outdoor exhibition of large-scale sculptures up and down the square and on Na Příkopě.

Gestapo Headquarters

Politických vězňů 20 (224 262 874). Metro Můstek. **Open** 8am-1pm daily. **Map** p125 E1 ⑭

Many Czechs were tortured here during the German occupation. Tours of the grim SS interrogation chambers can be booked one week in advance. The street on which the Gestapo HQ lies translates as 'Political prisoners', and still has bad karma (a block north lies the home of the Communist Party of Bohemia and Moravia).

Langhans Galerie

Vodičkova 37 (222 929 333/www. langhansgalerie.cz). Metro Můstek. **Open** 1pm-7pm Tue-Sun. **Admission** 60 Kč; 30 Kč reductions. **Map** p125 D1 ⑮

Once home to the Jan Langhans Atelier, where anyone who was anyone in interwar Prague had their portrait made. Now the emphasis is on historical shows, mixed in with work by established and emerging photographers.

The recurring theme of memory has made for some haunting exhibitions.

Laterna Magika

Národní třída 4 (224 931 482/ www.laterna.cz). Metro Národní třída. **Map** p124 A1/A2 ⑯

The 'Magic Lantern', a frosted-glass monstrosity, was built between 1977 and 1981 as a communist showpiece; the interior of the 'non-verbal' theatre, filled with imported marble and leather, is well-worn and patched. The black light shows that play here aren't worth the admission, perhaps in keeping with an unintentionally ironic socialist relic, but the building holds historical interest.

Leica Gallery

Školská 40 (608 963 523/www.lgp.cz). Metro Můstek. **Open** 11am-9pm Tue-Sun. **Map** p125 D2 ⑰

This respected and innovative photography gallery, run by the same folks who put a travelling show into a train car last year, is back in a new location. The venerated Leica Gallery lost its lease at Prague Castle and has now set up shop across the river, along with a new line-up of Czech and international stars.

Leica Gallery p129

Lucerna Pasáž

Vodičkova 36 (www.lucerna.cz). Metro Můstek. **Map** p125 D1 ⑱

Built from 1907 to 1921, this art nouveau arcade is a remarkable island of character on Wenceslas Square. Inside, where you'll find shops, concert halls, theatres and obscure offices, are faux-marble pillars, arches and grand stairs. Hanging prominently in the largest section is satirist/artist David Černý's take on St Wenceslas, with his horse inverted and dangling from a rope.

Main Station

Hlavní nádraží
Wilsonova 8 (840 112 113). Metro Hlavní nádraží. **Map** p125 F1 ⑲

Undergoing a confusing remake to convert the city's main rail hub into a German-style slick retail centre, the station – also known as Wilsonovo nádraží, or Wilson Station – also hosts scores of seedy types. Its lower levels still feature tons of typical 1970s communist architecture. A glimpse of its art nouveau former self is visible in the Fanta Kavárna, the upstairs café overlooking the main passenger corridor to the platforms.

National Museum

Národní muzeum
Václavské náměstí 68 (224 497 111/ www.nm.cz). Metro Muzeum. **Open** *May-Sept* 10am-6pm daily. *Oct-Apr* 9am-5pm daily. **Admission** 150 Kč; 200 Kč family; free under-6s.
Map p125 E2 ⑳

The iconic neo-Renaissance museum at the top of Wenceslas Square has done more than just take Soviet bullets in 1968; its displays have finally been modernised, with interactive exhibitions on new media now running alongside the older cases of fossils, geodes and stuffed animals. There's still a lack of labels in English but an audio guide is available for an extra 200 Kč.

New Town Hall

Novoměstská radnice
Karlovo náměstí 23 (224 948 229/ www.novomestskaradnice.cz). Metro Karlovo náměstí.
Map p124 C2 ㉑

Dating back to the 14th century, this tower established the Czech form of civil protest known as defenestration when local burghers tossed occupying Habsburg officials to their deaths from a high window in 1419. The Town Hall's current incarnation was built during the 19th and early 20th centuries.

Nová síň

Voršilská 3 (224 930 255/www. novasin.cz). Metro Národní třída. **Open** 11am-6pm Tue-Sun. **Admission** 20 Kč.
Map p124 B1 ㉒

The 1934 product of the Union of Creative Artists is still a central plank of the Prague art scene. The space is a skylit white cube in which many artists rent space and curate their own shows. It's also home to a culture club in which anything from Italian food events to Czech rock'n'roll can take over by night.

Our Lady of the Snows

Kostel Panny Marie Sněžné
Jungmanovo náměstí. Metro Můstek.
Map p124 C1 ㉓

New Town Hall

The towering black-and-gold Baroque altarpiece is awe-inspiring. Also worth seeking out is the church's side chapel, where you can gawp at the trio of gruesome crucifixes. Outside is the world's only Cubist lamp-post.

Paul's Tours

Václavské náměstí (602 459 481/ www.walkingtoursprague.com). Metro Muzeum. **Open** *Tours* 12.30pm Mon, Wed, Fri, Sat. **Map** p125 E2 ㉔

One of the more popular walking tours, Paul's Tours conducts three-hour strolls leading to the Castle. They depart from the equestrian statue of St Wenceslas daily, led by the clever and entertaining Paul and Michal, who charge 300 Kč a head for their historical/pop culture schtick. Pub breaks fill out the sights.

Police Museum

Muzeum policie ČR
Ke Karlovu 1 (974 824 845). Metro IP Pavlova. **Open** 10am-5pm Tue-Sun. **Admission** 30 Kč; 50 Kč family. **Map** p125 D5 ㉕

Sadly, Brek – the stuffed wonder dog responsible for thwarting the defection of several hundred dissidents – has been given a decent burial, but there are still plenty of gruesome exhibits to delight those with a morbid fascination, such as killer lighters and pens.

Slovanský Island

Masarykovo nábřeží. Metro Národní třída. **Map** p124 A2 ㉖

In the days before slacking became an art form, Berlioz was appalled at the 'idlers, wasters and ne'er-do-wells' who mingled here. Today, it's hard to resist the outdoor café or rowing-boats for hire.

St Wenceslas statue

Top of Václavske náměstí. Metro Muzeum. **Map** p125 E2 ㉗

The Czech patron saint, sitting astride his mount, is still the most popular meeting spot in Prague, surrounded by Saints Agnes, Adelbert, Procopius and Ludmila, Wenceslas's grandmother. A few steps below is a headstone with the images of Jan Palach and Jan Zajíc, who burned themselves alive here to protest the Soviet-led occupation of 1968.

Wenceslas Square

Václavské náměstí. Metro Můstek. **Map** p125 D1 ㉘

PRAGUE BY AREA

The modern hub of Nové Město, this broad, one-kilometre boulevard has been the backdrop to every major event of recent history, from the founding of the Czechoslovak Republic in 1918 to the 1989 Velvet Revolution.

Eating & drinking

Alcron

Štěpánská 40 (222 820 038/www. alcron.cz). Metro Můstek. **Open** 5.30-10.30pm Mon-Sat. **$$$$**. **Seafood**. **Map** p125 D2 ㉙

Before World War II, the Alcron was a byword for a top-class night on the town. The name was borne by the predecessor to what is now the SAS Radisson hotel, where the restaurant lurks in a side room off the lobby. Over just seven tables, seafood master Roman Paulus casts lobster bisque and smoked eel with black truffles and savoury sauces. Lunch is by prior arrangement only.

Banditos

Melounova 2 (224 941 096/www. banditosrestaurant.cz). Metro IP Pavlova. **Open** 9am-12.30am Mon-Sun. **$$**. **Americas**. **Map** p125 D4 ㉚

With an expat-friendly, café-style atmosphere, the food runs to Tex-Mex and Southwestern favourites. Try the spicy chicken sandwich, the Caesar salad or the cheeseburgers. Off the beaten path on a small street, but a great gathering point for margarita and bull sessions.

Bredovský dvůr

Politických vězňů 13 (224 215 428). Metro Můstek. **Open** 11am-midnight Mon-Sat; 11am-11pm Sun. **$$**. **Czech**. **Map** p125 E1 ㉛

An open secret among office workers around Wenceslas Square, at this resolutely Czech dining room gruff waiters serve up traditional food and you can sample some of the best Pilsner in town, courtesy of the beer tank – which preserves body and flavour. Hearty pork knuckle, sauerkraut and dumplings are stars.

Café Louvre

Národní 22 (224 930 949/ www.cafelouvre.cz). Metro Národní třída. **Open** 8am-11.30pm Mon-Fri; 9am-11.30pm Sat, Sun. **Café**. **Map** p124 B1 ㉜

Popular since its founding in 1902, this lofty café manages to get away with a garish cream-and-turquoise colour combination, perhaps because it leads to a fine backroom with pool tables. Here, you'll find solid weekend breakfasts and vested waiters. There's also a non-smoking room off to the left side of the bar and a more modern terrace one level below with free Wi-Fi.

Cicala

Žitná 43 (222 210 375/trattoria. cicala.cz/cz). Metro IP Pavlova. **Open** 11.30am-10.30pm Mon-Sat. **$**. **Italian**. **Map** p125 D3 ㉝

A substitute for home to the local Italian community, this warm, low-key cellar features the freshest weekly specials the owner can create or import, presented like works of art. An easily missed two-room restaurant on an otherwise unappealing street, Cicala is worth seeking out.

Deminka

Skřetova 1 (224 224 915/www. deminka.com). Metro IP Pavlova. **Open** 11am-11pm daily. **$**. **Czech**. **Map** p125 E3 ㉞

This celebrated café has changed much since opening in 1886, and at least twice since 1989. These days it's settled on a classically renovated space and menu of upmarket Bohemian classics mixed with quality Italian cuisine. Known recently as Il Conte Deminka, it's reverted to its old moniker. Free Wi-Fi.

Dynamo

Pštrossova 29 (224 932 020/www. dynamorestaurace.cz). Metro Národní třída. **Open** 11.30am-midnight daily. **$$$**. **Continental**. **Map** p124 A2 ㉟

This sleek designer diner typifies the renaissance of the area to the south of the

National Theatre. Steaks and pasta keep up with the decor; don't miss the wall of single-malt scotches, but don't mix them with the lunch specials if you need to be productive. Friendly and speedy.

Hot

Václavské náměstí 45 (222 247 240/ www.hotrestaurant.cz). Metro Muzeum. **Open** 6.30pm-1am daily. **$$. Central European**. Map p125 D1 ③⑥

Hot offers a cool if not exactly peaceful refuge on Wenceslas Square in the lobby of the remade classic Hotel Jalta. The programme's changed from Thai and seafood, but Prague restaurateur Tommy Sjöö now offers a menu high on tender ribs and steaks.

Jáma

V Jámě 7 (224 222 383/www. pub.cz). Metro Můstek. **Open** 11am-1am daily. **$. Czech/Americas**. Map p121 D2 ③⑦

Still a lunch and brunch fave after all these years, American-owned and out-fitted Jáma draws scenesters by day and young business types by night. Lunch specials and happy-hour deals are a big pull, as is the Mex menu. There's a patio space and a children's playground out back, and a bank of internet terminals.

Lemon Leaf

Myslíkova 14 (224 919 056/ www.lemon.cz). Metro Karlovo náměstí. **Open** 11am-11pm Mon-Thur; 11am-12.30am Fri; 12.30pm-12.30am Sat; 12.30-11pm Sun. **$$$. Thai**. Map p124 B3 ③⑧

Well-cooked Thai cuisine, with bargain lunch specials, served in a warm, yellow and dark-wood setting. Lemon Leaf serves the real deal with no compromises for the spice-phobic Czechs. Street tables may appeal.

Modrý Zub

Jindřišská 5 (222 212 622/ www. modryzub.cz). Metro Můstek. **Open** 11am-11pm daily. **$. Thai**. Map p125 D1 ③⑨

With chef Denis Baptiste in the kitchen, along with Asian colleagues who fuss over their curries and satés, Modrý Zub is a popular, reasonably priced, quick and healthy non-Czech lunch option for the Wenceslas Square crowd, who flock here for spicy Thai noodles, a modern casual streetside setting and take-away service at the back.

Musso

NEW *Vodičkova 32 (www.musso-praha. com). Metro Můstek* **Open** 8am-7pm Mon-Sat. **Café**. Map p125 D1 ④⓪

In a new incarnation after opening last year in the Vinohrady district, artisan chocolatier Jean-François Musso's beloved shrine to sweet, dark temptation is drawing more minions than ever with original creations using Valrhona products. Aside from the decadent *religieuse*, Musso also lays on light, healthy lunches.

Myšák

NEW *Vodičkova 31 (731 653 813/ www.gallerymysak.cz). Metro Můstek.* **Open** 8am-8pm Sun-Fri; 9am-8pm Sun. **Sweetshop**. Map p125 D1 ④①

This historic *cukrárna*, which was established in 1903, but reopened in 2009 following 16 dark years, has brought a warm glow to Czech hearts in a newly restored Rondo-cubist building featuring exteriors designed by an avant-garde architect of the time. Excellent ice-creams, sundaes and cakes are already tempting a new generation to abandon their diets.

Novoměstský Pivovar

Vodičkova 20 (222 232 448/ www.npivovar.cz). Metro Můstek. **Open** 10am-11.30pm Mon-Fri; 11.30am-11.30pm Sat; noon-10pm Sun. **$$. Czech**. Map p124 C2 ④②

One of surprisingly few brewpubs in Prague, this is an underground warren with great beer and pub grub, but also busloads of tourists and all the slack service and dodgy maths that accompany them. Some diners swear that its pork knuckle is definitive, and the massive goose platters (order ahead) are a hit with groups of visitors.

Oliva

Plavecká 4 (222 520 288/
www.olivarestaurant.cz).
Metro Karlovo náměstí.
Open 11.30am-3pm, 6pm-midnight Mon-Fri; 6pm-midnight Sat. **$$$**.
Mediterranean. Map p124 D2 ㊸
From Moroccan lamb couscous to veal in mathurini sauce, the Mediterranean accents at Oliva are sumptuous, confident and a wake-up call to the senses. Zingy starters such as mango gazpacho set the tone, and desserts like pain d'épices are hard to resist. The wine list features affordable amd quality choices. Fresh decor and welcoming staff.

The Pack

Ve Smečkách 21 (222 210 280/
www.thepack.cz). Metro Muzeum.
Open 11am-1am daily.
Sports pub. Map p125 D2 ㊹
Perhaps named after the mobs of yobs who were anticipated as customers, the Prague version of Hooters offers buffalo wings and hangover breakfasts served by girls in tight sweaters.

Pivovarský Dům

Lípová 15 (296 216 666/www.
npivovar.cz). Metro Můstek.
Open 11am-11.30pm daily. **$$**.
Czech. Map p124 C4 ㊺
This modern microbrewery should be top of the agenda for any serious beer fan. It makes and sells excellent traditional lager, possibly Prague's best *pivo*, and the various wheat, cherry, champagne and coffee varieties are novelties, which are actually worth trying. There's an affordable menu of traditional Czech cuisine as well.

Pizza Coloseum

Vodičkova 32 (224 214 914/www.
pizzacoloseum.cz). Metro Můstek.
Open 11am-11.30pm daily. **$**. **Pizza**.
Map p125 D1/D2 ㊻

Located just off Wenceslas Square, this top Prague pizzeria serves excellent bruschetta and big, saucy pastas with good wines; there's also a familiar range of steak and fish. Pizzas are typical of the Prague style, with thin crusts but a wide range of zesty toppings that runs from grilled aubergine to classic sausage and tomato sauce.

Radost FX Café

Bělehradská 120 (224 254 776/www.
radostfx.cz). Metro IP Pavlova. **Open**
Restaurant 11am-2am Mon-Wed, 11am-3am Thur-Sun. *Club* 10pm-5am Thur-Sat. **$**. **Vegetarian**. Map p125 E3 ㊼
Prague's first vegetarian restaurant, serving pastas, couscous and meatless Mexican food, has the latest opening hours in town. Dishes are of variable quality and the ornamental tables bash your knees, but it's still as popular as ever. Don't miss the groovy, tassled backroom lounge.

Samurai

Londýnská 120 (222 515 330/
www.sushi-restaurace-samurai.cz).
Metro IP Pavlova. **Open** noon-11.30pm Mon-Sat; 6-11.30pm Sun. **$$**. **Sushi**.
Map p125 E3 ㊽
Taking the Prague sushi craze one step beyond, Samurai wins bonus points for its teppanyaki grill. Decor goes all the way to the max, and is complete with tatami mats and sliding paper panels. It's not just about good looks, though: the seafood and sashimi are both excellent.

Universal

V Jirchářích (224 934 416/www.
universalrestaurant.cz). Metro Národní
třída. **Open** 11.30am-midnight Mon-Sat; 11am-midnight Sun. **$**.
Continental. Map p124 B2 ㊾
With old French advertisements on the wine-coloured walls, an interior inspired by train cars, servers who know their stuff, and appealing daily specials (cod in white sauce, flank steak and rolled veggie lasagne), Universal is

Club classic

Rewind to your student days at the Radost FX Café.

OK, so many members of the youngest, über-hip generation of Prague clubbers would never be dragged to such a popular place as the **Radost FX Café** (p134) these days. After all, everyone's heard of it, the place has been all but an institution since 1991 and even some of its hit party nights, such as Soul Train Weekender, now have a decade-long track record.

Clubbers pushing 40 turn out to shake their booty to the R'n'B tracks of DJ Rico, who has a web page (www.myspace.com/ricosoultrain) that attracts thousands of hits per month and counts grown-up Czech pop stars such as Dara Rolins among fans. Past guests have included Carl Cox and Moby, and the club has made it into the directory www.worldsbestbars.com.

Aside from go-go dancers, showy interior designs and the late-night vegetarian café, the club has a night dubbed 'Remember House', featuring veteran DJs with long Prague pedigrees: Loutka, Trava, Moskito and Groove Dan. Those looking for the latest anarchic buzz are more likely to head to the Holešovice district for a night at Cross Club (p153), they'll tell you with a sniff. Radost is 'too gay', in the words of one, and Duplex (p138) doesn't get the nod either. Both are building up a momentum of party nights for those who like to be seen at their most glam.

This latter club, in a soaring space above Wenceslas Square, has a membership loyalty card, hawks a CD compilation of its scratchers and hosts nights with themes such as Starlight, Moulin Rouge and Dirty Dancing. It even caters for corporate events.

So what's become of the days when you could find starving art students, substances for aiding mind expansion and all manner of decadence at Nové Město clubs? Well, maybe joining the European Union killed all the fun. Or the booming economy, which turned all those art students into middle managers. But do not worry – with world markets in the doldrums, perhaps the gritty days of hiding out from the grim Prague streets in clubs will make a comeback. If ageing DJs can, why ever not?

hard to fault. Sides are as impressive as mains: delectable fresh spinach or crispy gratin potatoes.

Zahrada v opeře

Legerova 75 (224 239 685/www.zahradavopere.cz). Metro Muzeum. **Open** 11.30am-1am daily. **$$.**
International. Map p125 E2 ⓺⓪
The entrance to the Opera Garden is hard to find, at the back of an office building. But the food at this Czech and international dining room makes it worth the effort. Tuna steak in ink is a delight, in keeping with the minimalist decor and quietly gliding waiters.

Zlatá Hvězda

Ve Smečkách 12 (296 222 292/www.sportbar.cz). Metro Muzeum. **Open** 11am-11pm Mon, Tue; 11am-11.30pm Wed, Thur; 11am-1.30am Fri-Sun. **Sports bar**.
Map p125 D2 ⓼①
An oldie but sometimes a goodie. Scuffed interior, poor service and very mediocre pizzas have done nothing to chase off the sports fans who gather here to watch all the games on the battered big-screens.

Zvonice

ⓝⓔⓦ *Jindřišská věž, Jindřišská Ulice (224 220 009/www.restaurantzvonice.cz). Metro Můstek.* **Open** 11.30am-midnight daily. **$$. Central European**. Map p125 D1 ⓼②
Věž means tower in Czech, and here you can dine amid belfry timbers, with the St Maria bell (circa 1518) hanging overhead. It's more than a gimmick, with the likes of delicate rump steak and bacon-wrapped asparagus spears on the menu and good-value lunch specials.

Shopping

Antikvariát Galerie Můstek

Národní 40 (224 949 587). Metro Národní třída. **Open** 10am-7pm Mon-Fri; noon-4pm Sat; 2-6pm Sun. Map p124 C1 ⓼③

A discriminating *antikvariát*, where you'll find a fine selection of old books and a reliable stock of the major works on Czech art.

Antikvariát Kant

Opatovická 26 (224 934 219/www.antik-kant.cz). Metro Národní třída. **Open** 10am-6pm Mon-Fri.
Map p124 B2 ⓼④
Impressive variety and layout make Antikvariát Kant an enjoyable place in which to shop. The entry room has books at 5-15 Kč, many drawings, boxes to poke through and English books. Photographs in boxes by the counter have random subject matter – such as an operating theatre with victim on the table.

Bazar Antik Zajímavosti

Křemencova 4 (no phone). Metro Národní třída . **Open** 11am-6pm Mon-Thur; 11am-5pm Fri.
Map p124 B2/B3 ⓼⑤
Heavy on the glass, this is your typical bazaar. Teacup collectors will think they've found paradise, and other shoppers will appreciate the linens and small collection of paintings and unique lamps.

Beruška

Vodičkova 30 (224 162 129). Metro Můstek. **Open** 10am-6.30pm Mon-Fri; 11am-4pm Sat. Map p125 D2 ⓼⑥
Beruška is a small shop that's filled with toys for young and older children: you'll find a good selection of stuffed animals, clever wooden toys, and all sorts of puzzles and games.

Cellarius

Lucerna Passage, Štěpánská 61 (224 210 979/www.cellarius.cz). Metro Můstek. **Open** 9.30am-8pm Mon-Sat; 2-8pm Sun. Map p125 D1 ⓼⑦
A huge selection of wines is crammed into a small and maze-like space at Cellarius: there are local labels and nice imports, including wines from France, Bulgaria and Chile.

Foto Škoda

Palác Langhans, Vodičkova 37 (222 929 029/www.fotoskoda.cz). Metro Můstek. **Open** 8.30am-8.30pm Mon-Fri; 9am-6pm Sat. **Map** p125 D1 ❸

Sales, repairs, developing and supplies make this shop great for professionals. But amateurs will find what they need as well: a great collection of lights, bags and second-hand lenses. The best pick of things photographic in Prague.

Globe Bookstore & Coffeehouse

Pštrossova 6 (224 934 203/www. globebookstore.cz). Metro Národní třída. **Open** 9.30am-midnight daily. **Map** p124 B2 ❸

The original version of this bookstore was a magnet for literary types from Richard Ford to the beat poets. Today the Globe is handy for buying paperbacks and getting online with a light menu of soups and salads. No beef there; just don't expect to feel like Hemingway.

Hamparadi Antik Bazar

Pštrossova 22 (hamparadi.prodejce.cz). Metro Národní třída. **Open** 2.30-6.30pm daily. **Map** p124 B2 ❻

Take your time to sift through goods here: it can resemble a charity shop, but that's half the fun. The stock is heavy on porcelain and glass, but sometimes includes fun finds like old toys.

Le Patio

Národní 22 (224 934 853/ www.lepatio.cz). Metro Národní třída. **Open** 10am-7pm Mon-Sat; 11am-7pm Sun. **Map** p124 B1 ❶

Le Patio's eclectic stock has colonial, leather and iron furniture, amazing light fixtures and great table settings.

Terryho ponožky

NEW Vodičkova 41 (244 946 829/ www.terryhoponozky.cz). Metro Můstek. **Open** 10am-8pm daily. **Map** p125 D1 ❷

The name, 'Terry's socks', is derived from the leggings that Terry Gilliam

once left to the attached art film club (the shop's in the Světozor cinema). The place sells no hosiery, but lots of posters and lobby cards of Czech and international films, new and vintage.

Tesco

Národní třída 26 (222 003 111). Metro Můstek or Národní třída. **Open** *Department store* 8am-9pm Mon-Sat; 9am-8pm Sun. *Supermarket* 7am-9pm Mon-Sat; 9am-8pm Sun. **Map** p124 B1 ❸

Always packed, and occasionally headache inducing, Tesco nonetheless probably has what you need. Purchase your items separately on each floor: the basement is groceries; the ground floor has cosmetics and beauty supplies, along with a small *potraviny*, or grocer's, and some souvenirs and gifts. Ascending, you'll find men's, women's and children's clothing, home stuff, sport goods and, finally, electronics.

Nightlife

For **Radost FX Café**, see p134.

Be Kara OK!

Legerova 78 (222 240 035/ www.karaokebox.cz). Metro IP Pavlova. **Open** 6pm-2am Mon-Thur; 6pm-5am Fri, Sat. **Map** p125 E3 ❹

Billing itself as the first karaoke box club in the Czech Republic, the collection of padded cellar rooms (with attached sushi bar, natch) has proven a sensation for song-loving Czechs. With fully equipped and miked box rooms available for 400-1,500 Kč per hour, it's okay to wail drunkenly in semi-public. Just swipe the bar-coded songlist with 9,000 tunes in five languages to throw the track you want onto the plasma screen, and sing your heart out.

Darling Club Cabaret

Ve Smečkách 32 (732 250 555/ www.kabaret.cz). Metro Muzeum. **Open** 8pm-5am Wed; noon-5am Thur-Tue. **Map** p125 D2 ❺

The biggest bacchanalia in town and a stopover for travelling 'entertainers' from all over, Darling attracts patrons with three plush bars and loads of improbably beautiful women. It wins out over Cabaret Atlas among aficionados, even though it offers the same prices and services.

Duplex

Václavske náměstí 21 (732 221 111/www.duplex.cz). Metro Můstek. **Open** 10pm-5am Wed-Sat. **Map** p125 D1 ⑥⑥

With themes such as Dirty Dancing and Love Parade, Duplex doesn't blaze trails in original DJ programming. That said, the crisp sound system and eyrie of bars and dancefloors in a glass box high over Wenceslas Square make for a unique night out. Afro-Latin nights (as in many Prague clubs, the genre changes nightly) offer live music by the likes of local faves Son Caliente. Dining on site and a chill-out space on the terrace.

Hot Pepper's

Václavske náměstí 21 (724 134 011/www.hotpepprague.cz). Metro Můstek. **Open** 8.30pm-5am daily. **Map** p125 D1 ⑥⑦

A recent addition to Wenceslas Square's increasingly tawdry reputation, Hot Peppers is just for striptease and drinks extortion. For more, customers will have to look elsewhere.

Lucerna Music Bar

Vodičkova 36 (224 217 108/www.musicbar.cz). Metro Můstek. **Open** 8pm-3am daily. *Concerts* 9pm. **Map** p125 D1 ⑥⑧

Threadbare and scuffed interiors disguise this hot club beneath Wenceslas Square. Jazz acts join Czech blues groups and the likes of Ladytron to heat it up when they raise the stage and everyone leans over the balconies to catch a better look. Enter the venue from the faded 1920s Lucerna Passage. Disco nights take over on Fridays and Saturdays.

Nebe

Křemencova 10 (777 800 411/www.nebepraha.cz). Metro Národní třída. **Open** 6pm-2am Mon, Sun; 6pm-4am Tue-Thur; 6pm-5am Fri, Sat. **Map** p124 B2 ⑥⑨

It may not live up to its claim to have 'inimitable' atmosphere and 'delicious cocktails at very attractive prices', but 'Heaven' offers a good time for clubbers on a budget, many of whom are foreign students. Some 50 drinks under 100 Kč, DJs who know a good beat and no one objects to you snogging in a corner.

Rock Café

Národní třída 20 (224 933 947/www.rockcafe.cz). Metro Národní třída. **Open** 10am-3am Mon-Fri; 5pm-3am Sat; 5pm-1am Sun. *Concerts* 7pm. **Map** p124 B1 ⑦⓪

With a programme that ranges from the Frames to cult talents such as Roe-Deer, this spacious underground hall is one of the bastions of live rock and blues in the city. An impassioned local following, folk who appreciate its embrace of the strange, and its unpretentious bunker-like qualities.

Arts & leisure

Evald

Národní třída 28 (221 105 225/evald.cinemart.cz). Metro Národní třída. **Map** p124 B1/C1 ⑦①

Arrive here early for any hope of a seat if the film is a good title: this downtown arthouse is one of the best, but it's seriously space-challenged. The owners distribute films and often have exclusive bookings on various European art movies, independent American films and Czech flicks, which are sometimes shown with English subtitles.

Lucerna Cinema

Vodičkova 36 (www.lucerna.cz). Metro Můstek. **Map** p125 D1 ⑦②

It shows mainly Hollywood fare, but the Lucerna is also a hub for Czech independent cinema. An art nouveau wonder, it will remind you how magical going to the movies once was. Large windows in the elevated lobby bar allow you to gaze at the 1920s-era shopping arcade. The theatre has been steadily moving towards featuring more European films in recent years.

Lucerna Great Hall

Vodičkova 36 (224 212 003/www. lucpra.com). Metro Můstek.
Open *Concerts* start 7-8pm.
Map p125 D1/D2
Run independently from the Lucerna Music Bar (see p138), this massive, pillared, underground hall hosts big-time acts from Maceo Parker to the Cardigans. Its art nouveau ballrooms, balconies, grand marble stairs and wooden floors add a palatial feel to rock shows. There are no regular box office hours, so book ahead via an agent such as Ticketpro (www.ticketpro.cz).

MAT Studio

Karlovo náměstí 19 (224 915 765/ www.mat.cz). Metro Karlovo náměstí.
Map p124 B3
The smallest theatre in town shows a fair mix of offbeat films, Czech classics with English subtitles and archival stuff from Czech TV. The bar has movie props and old posters from Czech films. Buy tickets early – shows inevitably sell out.

National Theatre

Národní divadlo
Národní 2 (info 224 901 448/ box office 224 901 319/www.nd.cz). Metro Národní třída. **Map** p124 A1
Undergoing a badly needed restoration (which has not affected programming as yet), this symbol of Czech nationalism concentrates on Czech opera, drama and ballet. For every brilliant interpretation of Chekhov or Dvořák, there's some tatty, musty old warhouse trundled out from the wings, trailing exhausted performers hitting their lines or notes by rote. The ballet, under the artistic direction of Petr Zuska, fares best.

State Opera

Reduta

Národní třída 20 (224 933 487/ www.redutajazzclub.cz). Metro Národní třída. **Open** *Club* 9pm-midnight daily. *Concerts* 9pm. **Map** p124 B1
Part of Prague history since 1958, Reduta is not home to the young Turks, but has a distinctive vibe (even if it's a bit sad that it still touts Bill Clinton's visit with sax of so many years ago). Cramped bench seating hasn't changed in years, and the venue charges tourist prices but acts are as talented as any in Prague, if decidedly older and softer.

State Opera

Státní Opera
Wilsonova 4 (224 227 266/www.opera. cz). Metro Muzeum. **Open** *Box office* 10am-5.30pm Mon-Fri; 10am-noon, 1-5.30pm Sat, Sun.* **Map** p125 E2
Originally the German Theatre, opened in 1887, this was regarded as one of the finest German opera houses until World War II. Today, it's a separate organisation, and presents contemporary opera alongside standards from the Italian, German, French and Russian repertoires.

Světozor Cinema

*Vodičkova 39 (224 946 824/www.
kinosvetozor.cz). Metro Můstek.*
Map p125 D1 **78**

A new partner of the respected Aero
repertoire house, the Světozor books
consistently engaging and off-beat
independent and global cinema, and
has built up a loyal following of fans.
The kino bar is invariably full of
colourful characters.

Žofín

*Slovanský ostrov (224 934 400/
www.zofin.cz). Metro Národní třída.*
Map p124 A2 **79**

A newly restored cultural centre situated
on an island in the Vltava river,
this large yellow building dating from
the 1880s hosted tea dances and concerts
until just before World War II.
Today, you're more likely to find lectures
and concerts being held here,
alongside one of the sweetest riverside
beer gardens in Prague.

Vyšehrad

Sights & museums

Vyšehrad

*Soběslavova 1 (www.praha-vysehrad.cz).
Metro Vyšehrad.* **Map** below A2 **80**

These tenth-century hilltop castle ruins
feature a cemetery that holds a dozen of
the greats of Czech culture and the neo-
Gothic Saints Peter and Paul, whose
spires dominate the river's skyline.

Eating & drinking

Rio's

*Štulcova 2 (224 922 156/www.
riorestaurant.cz). Metro Vyšehrad.*
Open 10am-midnight daily.
Map below A2 **81**

Cuisine and service pass muster, there
is a good selection of seafood dishes and
pasta and a reasonable wine collection.
But the main draw is the view from
Prague's oldest hilltop castle ruins.

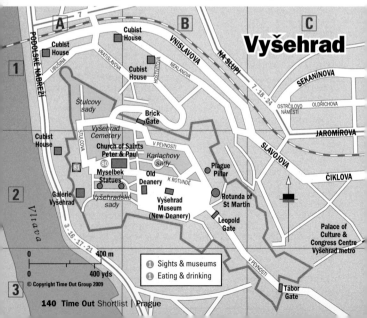

140 **Time Out** Shortlist | Prague

National Memorial p148

Vinohrady & Žižkov

Vinohrady

Once a separate town on what were then the outskirts of Prague, known chiefly as the city's vineyards, Vinohrady is today a stately district of 19th-century apartments, parks, elegant shaded lanes and more than a few great clubs and bars. Along with neighbouring Žižkov, it's the nexus of Prague's gay community and the locale for some of the city's most promising culinary openings.

Vinohrady's well-heeled young residents have cashed in on the Czech Republic's rapid rise in economic standards, which now match those of Western Europe. To meet their discerning tastes, the number of real-estate developers, boutique hotels, gourmet delis and clothiers has grown. The heart of the district is Náměstí Míru, a round 'square' spiked by St Ludmila's twin spires. Its main artery, Vinohradská, formerly called Stalinova třída, is lined with art nouveau façades.

Sights & museums

Church of St Ludmila
Kostel sv. Ludmily
Náměstí Míru (222 521 558). Metro Náměstí Míru. **Open** No official hours. **Map** p143 A2 ❶
Spooky and opulent, this neo-Gothic church marks a hub of the Vinohrady district, the point from which protesters started the march that brought down communism in 1989.

Eating & drinking

Café Medúza
Belgická 17 (222 515 107/www. meduza.cz). Metro Náměstí Míru. **Open** 10am-1am Mon-Fri; noon-1am Sat, Sun. **Café**. **Map** p143 A4 ❷
On a quiet Belgická street, you'll find one of the city's most serene, if threadbare, winter hideout spots, run by two sisters who serve warming soups and mulled wine to bookish regular patrons, along with a few light snacks and herbal liquers. Free Wi-Fi.

Café Sahara

Ibsenova 1 (222 514 987/www.sahara cafe.com). Metro Náměstí Míru. **Open** 11am-12.30am Mon-Fri; noon-12.30am Sat-Sun. **$$. Mediterranean. Map** p143 A2 ❸

Capacious rooms in cool sandstone shades, with big wicker chairs and fashionable waiters: this is a full-on café experience. Add to that a Middle Eastern menu of small plates and the view of Vinohrady's main square, and it's bound to appeal to style fans. The top quality is worth the investment.

La Grotta

Vinohradská 32 (222 520 060/www.la grotta.eu). Metro Náměstí Míru. **Open** 11am-midnight Mon-Sat. **$$. Italian/ seafood. Map** p143 B2 ❹

Having changed its name from Roca, this homely Italian hideout is still a local favourite, although it now features the Sofa Lounge, where karaoke is encouraged. You should be safe upstairs, however, in the non-smoking restaurant, which delivers hearty pastas in creamy sauces along with delicate shellfish and angler in spinach and pecorino. Service is genial, the decor rustic and casual.

Kaaba

Mánesova 20 (222 254 021/www. kaaba.cz). Tram 11. **Open** 8am-10pm Mon-Fri; 9am-10pm Sat; 10am-10pm Sun. **Café. Map** p143 A1 ❺

Filled with second-hand furniture, most of it looking fabulous and repainted in pastels, this neighbourhood café is a haven for local creative idlers. The great windows onto the Vinohrady street and decent wines by the glass from well-known domestic producers make it a good choice for long mornings of lazing with magazines and cheap coffee.

La Lavande

Záhřebská 24 (222 517 406/www.la lavande.wz.cz). Metro Náměstí Míru. **Open** noon-3pm, 5.30pm-midnight Mon-Thur; 5.30pm-midnight Fri-Sun. **$$$. International. Map** p143 B4 ❻

Another Prague contender for gourmet spot of the moment, La Lavande exudes a sense of laid-back charm and quietly efficient service in a semi-casual French farmhouse atmosphere. The Spanish-style rabbit, veal served with green olive and black truffle, fried anchovies with coriander and beef Rossini are all highly recommended.

Park Café

Riegrovy sady 28 (222 717 247). Metro Jiřího z Poděbrad. **Open** 11am-midnight daily. **Café. Map** p143 B1 ❼

One of the liveliest beer gardens in the area is always crowded with old-timers, children, dogs and expats. The beer is cheap and copious, and rock bands liven it up for the summer. Just watch where you step, the dogs leave deposits.

Passepartout

Americka 20 (222 513 340/www. passepartout.cz). Metro Náměstí Míru. **Open** 11am-11pm daily. **$$. Czech/ French. Map** p143 B4 ❽

This elegant but casual island of tasty Francophile fare caters to French property investors who are doing up Vinohrady. Come for quality bistro food, from Moroccan lamb stew to duck confit, preceded by fresh salads and followed by a tempting dessert cart and espresso.

Pastička

Blanická 25 (222 253 228/www. pasticka.cz). Metro Náměstí Míru. **Open** 11am-1am Mon-Fri; 5pm-1am Sat, Sun. **Pub. Map** p143 B1 ❾

The 'Little Mousetrap' is a beloved neighbourhood hangout that's always jumping with an eclectic crowd – especially on the summer terrace out back. They go in for pub grub, beer and cigarettes. Lots of 'em.

Popocafepetl

Italská 2 (777 944 672/www. popocafepetl.cz). Metro Náměstí Míru. **Open** 1pm-2am Mon-Fri; 4pm-2am Sat, Sun. **Café. Map** p143 A2 ❿

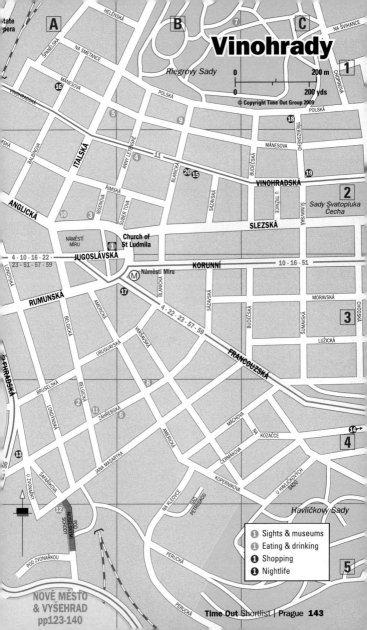

Vinohrady

Pastička p142

A stylish bar in a graceful old building that has long generated a buzz among locals. Food's on offer, but, apart from the grilled meats on the terrace, there's nothing terribly imaginative here. Still, a fine view of the Nusle valley rewards those sitting outside.

Shopping

Fra

Šafaříkova 15 (607 842 045/www. fra.cz). **Metro Náměstí Míru. Open** 9am-11pm Mon-Fri; 4-11pm Sat. **Map** p143 A4 ⓭

A bookshop and café specialising in small-press volumes and works in translation by Czech and Central European writers, with a studious crowd of characters who stage readings and occasional poetry nights.

Shakespeare & Sons

Krymská 12 (271 740 839/www. shakes.cz). **Metro Náměstí Míru. Open** noon-midnight daily. **Map** p143 C4 ⓮

Patterned on Paris's Shakespeare & Co, Prague's conception is considerably scaled down but features walls of well-chosen new and used books, as well as a calendar of publishing-related events and readings and Bernard beer on tap. Cosy, low-key and comfortable if you can find the backstreet it's on.

Nightlife

Bordo

Vinohradská 40 (728 229 554/ www.bordo.cz). **Metro Náměstí Míru. Open** 5pm-2am Mon-Thur; 5pm-4am Fri, Sat; 6pm-2am Sun. **Map** p143 B2 ⓯

Inside this multi-purpose building, your quarry is upstairs. Bordo is usually in a state of renovation but always generates a buzz, booking the coolest underground DJs and occasional bands. Inside its black-washed walls, you'll find infectiously fun nights organised by groups such as www.hiphopfest.cz.

A sister café to the one in Malá Strana (p88), this is the quieter, gentler Popo, but not by much. Regulars fill the space until the wee hours. They're not here for fine service or beers, but somehow the place has always got a buzz, with its mix of local bohemians and decadent expats.

Žlutá pumpa

Belgická 12 (608 184 360/www.zluta-pumpa.info). **Metro Náměstí Míru. Open** noon-12.30am Mon-Fri; 4pm-12.30am Sat, Sun. **$$$. Continental. Map** p143 A4 ⓫

The latest Prague trend, new angles on trad pubbing, finds Czech-Mex expression at the Yellow Pump. It's buzzy, colourful and local, but don't expect outlandishly memorable chow.

Zvonařka

Šafaříkova 1 (224 251 990/www. restauracezvonarka.cz). **Metro IP Pavlova. Open** 11am-midnight daily. **Bar. Map** p143 A5 ⓬

Le Clan

Balbínova 23 (222 251 226/www.
leclan.cz). Metro Náměstí Míru. **Open**
2am-10am Wed-Sat. **Map** p143 A1 ⑯
Offering that thrill of insider exclusiv-
ity yet with a surprisingly democratic
ethic, Le Clan only advertises itself at
street level with a small glowing cres-
cent moon and a red-lit buzzer. But it's
no den of illicit activity, just a comfortable, old-fashioned lounge bar hidden
two levels underground.

Retro Music Hall

Francouzská 4 (222 510 59/www.retro
praha.cz). Metro Náměstí Míru. **Open**
5pm-5am Thur-Sat. **Map** p143 B3 ⑰
With a capacity of 1,200, Retro has
revived a former party palace that
went off the radar for years. The bar
has been raised with some serious
international acts, but the programme
also features student parties (sometimes with foam) and consistency
seems an issue.

Saints

Polská 32 (222 250 326/www.prague
saints.cz). Metro Náměstí Míru. **Open**
7pm-4am daily. **Map** p143 C1 ⑱
A friendly, casual gay bar, with an
open atmosphere (dykes like it, too)
and a small but amusing dance space.
Saints is run by British owners who
excel at cocktails and it doubles as an
information hub for the community in
Prague (the website provides accom-
modation and entertainment listings).

TERmix

Třebízského 4a (222 710 462/www.
club-termix.cz). Metro Jiřího z Poděbrad.
Open 10pm-5am Wed-Sun. **Map** p143
C2 ⑲
Dedicated to the pure ideal of gay and
lesbian drinks, dancing and sex,
TERmix fulfils its obligations beautifully. Ring the bell and descend into the
sleek and chic club, past a long glass
bar, a widescreen TV, sofas and a car
parked in the wall. Two darkrooms,
cabins and a shower too.

Valentino

Vinohradská 40 (222 513 491/www.
club-valentino.cz). Metro Náměstí Míru.
Open 2pm-5am daily. **Map** p143 B2 ⑳
Prague's biggest gay disco is a big
production indeed, at least on the scale
of Czech clubbing. The Red Bar has
nightly oldies tunes and Czech classics; the Star Bar, blasting house and
pop, opens at weekends. Monthly
parties are equally over-the-top, but a
street level bar offers quieter space.
Welcoming yet ebullient.

Žižkov

Still notorious for being Prague's
rough-and-tumble party central,
Žižkov, which lies down the hill to
the north and east of Vinohrady,
offers an appealing contrast with a
concentration of pubs that's said to
be the world's greatest per capita.
Known for its struggling artists,
pleasure-seekers and large Romany
population, Žižkov makes for a
characterful pastiche of good times
and bad behaviour. Always a
working-class district, it's also
home to the greatest monument
to working-class hero Jan Žižka, the
one-eyed Hussite horseman general
and an impressive former signal-
jamming tower.

Sights & museums

Church of the Sacred Heart

Nejsvětější Srdce Páně
Náměstí Jiřího z Poděbrad (no phone).
Metro Jiřího z Poděbrad. **Map** p146
B4/B5 ㉑
Ecclesiastical modernism reaches new
heights in this fantastic (for 1928-32)
church, whose rose window features an
unbroken ramp that you could ascend
on a bicycle. It's one of the most inspiring structures in the city, designed by
Josip Plečnik, the pioneering Slovenian
architect who also redid Prague Castle
to make the mark of the First Republic.

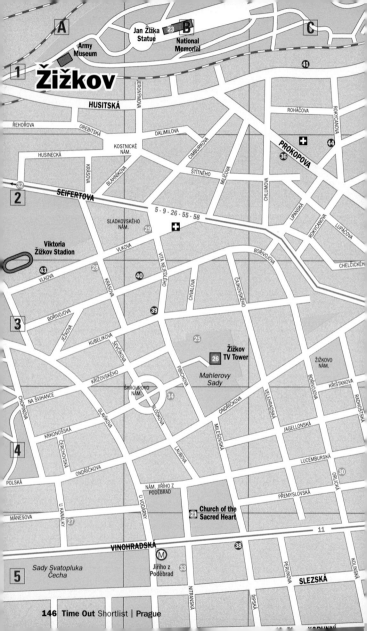

Žižkov

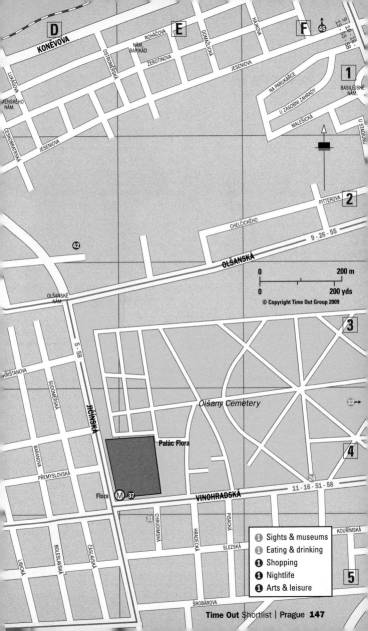

Jewish Cemetery

Židovské hřbitovy

Vinohradská and Jičínská (no phone).
Metro Želivského. **Open** 9am-6pm
daily. **Map** p147 F4 22

Not to be confused with the Old Jewish
Cemetery (p101) in Staré Město,
this neglected posthumous home to
Franz Kafka, founded in 1890, has ivy-
covered graves mainly thanks to the
Holocaust – few family members remain
to care for the graves, while those across
the street are lovingly weeded with fresh
flowers. For Kafka's grave, follow the
sign by the Želivského metro entrance;
it's approximately 200m (660ft) down
the row by the southern cemetery wall.

National Memorial

Národní památník

U památníku 1900 (222 781 676).
Metro Florenc. **Open** times vary
(booking required). **Admission**
varies. **Map** p146 B1 23

Undergoing a major rehab for most of
2009, this monumental mausoleum for
communist big-wigs, where Klement
Gottwald was encased in glass for a
time, is still a draw. Its façades feature
Soviet war heroes and it's topped by
one of Europe's great equestrian statues, a 16.5-ton effigy of Hussite hero
Jan Žižka.

Olšany Cemetery

Olšanské hřbitovy

Vinohradská 153/Jana Želivského
(272 011 113). Metro Flora or
Želivského. **Open** dawn-dusk daily.
Map p147 F4 24

The Garden of Rest honours Red Army
soldiers who died in Czechoslovakia.
To the right of the entrance, is the
grave of anti-communist martyr Jan
Palach, the student who set fire to himself in Wenceslas Square in 1969.

Žižkov Jewish Cemetery

Fibichova (www.jewishmuseum.cz).
Metro Jiřího z Poděbrad. **Open**
9am-3pm Mon, Wed; 9am-1pm Fri.
Admission 50 Kč. **Map** p146 B3 25

Žižkov Tower

This is all that remains of the cemetery
that once covered this square, displaced
by the communist regime to make
way for its Western signal-jamming
transmitter, Žižkov Tower. A poignant
reminder of the not-too-distant past.

Žižkov Tower

Mahlerovy sady (242 418 778/www.
tower.cz). Metro Jiřího z Poděbrad.
Open 10am-11.30pm daily. **Admission**
150 Kč; free under-5s. **Map** p146 B3 26

The huge, thrusting, three-pillared
television tower in Žižkov has long
been dubbed the Pražský pták, or
Prague Prick, by locals. Completed
early in 1989 as a foreign signal-jamming transmitter, it now broadcasts
reality TV shows to eager Czechs. A
lift flies up to the eighth-floor viewing
platform; alternatively, take a drink in
the fifth-floor café of this 216m (709ft)
monstrosity. The intriguing, rather
disturbing babies on the side are the
work of Czech bad-boy artist and
satirist David Černý.

Eating & drinking

Aromi

*Mánesova 78 (222 713 222/www.
aromi.cz). Metro Jiřího z Poděbrad.*
Open noon-11pm Mon-Sat; noon-10pm
Sun. **$$$**. **Italian**. **Map** p146 A5 ㉗
This top Italian restaurant lies quietly
off the tourist radar. Rough wood and
brick interiors bely authoritative kitchen
staff, whose fine dishes include veal on
saffron risotto and a six-seafood antipasti
platter. Excellent wines are fairly priced.

Blind Eye

*Vlkova 26 (no phone/www.blindeye.cz).
Metro Jiřího z Poděbrad.* **Open** 7pm-
4am daily. **Bar**. **Map** p146 A3 ㉘
A late-night hideout for sleep-starved
bohemians, the Blind Eye offers ram-
bling conversations at the wavy iron-
top bar, beer at a booth table and is
popular with student parties.

Café Pavlác

NEW *Víta Nejedlého 23 (222 721 731).
Trams 5, 9, 26.* **Open** 11am-midnight
daily. **Café**. **Map** p146 B2 ㉙
A new centre for the district's latest gen-
eration of creatives and media types,
with the usual brace of quality coffees,
light pesto toasts and a buzzy, urbane
space for trading tips and portfolios.

Hapu

*Orlická 8 (no phone). Metro Jiřího
z Poděbrad.* **Open** 6pm-2am Mon-Sat.
Bar. **Map** p146 C4 ㉚
This one-room cellar with beaten-up
sofas and a small bar has been a living-
room bar to the neighbourhood for years.
That's because it whips up top cocktails
but mixes in none of the pretence often
found in cocktail bars. It usually hosts a
fun crowd of international raconteurs.

Infinity

*Chrudimská 7 (272 176 580/www.
infinitybar.cz). Metro Flora.* **Open**
11am-4am Mon-Thur; 11am-4am Fri;
noon-4am Sat; noon-midnight Sun.
Bar. **Map** p147 E4/E5 ㉛

Hip hangs

For a creative rendezvous, try the zesty Café Pavlác

Every season, a new meeting
spot for Prague's insiders,
media moguls, creatives and
their acolytes. This year, it's
Café Pavlác (p149), which lies
just outside the centre but is not
so far away that it requires any
travel commitment to get to.

Its leafy patio is all but essential
for any urban hub of hip in Prague,
given the limited summers. The
menu is short and sweet, with
favourites like toasts, soups and
smoked salmon, but a sprinkle
more zest – a touch of pesto
here, a vegetarian-friendly tofu
platter there, a reliable supply of
Arabica coffees and friendly staff.

Pavlác is also refreshingly
unpretentious, exhibiting classic
wooden benches and a good dose
of artistry in the custom-made bar.
On the cocktail well, geometrical
patterns intermingle music
scores and blueprint designs;
the vibe is energetic but low-key.
Photographs of urban scenes
hang on mustard-coloured walls
and the clientele is a mix of the
studenty and professional.

In short, it has that intangible
magic touch which makes a great
neighbourhood bar. Until now, the
district only had the **Akropolis**
(p150) as an alternative for urban
trendsetters. Happily, that venue
is also looking up. Its renovated
interior is complete with surrealist
motifs by František Skála and a
cosy, cave system of bars entices
its theatre goers. The fishbowl,
street-level diner is popular among
Praguers on the edge. Looks like
a grand day for a drink in Žižkov.

PRAGUE BY AREA

Infinity draws a dressy crowd for parties and general carousing, and has added a light menu of antipasti and treats such as lamb carpaccio. Its nooks, recessed lighting, brick and red-washed interiors make for mellow sipping, with DJ action after 10pm.

Manni Restaurant

NEW *Seifertova 11 (222 511 660). Trams 5, 9, 26.* **Open** 11am-10pm Mon-Sat. **$. Pakistani. Map** p146 A2 **32**

An affordable, quick and friendly spot for all your tikka, korma, madras and vindaloo needs in a simple, no-fuss setting. Well situated for lunches or rocket-fuel dinners before hitting the local bars and clubs.

Mozaika

Nitranská 13 (224 253 011/www. restaurantmozaika.cz). Metro Jiřího z Poděbrad. **Open** 11.30am-midnight Mon-Fri; noon-midnight Sat; 4pm-midnight Sun. **$. International. Map** p146 B5 **33**

A favourite among locals, friendly, Mozaika offers solid value. Above-average comfort food: praise-worthy hamburgers with fresh mushrooms, home-made pâté and Philly cheesecake are served with speed and cheer, earning Mozaika a loyal following.

U Sadu

Škroupovo náměstí 5 (222 727 072/ www.usadu.cz). Metro Jiřího z Poděbrad. **Open** 8am-4am Mon-Fri; 9am-4pm Sat-Sun. **$. Czech. Map** p146 B4 **34**

A classic Czech pub-restaurant that's popular with students and holds its own against the many earthy pubs. Chilli goulashis are a treat, the Pilsner and Gambrinus well-poured and service gruff. It doesn't get more authentic.

Sonora

Radhošťská 5 (222 711 029/www. sonoras.cz). Metro Flora. **Open** 11am-midnight daily. **$. Mexican. Map** p147 D4 **35**

Inspired efforts in Mexican food: mole, taco salads, beef burritos and tasty quesadillas. All are complemented by cheap Czech beer and a wall-size map of North American Indian tribes.

Shopping

La Lagartija

NEW *Prokopova 13 (776 622031/www. lagartija.cz). Trams 5, 9, 26.* **Open** 11am-7pm Mon-Fri. **Map** p146 C2 **36**

With a vibrant collection of handmade ceramics, featuring inspiring colours, patterns and ethnic influences from eastern and southern Europe, this offers great touches for the home or office.

Palác Flora

Vinohradská 151 (255 741 707/www. palacflora.cz). Metro Flora. **Open** 8am-midnight daily. **Map** p147 E4 **37**

Yet another major installation in the tidal wave of Czech malls. This one's admittedly handy and attracts young couples who love to hang out in its cafés and bars. You can also pick up another winter layer or two, or catch a movie.

Pour-pour

NEW *Vinohradská 74 (777 830 078/ www.pourpour.com). Metro Jiřího z Poděbrad.* **Open** 11am-7pm Mon-Fri. **Map** p146 B5 **38**

A hip collection of streetwear, casual, colourful, youthful separates, accessories and hats. It's small, personal, indie and highly fashionable, without trading off practicality – and this little boutique remains priced for the masses. No wonder it's the hit of the season.

Nightlife

Akropolis

Kubelíkova 27 (296 330 911/www. palacakropolis.cz). Metro Jiřího z Poděbrad. **Open** *Divadelní Bar* 7pm-5am daily. *Malá Scéná Bar* 7pm-3am daily. *Concerts* 7.30pm. **Map** p146 B3 **39**

Still the city's most soulful venue, this 1927 art deco theatre and coffeehouse features a line-up of avant-garde plays, indie rock and world music, as well as hosting book groups on the main basement stage. The Divadelní Bar (theatre bar) has nightly DJs and occasional MCs, all for free, while the Malá Scena features live jams and red-lit sofas.

Bukowski's

Bořivojova 86 (no phone). Metro Jiřího z Poděbrad. **Open** 6pm-midnight daily. **Map** p146 B3 ⓴
This self-billed dive bar is a magnet for mischievous expats and bohemians . Owner Glen Emery, a Prague bartending legend, makes good times just about guaranteed at this rollicking little joint, done in British pub style.

Matrix

Koněvova 13 (776 611 042/www. matrixklub.cz). Metro Florenc. **Open** 8pm-4am Tue-Sat. **Map** p146 B1/C1 ㊶
As underground as Neo himself, this former frozen meat plant knows its breaks, booking hip DJs and other fringe acts. It draws a young crowd of adventurers, who appreciate the noise, the shadows and the Gambrinus beer on tap.

Parukářka

Olšanská & Prokopova (776 366 410/ www.parukarka.cz). Metro Flora. **Open** *Pub* 1pm-1am daily. *Club* varies. **Map** p147 D2 ㊷
This rustic old pub atop a grassy hill is an attraction indeed, playing host to occasional live bands and a dedicated crowd of characters. But the club in the old bunker, deep inside the hill, is the highlight. Usually open at weekends, you go down spiral stairs once you've found the curved door above Prokopská street.

Sedm Vlků

Vlkova 7 (222 711 725/www. sedmvlku.cz). Metro Jiřího z Poděbrad. **Open** 5pm-3am Mon-Sat. **Map** p146 A3 ㊸
With surrealist art, low light and bendy ironwork, the Seven Wolves remains an appealing art bar and club space. The

Akropolis

decks dispense hot and cold running jungle, but there's really only beer to slake a thirst. Solid sound system, though.

XT3

Rokycanova 29 (222 783 463/ www.xt3.cz). Metro Jiřího z Poděbrad. **Open** 6pm-5am daily. **Map** p146 C2 ㊹
XT3 dishes up breakbeat, lots of smoke and cheap beer, all in a venue that's unlikely to be stumbled upon by foreigners. Mixing starts at eight. Don't forget your skateboard.

Arts & leisure

Karlín Studios

Křižíkova 34 (no phone/www.karlin studios.cz). Metro Křižíkova. **Open** *Public gallery* noon-6pm Tue-Sun. **Map** p147 F1 ㊺
A wonderfully industrial art space, this vast complex of studios hosts year-round shows by some of the best Czech creatives and holds regular open days for them. It's the traditional home of the Prague Biennale, the contemporary art event.

DOX p160

Holešovice

The district most likely to overtake Old Town for rapid transformation (and with much less historic preservation to hold it back) is clearly Holešovice. The former centre for slaughterhouses, breweries and freight train terminuses still has some way to go, of course. But, with its complement of inviting public parks, fairgrounds, the new **DOX** arts centre and rising numbers of creative but unpretentious food and drink options, progress is well under way. Situated across the Vltava river to the north of Old Town, this area is shaking off years of industrial neglect and still features grimy façades alongside smart cafés, plugged-in theatres, sports centres and galleries. Those arriving by train may well enter the city here: the area hosts one of Prague's two international train stations, Nádraží Holešovice, which remains a striking example of the old Holešovice. The newer attractions can be seen at DOX, the **Cross Club** art bar, the climbing wall at **Boulder Bar**,

Stromovka Park and Letná, where young families and skaters vie for control of the paths.

Holešovice's main drag, Dukelských hrdinů, has a sleek constructivist building, **Veletržní palác**, a modern art mecca of the National Gallery. Výstaviště, up the street, is an appealing exhibition ground, with a lapidarium and aquarium housing the original saints from Charles Bridge, and a funfair – Lunapark – behind its glorious main hall. Stromovka, a park to the west, laid out by Rudolf II in the 16th century, provides green space, as does Letná to the south. In between are lifestyle-conscious bars, such as **La Bodega Flamencaa** and **Fraktal**. On the eastern side, Mecca is a classic club for thirtysomethings.

A ten-minute walk north of Stromovka via the bridge (or by Bus No.112 from Metro Nádraží Holešovice) brings you to **Zoo Praha**, which continues to expand its facilities every year, and makes for a great family day out.

Sights & museums

Lapidárium

Výstaviště (233 375 636/www.nm.cz).
Metro Nádraží Holešovice. **Open** noon-
6pm Tue-Fri; 10am-6pm Sat, Sun.
Admission 40 Kč; 80 Kč family.
Map p155 D1 ❶

Following a badly needed reconstruction
phase in the spring of 2009, this
Victorian-era hall has regained lustre.
Only fitting for the home of the original
stone saints from Charles Bridge (those
on the bridge itself are nearly all replicas).
The pantheon rests peacefully here,
along with outstanding Czech stone
sculptures from the 11th to 19th centuries, including baroque works by masters like Matthias Braun and Jan Brokoff.

National Gallery Collection of 19th-, 20th- & 21st-Century Art

Sbírka moderního a současného umění
Veletržní palác, Dukelských hrdinů 47
(224 301 122/www.ngprague.cz). Metro
Vltavská. **Open** 10am-6pm Tue-Sun.
Admission 200 Kč; family 300 Kč;
half-price after 4pm. Temporary
exhibitions 50 Kč; free under-10s.
Map p155 D2 ❷

This functionalist building, designed by
Oldřich Tyl and Josef Fuchs and opened
in 1929, houses the National Gallery's
collections of modern art, including
paintings by Karel Purkyně and 19th-
century symbolists Max Švabinský and
František Bílek. The pioneering abstract
artist František Kupka is well represent-
ed here, along with Czech Cubists.

Výstaviště

Za Elektárnou 49 (220 103 111/www.
incheba.cz). Metro Nádraží Holešovice.
Open *Grounds* 9am-9pm daily. *Water*
World 10am-7pm daily. **Admission**
Grounds free. *Water World* 240 Kč;
145 Kč under-12s; free under-4s. **Map**
p154 C1 ❸

Filigree exhibition hall towers mark this
out as a retro gem of the district. It was
built for the Jubilee Exhibition (circa

1891) and signalled the birth of Art
Nouveau in Prague. A recent fire damaged the west wing but rebuilding has
been swift. The grounds around, alas,
are sleepy except during the midwinter
carnival Matějská pouť, when high-tech
German and Dutch attractions are rolled
in. The area features a time-worn fountain with a musical light show and an
aquarium, Water World, which draws
the kiddies.

Zoo Praha

U Trojského zámku (296 112 111/
www.zoopraha.cz). Metro Nádraží
Holešovice. **Open** *Mar* 9am-5pm daily.
Apr, May, Sept, Oct 9am-6pm daily.
June-Aug 9am-7pm daily. *Nov-Feb* 9am-
4pm daily. **Admission** 150 Kč; 450 Kč
family; free under-3s. **Map** p154 A1 ❹

Praguers have rallied around their
newly remodelled zoo, which now
hosts 665 species and some 4,300
animals (at the last count). Scientists
here also conduct important research
on breeding. The children's area is a
hit, as are the outdoor exhibition
grounds for Sumatran orangutans.
There's a list of feeding and exercise
times (in English) on the website.

Eating & drinking

La Bodega Flamenca

Šmeralova 5 (233 374 075/www.la
bodega.cz). Metro Vltavská. **Open** 4pm-
1am Mon-Thur, Sun; 4pm-3am Fri, Sat.
$. Spanish. **Map** p154 B3 ❺

The easily missed entrance to this
cellar tapas bar conceals a perpetual
sangria party. Owner Ilona oversees
the bar, serving up tapas such as marinated olives and garlic mushrooms.
Bench-style seats line the walls and fill
up fast. In true Spanish style, things
only really start hotting up after 1am.

Bohemia Bagel

NEW *W Dukelských hrdinů 48 (220 806*
541). Metro Vltavská. **Open** 7am-mid-
night Mon-Fri; 8am-midnight Sat-Sun. **$$.**
Americas. **Map** p155 D2 ❻

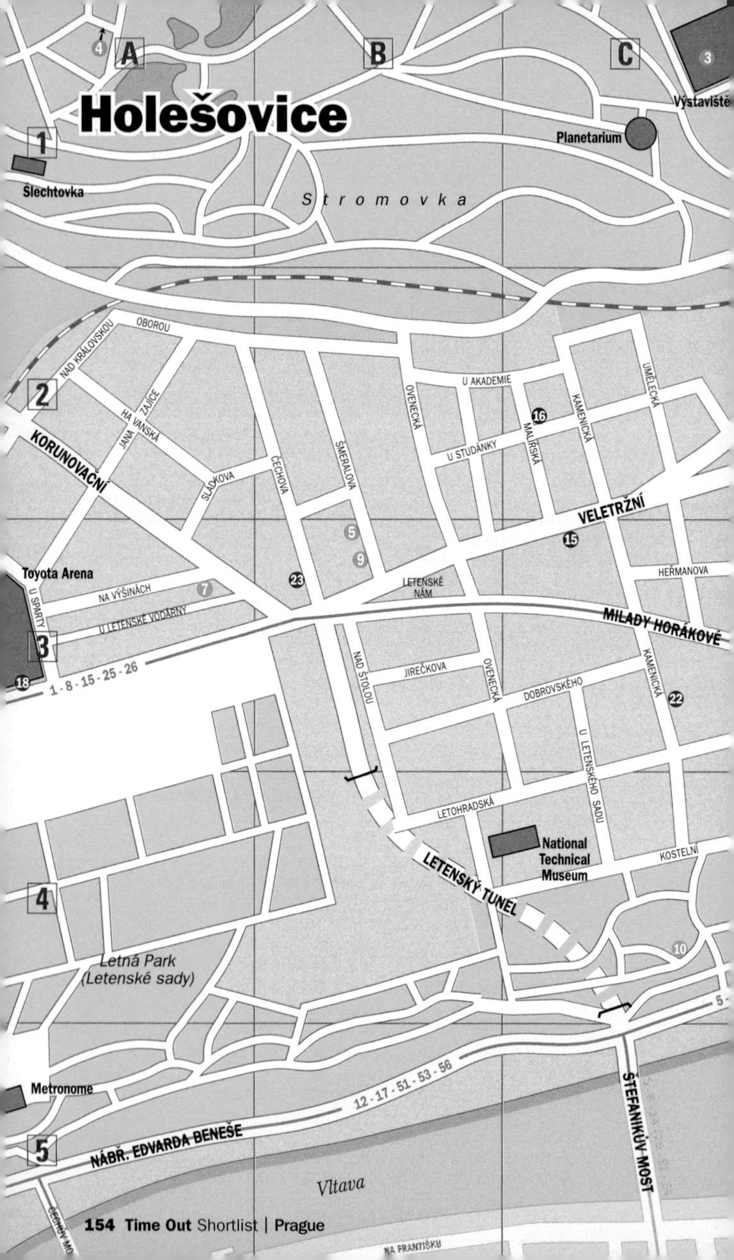

Holešovice

Šlechtovka

Stromovka

Výstaviště

Planetarium

OBOROU

NAD KRÁLOVSKOU

KORUNOVAČNÍ

JANA VANŠKA

HA ZAJÍCE

SLÁDKOVA

ČECHOVA

ŠMERALOVA

OVENECKÁ

U AKADEMIE

U STUDÁNKY

MALÍŘSKA

KAMENICKÁ

UMĚLECKÁ

VELETRŽNÍ

HERMANOVA

Toyota Arena

U SPARTY

NA VÝŠINÁCH

U LETENSKÉ VODÁRNY

1 - 8 - 15 - 25 - 26

LETENSKÉ
NÁM.

NAD ŠTOLOU

JIREČKOVA

OVENECKÁ

DOBROVSKÉHO

U LETENSKÉHO SADU

KAMENICKÁ

MILADY HORÁKOVÉ

LETOHRADSKÁ

National
Technical
Museum

KOSTELNÍ

LETENSKÝ TUNEL

Letná Park
(Letenské sady)

Metronome

12 - 17 - 51 - 53 - 56

ŠTEFÁNIKŮV MOST

NÁBŘ. EDVARDA BENEŠE

Vltava

NA FRANTIŠKU

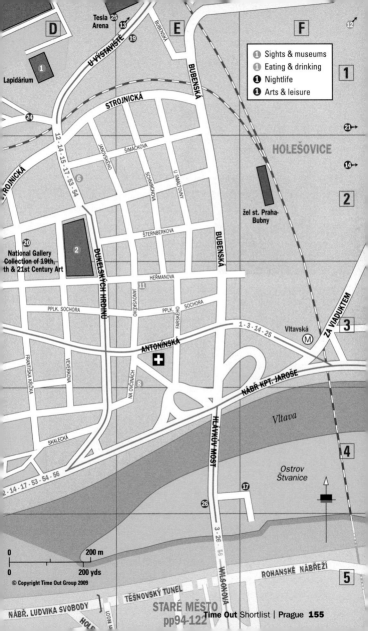

Burgermaster

Scott Kelly reveals the secrets of his culinary success.

Chef **Scott Kelly**, co-owner of Bohemia Bagel (p153) and founder of Fraktal (p155), is a veteran of the Culinary Institute of America, New York, the four-star Gustav Anders Restaurant in Southern California. He has run kitchens in Beirut, Moscow and Prague, including Pálffy Palác (p47). Here, he reveals the art behind his latest venture's burgers, which have won honours as the city's best.

Time Out (TO):
What is the essence of a great cheeseburger?

Scott Kelly (SK): There is no one thing that makes a great burger, but one must have fresh ingredients and stick to the basics: nice beef with the right amount of fat (it's neither lean nor fatty), char-broiled preferably, fresh sesame bun gently toasted on the grill (we make our own and it is fresh daily), good-quality cheddar cheese, iceberg lettuce, tomatoes and onions; the better their quality the better the burger.

TO: Did you guys have to train a bakery to produce those great bagels, which Bohemia Bagel launched here a decade ago? What was that process like?

SK: We actually had to hire a British chef to help and it took us weeks of trial and error to produce the right kind of sponge dough, making it overnight in a two-stage process. First, you mix some of the flour with water, sugar and yeast, and let it rise and ferment overnight. In the morning you add more of the same ingredients and a few others, then bake. What you are getting is neither a sponge cake nor a sourdough bread.

TO: What was your greatest challenge to keeping up a consistent quality in the kitchen?

SK: Not being able to fly in Mexicans! More seriously, it's teaching people to make food they have never seen or tasted before.

TO: What can you say about sourcing your beef? Still difficult to get lean, tender stuff here?

SK: We owe our excellent burger beef to (the now defunct) Planet Hollywood. It was their imported chef who taught a local supplier to do the right kind of ground beef mix. We use the same supplier and will not divulge the name.

TO: What is your business strategy for dark economic times?

SK: Keeping up quality and not freaking out. People have to eat and they will continue to eat in places where they like the food, and where they feel as though they are getting good value for their money. We don't believe in discounting during times of crisis.

This branch of the Malá Strana-based company features the best menu, complete with an array of fresh-fired burgers and a cocktail bar that evokes an Edward Hopper painting, complete with local scenesters, of course.

Čajovna v věži

NEW *Na výšinách 1 (724 593 215). Metro Vltavská.* **Open** *May-Oct* 5pm-11pm daily. *Nov-Apr* 4pm-10pm daily. **$.** **Teahouse.** **Map** p154 A3 **7**

The best disguised of the many backroom teahouses in Prague. After a climb up several flights, the top of this historic tower reveals a candlelit spot for sipping fine whole-leaf brews, courtesy of Keemun Mao Feng.

La Creperie

Janovského 4 (220 878 040). Metro Vltavská. **Open** 9am-11pm Mon-Sat; 9am-10pm Sun. **$.** **Crêperie.** **Map** p155 E3 **8**

The French owner specialises in sweet and savoury crêpes for a pittance. Seating is in a comfy but closet-sized

basement, so it's probably not ideal for coach parties. Still, although the room is small, the portions are large. Above-average wine list and fresh croissants.

Fraktal

Šmeralova 1 (777 794 094/www. fraktalbar.cz). Metro Vltavská. **Open** 11am-midnight daily.**Café.** **Map** p154 B3 **9**

This comfy art bar is a trashy, convivial place where anything goes. Mojitos and tequila gold with orange and cinnamon cocktails are notable accompaniments to the improved menu of Czech-Mex dishes. It has been voted as serving the best burger in town. Free Wi-Fi and popular Sunday brunch are other attractions.

Letenský zámeček

Letenské sady 341 (in Letná Park) (233 375 604/www.letenskyzamecek. cz). Metro Hradčanská. **Open** *Beer garden* Apr-Oct 11am-11pm daily. *Restaurants* 11am-11.30pm daily. **$$.** **Czech.** **Map** p154 C4 **10**

Bohemia Bagel p153

A leafy enclave on the hill above the Vltava is arguably the city's finest summer beer garden. A local crowd gathers under the chestnut trees for cheap beer in plastic cups late into the evening during warmer months. The adjoining Restaurant Belcredi and Brasserie Ullman have gone upmarket, with modern designer interiors, a dressy crowd and Bernard beer on tap.

Ouky Douky
Janovského 14 (266 711 531/www. oukydouky.cz). Metro Vltavská. **Open** 8am-midnight daily. **Café**. **Map** p155 E3 ⑪
A bookstore café without much to read for English speakers, this is the original location of the Globe Bookstore and Coffeehouse. The owners haven't been too successful in copying its formula.

Pivovar U Bulovky
Bulovka 17, Libeň (284 840 650/ www.pivovarubulovky.cz). Metro Palmovka, then tram 10, 15, 24, 25. **Open** 11am-11pm Mon-Thur; 11am-midnight Fri; noon-midnight Sat. **Pub**. **Map** p155 F1 ⑫
Though it's well off the beaten track (and beyond the Holešovice district borders), critics from the *New York Times* have tracked down František Richter's pub, known to beer aficionados far and wide for its excellent microbrew beers, homemade sausage and unique flavouring inspirations. The Friday night blues bands play irregularly but add a jolt.

Nightlife

Cross Club
Plynární 23 (736 535 053/www.cross club.cz). Metro Nádraží Holešovice. **Open** 2pm-3am Mon-Fri; 4pm-5am Sat, Sun. **Map** p155 E1 ⑬
This club may look like a car spares shop, but don't be deceived. It's worth the hike north from the Metro station to find it. This magnet for arty types is a centre for music, film, dance and drink, and every surface has been

welded or moulded, gallery-style, into what is the city's hippest art bar – and a raw and laid-back one at that, altogether unpretentious.

Mecca
U Průhonu 3 (283 870 522/www. mecca.cz). Metro Vltavská. **Open** *Club* 10pm-5am Wed, Fri, Sat. *Concerts* 10pm; call for times. **Map** p155 F2 ⑭
These days, Mecca is a bit too slick for its own good, but it's still fun at times for its excesses. It was the first big club to set up in the burgeoning Holešovice district. Under new management, it still draws improbably beautiful people, but it all seems rather posed. However, it's still the biggest modern dance palace in the district, and does deliver powerful, clean sounds.

Misch Masch
Veletržní 61 (603 272 227/www. mischmasch.cz). Metro Vltavská. **Open** 8pm-4am Thur-Sat. **Map** p154 C3 ⑮
This big, loud club is where locals who love mixing Malibu into their drinks come out to play. If the pop tracks get tiresome (likely), there are other clever

Čajovna v věži p157

entertainments such as the Barmaid Flair Challenge or the annual Miss Misch Masch. Fascinating in its way, but only for the brave.

Wakata

Malířská 14 (233 370518/www.wakata. eu). Metro Vltavská. **Open** 5pm-3am Mon-Thur; 5pm-5am Fri, Sat; 6pm-3am Sun. **Map** p154 C2 ⑯

A down-and-dirty teenage wasteland, Wakata can deliver great jungle, but more often it feels as though you've unwittingly stepped out of Prague and onto the set of a cheap horror film. At least, it stays open way past official hours, has motorcycle seats for bar stools, and is away from it all.

Arts & leisure

I. ČLTK

Ostrov Štvanice 38 (222 316 317/www. cltk.cz). Metro Florenc or Vltavská. **Open** 7am-11pm daily. **Map** p155 F4 ⑰

Ten outdoor clay courts, three of which are floodlit, plus sparkling indoor facilities (four hard courts, two clay courts) are all up to scratch for Czech players who take the game

of tennis deadly seriously. Booking is essential at these facilities.

AC Sparta Praha

Toyota Arena, Milady Horákové 98, (296 111 400/www.sparta.cz). Metro Hradčanská. **Map** p154 A3 ⑱

Sparta has seen rivals emerging of late and doesn't always manage to set the pace these days in Czech football. But although it's comparatively poor in Europe too, this hasn't stopped it from pulling off some mighty upsets against wealthier opponents. Its 18,500-capacity stadium, also known at Letná, is one of the country's best.

Boulder Bar

U výstaviště 11 (220 514 540/www. boulder.cz). Metro Nádraží Holešovice, then tram 5, 12, 17. **Open** 3-11pm Mon, Fri; 9am-11pm Tue, Thur; 3-11pm Wed, noon-11pm Sat, Sun. **Map** p155 E1 ⑲

Having moved from their original location downtown, the rock is back, with 300 square metres of climbing wall space, some surfaces 4.3 metres high. Rallies, training, a gear shop, friendly pros and an easygoing café-bar.

PRAGUE BY AREA

Divadlo Alfred ve Dvoře

Františka Křížka 36 (233 376 997/
www.alfredvedvore.cz). Metro Vltavská.
Map p155 D2 **⑳**
Fare tends towards movement and non-verbal work; if something text-based is featured, it comes with English programme notes. A hub of alternative theatre, Alfred also co-produces new work with such groups as Chicago's Goat Island. Watch for Handa Gote research and development.

DOX

NEW *Osadní 34 (774 145 434/www.*
doxprague.org). Metro Vltavská. **Open**
11am-7pm Wed-Fri; 10am-6pm Sat-Mon.
Map p155 F1 **㉑**
The city's most exciting development in independent art is this sprawling industrial space for travelling shows, studios, cultural events and cross-pollination. Founded by Leoš Válka and partners, and developed for six years with a mission of integration and exchange, DOX is the new home for fresh photography, film and painting.

Hunt Kastner Artworks

Kamenická 22 (233 376 259/www.
huntkastner.com). Metro Vltavská.
Open 1-6pm Tue-Fri; 2-6pm Sat
or by appointment. **Map** p154 C3 **㉒**
This private gallery was set up to nurture the careers of a stable of more than a dozen Czech contemporary artists like Tomáš Vaník and Michael Thelenová, while at the same time helping to find collectors for their work and encourage development of the fledgling art market.

Skala Sport

Čechova 3 (605 258 670/www.skala
sport.wz.cz). Metro Vltavská. **Open**
10am-8pm Mon-Fri; 10am-1pm Sat,
Sun. **Map** p154 B3 **㉓**
Rent inline skates or bikes by the hour or the day to be kitted out for nearby Stromovka or Letná parks. Skis, boating, climbing and camping gear can be hired as well and the canny staff can do repairs on your gear.

Stromovka

U Výstaviště & Dukelských hrdinů.
Metro Nádraží Holešovice, then tram
5, 12, 17. **Map** p155 D1 **㉔**
Located just 15 minutes from downtown Prague, but with nary a hint of the city about it, this former royal hunting ground draws in runners, strollers, lovers, kids and dogs. After the initial sprint to try and avoid the Výstaviště crowds, you can have the meadows to yourself. See if you can hear the language of birds that alchemist John Dee claimed to have understood here.

Tesla Arena

Výstaviště, Za elektrárnou 319,
Holešovice (266 727 443/www.
tesla-arena.cz). Metro Nádraží
Holešovice. **Map** p155 D1/E1 **㉕**
A skating rink and the 70-year-old home of ice hockey team HC Sparta Praha (that is, when not a concert hall), this barn has all the acoustics that you would expect from such a place. However it's one of the few indoor spots in Prague that can accommodate thousands of spectators. Game and concert tickets can be purchased in advance from the box office at the entrance, or online through the Ticketpro agency (www.ticketpro.cz).

Zimní stadion Štvanice

Ostrov Štvanice 1125 (602 623 449/
www.stvanice.cz). Metro Florenc
or Vltavská. **Open** 10am-noon, 2.30-4.15pm Mon; 10.30am-noon, 3-5.30pm Tue, Thur; 10am-noon, 3-4.30pm, 8-9.30pm Wed; 10.30am-noon, 3-5.30pm, 8-9.30pm Fri; 9am-noon, 2-5pm, 8-10pm Sat; 9am-noon, 2-5pm Sun.
Map p155 E4 **㉖**
This rickety-looking structure houses two ice-skating rinks, with reasonably generous opening hours, on an island situated in the Vltava river. True old-school Prague, complete with eccentric, inconvenient opening hours. Make sure that you bring a Czech friend along – little English is spoken.

Essentials

Kempinski Hybernská Prague p172

Hotels

Most say the Czech Republic avoided the worst of the great economic crash of 2008, yet it's a buyer's market in the hostelry biz. A recent boom in more lavish hotels means that there's more choice than ever and, if you shop around, an inevitable deal. From Philippe Starck appointments to boutique stays with timbered ceilings, smaller hotels and inns are giving the major venues a run for their money. Service has improved by miles, as have the handy and cool amenities. Wi-Fi is ubiquitous, while tour packages are often thrown in as incentives, and hotel restaurants, such as the Kempinski Hybernská Prague's Le Grill and the Michelin star-winning Four Seasons' Allegro, continue to blossom.

Even so, the free market is not yet a generation old, so you should be forewarned that lax attitudes towards customers are far from extinct, especially at larger hotels. Places like the **Buddha-Bar Hotel** are endeavouring, fairly successfully, to be many things to many people (you would almost be forgiven for not venturing out). Other hotels, such as the **Icon**, **987 Prague** and **Hotel Josef**, are good examples of affordable style. Backpackers will appreciate the cool bar at **Sir Toby's Hostel** and may forget the **Czech Inn** is a hostel at all.

Great bargains are best found on hotel web pages and particularly during the off season. That said, Prague doesn't really have an off season, although it can look more romantic when the summer hordes aren't to be seen and heard. Adventurous (or simply practical) travellers can always share a spare room with a family or stay in basic pensions, in which agencies like Stop City (www.stopcity.cz) specialise. A newer generation of apartment bookers such as

www.apartments-in-Prague.org
and www.toucanapartments.com
carry homely places with cooking
facilities and amazing locations.

Remember that you can often
score a room in a restored palace,
a dreamy villa or a 17th-century
inn for the same rate as the Best
Western if you book ahead, to take
advantage of the city's stunning
architecture. Family facilities are
common now, with babysitting
services or free rates for kids who
share your room more evident.

Money matters

Many hotels quote their rates
in euros and, although the Czech
Republic has not yet joined the euro
zone, will happily take them. Note
that if you pay in Czech crowns, the
price often won't be calculated at
the official exchange rate and you'll
take a hit. Many places, however,
offer discounts for cash, so it may
be worth proffering euro notes.
Many hotels quote room prices
exclusive of VAT. Always check.

Hradčany

U Červeného Lva

*Nerudova 41 (257 533 832/www.hotel
redlion.com). Metro Malostranská.* **$$$**.
There are few small hotels on the
royal route leading to Prague Castle
that can boast such authentic 17th-cen-
tury decor, including hand-painted
vaulted ceilings. This reconstructed
burgher's house with just eight rooms
gives guests a sense of Renaissance
Prague, but its service is more ade-
quate than standout.

Golden Horse House

*Úvoz 8 (777 130 286/www.goldhorse.cz).
Tram 20, 22* **$**.
It can't compete with other posh inns
for creature comforts, but the Golden
Horse beats them handily in terms of
value for location. These ten, en suite

ESSENTIALS

1000 ways to
spend your
weekends

1000 things to do in Britain

1000 things to do in New York

1000 things to do in London for under £10

1000 things to do in London

1000 things for kids to do in the holidays

From £12.99/ $19.95

rooms, are warm and clean. Service is amiable, breakfast is on offer for an extra 125 Kč, and the inn is next door to a hip pub (U Zavěšenyho Kafe), where musos and actors hang out. You can cook on site and Wi-Fi is available.

Hotel Neruda

Nerudova 44 (257 535 556/www.hotel neruda.cz). Metro Malostranská. **$$$$**.
In this atmospheric building, elements of which date from 1348, the style is old-world charm meets airy modern. Czech star designer Bořek Šipek oversaw the expansion, which has increased the number of rooms from 20 to 43. Service is friendly and you're right on the main lane leading up to Prague Castle. Terrace restaurant with Wi-Fi.

Hotel Questenberk

Úvoz 15 (220 407 600/www. questenberk.cz). Tram 20, 22. **$$$**.
Converted in 2002 from a neglected monastery (there is a stone crucifix in the entrance), the 30 rooms of this quaint Baroque building, just 500 metres away from the Castle, are definitely too comfy for monks and come with Wi-Fi. But they're not as plush as you would expect for the price, and the enthusiastic staff can appear a little flustered. An only-in-Prague effect.

Hotel Savoy

Keplerova 6 (224 302 430/www. hotel-savoy.cz). Tram 20, 22. **$$$$**.
With an award-winning dining room on site, the Savoy impresses visitors with its quiet competence, as evidenced by the library, fireplace and gliding service. Then you notice a rock star in the elevator and spot a Hollywood idol in the breakfast room. The 61 well-appointed, if not huge, rooms keep the biz and showbiz crowd coming back.

U Krále Karla

Úvoz 4 (257 532 869/www.romantic hotels.cz). Metro Malostranská. **$$$**.
Solid oak furnishings, painted vaulted ceilings, stained-glass windows and

Baroque treasures lend this 19-room inn the feel of an aristocratic country house, even though it was once owned by the Benedictine order. There are discounts for cash payment and a Bohemian restaurant on site.

Romantik Hotel U Raka

Černínská 10 (220 511 100/www. romantikhotel-uraka.cz). Tram 20, 22. **$$$**.
Booking well ahead is the only way to land one of these six rooms, which date back to 1739. It's a small, rustic pension suited to couples with time to spare and located on a quiet Hradčany backstreet within earshot of the bells of the Loreto. Unique but also backed by polished service. Enchanting breakfast/reading room with brick hearth. No children under 12 but pets welcome.

U Velké Boty

Vlašská 30 (257 532 088/www.dumu velkeboty.cz). Metro Malostranská. **$$**.
In a Renaissance-era burgher house rebuilt by Santini de Bossi before 1669, the Rippl maintains this hotel, favourite of artists and writers. The family won back their house from the state after 1989 and opened the 'House at the Big Boot' to fund its restoration. Expect tasteful period furniture and mod-cons. It's a bargain and offers one of the most rewarding stays in the area. Family suites may include a kitchen. Breakfast is an extra 200 Kč and Wi-Fi is available.

Malá Strana & Smíchov

Alchymist Grand Hotel & Spa

Tržiště 19, Malá Strana (257 286 011/ www.alchymisthotel.cz). Metro Malostranská. **$$$$**.
Humbly ensconced in the Baroque U Ježišek Palace, the Alchymist works its magic on more than your wallet. Mottled walls, vaulted ceilings, frescoes, four-poster beds and spoiling

ESSENTIALS

service are complemented by one of Prague's hottest wellness centres, with Balinese massage and pool. The US embassy is next door.

Alchymist Residence Nosticova

Nosticova 1, Malá Strana (257 312 513/www.nosticova.com). Metro Malostranská. **$$$**.

Completely revamped into one of the city's most talked-about boutique hotel developments, this Baroque 'residence' now features the latest in everything. It's on a quiet lane just off Kampa Island. The ten suites range from ample to capacious and come with antiques, huge bathrooms and kitchenettes. Two have working fireplaces and one has a rooftop terrace. A sauna, massages and a sushi bar add to the decadence.

Aria Hotel

Tržiště 9, Malá Strana (225 334 111/www.ariahotel.net). Metro Malostranská. **$$$$**.

The Aria has broken new ground and set the standard for boutique hostelry in Prague, with its amenities, service and location. The oddly shaped rooms (the building was a post office) are classically designed and jammed with audiophile toys; computers, DVD players and serious speakers are standard. Each room is dedicated to a musician, whose biography and songs are available on your hard drive, and there's a music library (great books and DVDs) in the lobby. The roof terrace offers a wonderful view of the city. Request a room facing the Baroque gardens. There's a free airport shuttle, gym and a much-lauded lobby piano café/bar.

Best Western Kampa Hotel

Všehrdova 16, Malá Strana (257 320 508/www.praguekampahotel.com). Metro Malostranská. **$$$**.

Located on a quiet backstreet in Malá Strana, the Kampa Hotel has retained its 17th-century architecture and style

through recent renovations, and rooms are elegantly arranged. The vaulted 'Knights Hall' dining room and adjacent pub is a huge hit with frustrated knights. Fret not for lack of the grail, there are mugs of 60 Kč beers a plenty.

Hostel Sokol

Nosticova 2, Malá Strana (257 007 397/ www.sokol-cos.cz/hostel.html). Metro Malostranská. **$**.

Find Hostel Sokol (the entrance is accessible via the yard behind the Sokol sports centre) and you've found the student travel nerve centre of Prague. It has a great terrace for beer-sipping with a view; bunks are situated in a large gymnasium. The hostel lies within easy reach of the Castle and Charles Bridge. Breakfast is not included. Book ahead via phone, or email hostel@sokol-cos.cz.

Hotel Hoffmeister

Pod Bruskou 7, Malá Strana (251 017 111/www.hoffmeister.cz). Metro Malostranská. **$$$$**.

Filled with original images by Adolf Hoffmeister, an inveterate chronicler of the Jazz Age in Prague, this hotel offers suitably decadent and classy rooms, a fine terrace restaurant with an impressive wine cellar and a wellness centre that has won praise from the most demanding travellers. Book well ahead to get the best deals.

Hotel U Kříže

Újezd 20, Malá Strana (257 312 523/www.ukrize.com). Tram 6, 9, 12, 20, 22. **$$**.

Quaint enough, with 22 pleasant rooms as well as great value for money. Strategically located across the street from Petřín hill, a quick walk from Kampa Island, one tram stop to the National Theatre and two stops to Malostranská náměstí. Ask for a room facing the atrium; those looking out towards the hill tend to get rattled by the street trams going past. Free coffee and cake can be taken in the bar all day. Pet friendly.

Hotel U Zlaté Studně

Mandarin Oriental

Nebovidská 1, Malá Strana (233 088 888/www.mandarinoriental.com/prague) Tram 6, 9, 12, 20, 22. **$$$$**.

The hotel event of 2006 was the opening of this 99-room gem three blocks away from Charles Bridge. The former 14th-century monastery has custom rooms, a spa with holistic treatments and a grand restaurant with fine Asian and continental fare. Modern and high-tech yet cosy rooms with royal blue accents. Excellent service.

Hotel William

Hellichova 5, Smíchov (257 320 242/ www.euroagentur.com/cz/ea-hotel-william). Tram 6, 10, 12, 20, 22. **$$**.

Opened in 2001, this inconspicuous hotel of 42 rooms occupies a great location, a quick walk away from the funicular up Petřín hill, and just one tram stop from Malostranské náměstí, the main square of the district. Decorators went a little bit overboard trying for a 'castle feel' but rooms are comfortable and good value for money. Ask for one at the back of the hotel, which will offer you peace and quiet, away from the noise of the trams.

Hotel U Zlaté Studně

U Zlaté studně 4, Malá Strana (257 011 213/www.zlatastudna.cz). Metro Malostranská. **$$$**.

This 20-room inn is nestled along a secluded street on a Malá Strana hill below the Castle. Rooms feature wood floors and ceilings and stylish furniture. If you could use a soak, ask for one of the rooms with a huge tub. Breakfast on a terrace goes with a stellar view of the city. The view from the indoor dining area is tremendous.

Julian

Elišky Peškové 11, Smíchov (257 311 150/www.julian.cz). Tram 6, 9, 12, 20, 22. **$$**.

A splash of luxury in Smichov, the Julian features a drawing room with fireplace and library and a non-smoking lobby bar, a rarity in Prague. Room decor is light and understated and there are apartments with kitchenettes as well as a family room, complete with toys. Even though it is not quite in the centre, it's an easy tram or metro ride away from Old Town. Airport/railway station shuttle, gym, sauna, whirlpool, massage and Wi-Fi.

ESSENTIALS

Airline flights are one of the biggest producers of the global warming gas CO_2. But with **The CarbonNeutral Company** you can make your travel a little greener.

Go to **www.carbonneutral.com** to calculate your flight emissions then 'neutralise' them through international projects which save exactly the same amount of carbon dioxide.

Contact us at **shop@carbonneutral.com** or call into the office on **0870 199 99 88** for more details.

CarbonNeutral®flights

U Karlova mostu

Na Kampě 15, Malá Strana (257 531 430/www.archibald.cz). Metro Malostranská. **$$.**

Formerly named Na Kampě 15, the inn named 'At the Charles Bridge' in Czech affords fine views of the bridge and Old Town, yet stands at a sufficient distance to offer peace and quiet. The former 15th-century tavern that brewed one of the city's pioneering beers still has wood floors, exposed beams and garret windows, but now features modern furnishings. The two cellar pubs and the beer garden out the back offer Czech trad grub and well-tapped beer.

Mövenpick

Mozartova 1, Smíchov (257 151 111/ www.movenpick-prague.com). Metro Anděl/tram 4, 7, 9. **$$.**

The not so easily accessible location is more than set off by the surrounding beauty and Mövenpick-standard service. Actually two buildings (the executive wing accessible only by cable car), it's family-friendly too and has fine dining restaurants frequented by many Praguesters. Rooms are fairly standard-issue, but deep discounts are available off-season and a verdant park is next door. Good concierge and business services plus babysitting.

Pension Dientzenhofer

Nosticova 2, Malá Strana (257 311 319/www.dientzenhofer.cz). Metro Malostranská. **$$.**

This popular inn facing Kampa Island has a quiet courtyard and back garden that offer a lovely respite in the midst of Malá Strana. The ten rooms are bright, and the staff are efficient and friendly. Baroque architect star Kilian Ignaz Dientzenhofer was born in the 16th-century building and his work fills this quarter of the city.

Rezidence Lundborg

U Lužického semináře 3, Malá Strana (257 011 911/www.lundborg.se). Metro Malostranská. **$$$.**

With a prime view of Charles Bridge, located on the site of the old Juditin Bridge, this Scandinavian-owned hotel of 13 suites exudes luxury and charm. Lundborg pampers stressed guests with apartments that successfully blend reconstructed Renaissance with business amenities. A major splash out, but every need is anticipated, from providing a wine cellar to arranging golf programmes in Karlštejn or Konopiště resorts during summer.

Riverside Hotel

Janáčkovo nábřeží 15, Malá Strana (234 705 155/www.riversideprague. com). Metro Malostranská. **$$$.**

A luxe little retreat that's a fave with actors seeking to escape the bright lights while in Prague, this gem of the MaMaison group is ensconced in a Baroque townhouse whose east-facing rooms overlook the Vltava. Spacious bathrooms, Wi-Fi, DVD library and other extras helped make Riverside an award-winner in its first year.

Staré Město

Buddha-Bar Hotel

NEW *Jakubská 8 (221 776 300/www. buddha-bar-hotel.cz). Metro Náměstí Republiky.* **$$$.**

The promo line 'Not just another hotel, it's a lifestyle' can be forgiven for the sheer zest with which this Prague satellite of the Paris-based Buddha Bar group began life in early 2009. With the aim of electrifying the city's nightlife with an epic DJ bar and Asian/Pacific Rim resto, while also setting the standard for cool hostelry, the company is aiming high. Time will tell whether they bring it off but introductory deals make it worth considering. Spa, hamman steam, wellness and high-tech fitness centres help with your conversion.

Cloister Inn

Konviktská 14 (224 211 020/ www.cloister-inn.com). Metro Národnítřída. **$$.**

ESSENTIALS

Buddha-Bar Hotel p169

Resting behind the cheaper Pension Unitas, the Cloister Inn has attentive staff, a great location, good prices and a nearby house full of nuns should you need redemption. Bright, cheery rooms and a lobby computer with free internet, plus free coffee and tea and a lending library. Prices have risen of late, but the website offers deals.

Euro Agentur Hotel Royal Esprit

Jakubská 5 (224 800 055/www.euro anentur.com/cz/ea-hotel-royal-esprit). Metro Náměstí Republiky. **$$$**.
Until recently known as the Hotel Mejstřík, this hotel in the heart of Old Town was founded in 1924. Now chain-licensed, it still has 30 individually decorated rooms that are a hybrid of modern hotel decor and 1920s style. Art deco accents and wood trim are a nice touch, and corner rooms offer great vantages for spying on streetlife and gables. Some no-smoking, disabled-adapted rooms and a trad Czech restaurant.

Floor Hotel

Na Příkopě 13 (234 076 300/www. floorhotel.cz) Metro Můstek. **$$**.
An affordable addition to Prague's marquee shopping promenade but the venture capitalists kept it simple with 43 rooms over four storeys, half of which offer traditional luxury, the other half sleek and modern decor (jacuzzis optional). The upscale fusion eaterie has an impressive menu, and there's a large, crystal chandeliered conference room for the business crowd.

Four Seasons Hotel Prague

Veleslavínova 2A (221 427 000/www. fourseasons.com/prague). Metro Staroměstská. **$$$$**.
The only fault to be found with the Four Seasons is that it's perhaps too 'perfect'. While it's a seamless melding of restored Gothic, Baroque, Renaissance and neo-classical buildings, guests will be hard-pressed to catch even a whiff of musty history. Of course, there's no shortage of that just outside the walls,

so you might as well enjoy the luxury, the service and the country's only Michelin-star resto, Allegro. Vista seekers should reserve the top-flight rooms with sweeping views of Prague Castle and Charles Bridge. In-room massage and pedicures go a long way to restoring Castle-worn lower extremities.

Hostel Rosemary

Růžová 5 (222 211 124/www.prague cityhostel.cz) Metro Můstek. **$**.
Far cleaner and better run than you might expect a hostel to be, the Rosemary is the latest generation, offering some private rooms with en suite baths starting at 34 euros and twins at 17 euros per person with nary a curfew. Breakfast isn't included, but free internet access is, credit cards are accepted and the location can't be beaten – it is situtated just off historic Wenceslas Square. A good new option for backpackers, with more beds available at sister hostel U Melounu.

Hotel Černý Slon

Týnská 1 (222 321 521/www.hotel cernyslon.cz). Metro Staroměstská. **$$**.
With an incredible location in the shadow of the Tyn church just off Old Town Square, this cosy 16-room inn is ensconced in a 14th-century building that's on the UNESCO heritage list. Gothic stone arches and wooden floors go with the smallish, but comfortable rooms laid out with basic amenities. Windows look out onto the cobbled mews in the quieter part of Old Town, although they still offer a constant parade of characters.

Hotel Josef

Rybná 20 (221 700 111/www.hoteljosef. com). Metro Náměstí republiky. **$$$**.
A renovated fitness centre and sauna help make the Josef one of the hippest designer hotels in Old Town, and it has been a trendsetter ever since it opened in 2002. Flash modernist interiors and unique fabrics and glass bathrooms (superior-class rooms only) are the work of London-based Czech designer Eva Jiřičná. All this in the thick of the historic centre, with the top-floor rooms in the 'Pink House' having the best views. There's no real designer bar, alas, just the overlit lobby one, but you do feel sleek here. Kids under six are free.

Hotel Paříž Praha

U Obecního domu 1 (222 195 195/ www.hotel-pariz.cz). Metro Náměstí Republiky. **$$$**.
If any hotel captures the spirit of Prague's *belle époque*, it's this one. Immortalised in Bohumil Hrabal's novel *I Served the King of England* (the film version of which was released in 2006) the Paříž is ageing with remarkable grace. Guests who are weary of cookie-cutter hotels will appreciate the patina of the historic rooms and well-preserved jazz-age dining room and café. Money no object? Try the Royal Tower Suite, with its 360-degree view of the city. Nice wellness spa centre too.

Iron Gate p172

Hotel U Tří Bubnů

*U radnice 10 (224 214 855/www.
utribubnu.cz). Metro Staroměstská. $$.*
Just 50 metres from Old Town Square,
this hotel proves you can just about
sleep within the landmark sights of
Prague. Well-appointed rooms have a
rustic vibe, thanks to the wood furniture
and ceilings. The attic suites are huge –
perfect for a family. Quiet, despite the
location, due to thick ancient walls.
Service is worthy of the days of old as
well. Wi-Fi access and complementary
laptop and DVD player loan.

Inter-Continental Praha

*Náměstí Curieovych 5 (296 631 111/
www.icprague.com). Metro
Staroměstská. $$$$.*
With 32 years as Prague's flagship for
decadence, the Inter-Continental Praha
may at last be getting it right. While
traces of communist design were
expunged during a $50-million refur-
bishment in the 1990s, only recently
does the transformation seem to have
taken hold in earnest, with courteous
service following. All 372 rooms have a
dataport for your laptop and the entire
hotel has Wi-Fi. Still, one side faces a
garish casino, and it costs an extra 40
euros for a room facing the river. Kids
eat for free and the fitness centre, jacuzzi
and sauna attract Prague's elites.

Iron Gate

*Michalská 19 (225 777 777/www.iron
gate.cz). Metro Staroměstská. $$$.*
The city of Prague has recognised the
Iron Gate's historically senstive reconstruction in 2003, making use of buildings from the 14th and 16th centuries
and preserving the original painted
ceiling beams and frescoes. To
maintain the look, kitchenettes are
discreetly tucked inside antique
armoires. The Tower Suite is over the
top in more ways than one: stashed
away on three floors of the building,
it features a heart-shaped bed, jacuzzi
for two, and views of Old Town Hall
and Prague Castle.

Kempinski Hybernská Prague

NEW *Hybernská 12 (226 226 111/
www.kempinski-prague.com). Metro
Náměstí republiky. $$$.*
After a false start in Old Town, the
Kempinski group has opened a Prague
edition with characteristic style. Le
Grill restaurant is ambitious but the
neo-Baroque Two Steps bar is more
inviting, while rooms with dark wood
accents feature media panels, DVD
players on loan and capacious bath-
rooms. The staff aim to please and the
effect is comfort with professionalism.

Maximilian Hotel

*Haštalská 14 (225 303 111/www.
maximilianhotel.com). Metro Náměstí
republiky. $$.*
With bold design by Eva Jiřičná, these
71 rooms have won a loyal following
since the Maximilian opened and it
offers great value, especially in the off
season. With all the modcons, from free
Wi-Fi to massive showerheads, plus the
Asian wellness centre a place like this
simply must have these days, this is an
option worth seeking out.

U Medvídků

*Na Perštyně 7 (224 211 916/www.u
medvidku.cz). Metro Národní třída. $$.*
The iron doors on some rooms recall
Gothic dungeons, while the rudimenta-
ry bathrooms evoke the benighted
years of communism. The traditional
inn's also attached to a pub – one of the
first to serve Budvar – that keeps a con-
stant stream of tourists and locals fed
on roasted pig, beer-basted beef and
dumplings. Damn handy for carousing.

Pachtův Palace

*Karoliny Světlé 34 (234 705 111/www.
pachtuvpalace.com). Metro Národní
třída. $$$$.*
With 50 deluxe apartments designed by
Jane Wilson, and country managers
already moving in, you'll be in power-
ful company here. The former residence
of Count Jan Pachta is a swanky stay,

Lotus speak

Experience Zen-inspired luxury at the Buddha-Bar Hotel.

The effusive press releases began rolling out in 2009. 'After Beirut, New York, Dubai, Kiev, São Paulo, London and Jakarta, the world-famous Parisian restaurant and bar has now opened its doors in Prague,' it read. So the city's officially on the map? So the **Buddha-Bar Hotel** (p169) thinks.

The place informs visitors it's not a hotel, but a lifestyle (sigh), and has transformed a block of Staré Město that was for years a focal point of backpackers who came to throw back absinthe at dive bars like the Marquis de Sade (now closed). It was aptly named.

Such exploits are unimaginable now that the Buddha-Bar has landed, complete with fabulous interiors, a menu card suitable for the fussiest of guests and a slick PR phalanx ('a unique urban resort that will redefine lifestyle within the Hospitality Industry' is a classic).

The project features two floors covering 800 square metres, with a standard nightly dinner capacity at 150, a gamut of Asian and Pacific-Rim fusion cuisine, a mezzanine bar and lounge for 100 more, complete with DJ tracks 'to infuse each night with energy and sensuality', just as the formula from the Paris original dictates. As for the settings, Siddharta Café developer George V assures us it creates a Pop art 'Eatmosphere', with sofas, chandeliers and 'modern Buddha-inspired paintings'. The DJ tracks start at noon and run late, and the lounge/bar stays open 24/7, which truly gives it an edge.

So is Prague ready for such splendour? Or, more to the point, are its visitors? Room rates are up there with those of the city's posh pads and, despite great cuisine and lunch specials, Buddha's menus are expensive. Had the investors forecasted the dramatic drop in tourism that the city is seeing, we might well have had to wait far longer to achieve such enlightenment. As it is, they are no doubt counting every dime from the sale of T-shirts at the Buddha-Bar Hotel Boutique.

where biz amenities, a classy bar and babysitting go along with the timbered rooms and, well, palatial public areas.

Pension Accord

Rybná 9 (222 328 816/ www.accordprague.com). Metro Náměstí republiky. **$$.**

The convenient location just three blocks from Old Town Square makes for outstanding value, as do the spring and summer double rates of 110 euros including breakfast (32 less in winter). This clean, basic place follows the Central Europe efficiency model but for budget travellers who won't be in their rooms much, you could do far worse.

Residence Řetězová

Řetězová 9 (222 221 800/www. residenceretezova.com). Metro Staroměstská. **$$$.**

A labyrinth of restored Renaissance rooms, some with timbered ceilings and lofts, make up this easy-to-miss Old Town gem. Genial service, an incredible location and a homely feel make it easy to imagine retiring to this abode to live a quiet life. The significant spread in rates reflects, aside from deep seasonal discounts, a variety of room sizes – all tastefully appointed charmers.

Travellers' Hostel

Dlouhá 33 (224 826 662/www. travellers.cz). Metro Náměstí Republiky. **$.**

No lock-out nonsense, all branches open 24 hours, dorm rooms starting at 300 Kč per person, breakfast included, and, at this location, the hottest club in Old Town (the Roxy, p120) right next door. There's a romantic suite with beamed ceilings, plus free Wi-Fi. Both apartments and the suite feature kitchens, but book ahead. This is also the booking office for a network of hostels (www.czechhostels.com). The seventh night is free of charge.

Ventana Hotel

Celetná 7 (221 776 600/www.ventana-hotel.net). Metro Staroměstská. **$$.**

From the Italian marble-filled lobby on, it's clear this recent addition to Old Town hostelry is a classy indulgence. A design hotel for grown-ups, the genteel Ventana has a five-storey atrium and plush rooms, many with exposed beams and Philippe Starck bathtubs. Its bar and library are particularly elegant.

U Zlaté studny

Karlova 3 (222 220 262/www.uzlate studny.cz). Metro Staroměstská. **$$.**

Mystery abounds in this 16th-century building named for the well in its cellar. Exquisitely furnished with Louis XIV antiques and replicas, the four suites and doubles are vast by Old Town standards. The UNESCO heritage building is halfway between Charles Bridge and Old Town Square on the Royal Route.

Nové Město & Vyšehrad

987 Prague Hotel

Senovážné náměstí 15 (255 737 200/www.987praguehotel.com). Metro Hlavní nádraží. **$$.**

Modern, affordable and friendly, the 987 Prague Hotel was transformed by Philippe Starck from a 19th-century apartment building, the façade of which is the only aspect unchanged. Interiors are infused with contemporary brilliance and have a sleek, comfy 1960s feel. A good option for late rail arrivals.

Andante

Ve Smečkách 4 (222 210 021/www. andante.cz). Metro Muzeum/IP Pavlova. **$$$.**

A fairly spartan modern exterior hides a warm interior. A recent revamp has improved the decor and infrastructure; it's clean and simple. The great location and super staff are the main draw. The 32 rooms are small, but you're a block from the liveliest street in town. A bookish retreat it ain't, though rooms are quiet. Concierge and airport transit.

Carlo IV

Senovážné náměstí 13 (224 593 111/ www.boscolohotels.com). Metro Hlavní nádraží. **$$$**.

An epic-looking place, considering the location just yards from the main train station, but that doesn't hold back the Italian owners. With a lobby worthy of a Stanley Kubrick flick, Boscolo Hotels welcomes visitors to this former bank with opulence, complete with cigar bar, pool, gym, wooden floors and a colour-palette of sage, gold and mahogany. Service is classic Mediterranean, alas. There's also an impressive spa.

Hotel Adria Prague

Václavské náměstí 26 (221 081 111/ www.hoteladria.cz). Metro Můstek **$$**.

In olden times a nunnery for the Carmelites, the Adria now lies in sin city central on Wenceslas Square, the only sign of its virtuous days being the Franciscan Gardens. Newly modernised, like so much of Prague, with young and eager staff, plus a memorable restaurant and bar with fairly standard-issue offerings. Concierge, sauna, massage and summer garden are further draws.

Hotel Elite

Ostrovní 32 (224 932 250/www.hotel elite.cz). Metro Národní třída. **$$**.

A reliable winner of accolades over the years, the family-run Elite is part of the Small Charming Hotels group, and fits nicely with the brand. The 14th-century volume, carefully revamped to retain its character, is protected by the Town Hall as a historical monument and the former barracks is right downtown with loads of hip restaurants and bars nearby.

Hotel Palace Praha

Panská 12 (224 093 111/www.palace hotel.cz). Metro Můstek. **$$$$**.

Just off Wenceslas Square, yet still close to everything, especially the city's tonier high street, Na příkopě. The Palace seems a world apart with understated, old-style formal service and solid creds among business travellers. Along with

Carlo IV

its award-winning Gourmet Club restaurant, there's a meeting centre, no-smoking floors and a sauna.

Ibis Praha City

Kateřinská 36 (222 865 777/www. hotelibis.cz). Metro IP Pavlova. **$$**.

For familiarity and reliability (read predictability?) in travel, the Ibis does offer deals on clean, new rooms in good locations – and recently launched another 271-room branch on handy Na Poříčí just east of Old Town. Unlike many wannabe exclusive places in Prague, it also knows its customer service. There's disabled access, a gym and an all-night restaurant.

Icon Hotel

V jámě 6 (221 634 100/www.icon hotel.eu). Metro Můstek **$$**.

One of the most successful of Prague's new design hotels, the Icon stands apart for its service, amenities and thoughtful touches. With the attached Jet Set bar, a cousin of this cool scenesetter originally installed in Smíchov, even the lobby makes for a good hangout. Pampering wellness centre, of course.

Radisson SAS Alcron
Štěpánská 40 (222 820 000/www. radisson.com/praguecs). Metro Muzeum. **$$$$**.
Originally known as a jazz hotel when built in 1930, the Alcron celebrates the heritage of Duke and Satchmo, who both passed through, with art deco motifs. It's also kept up its rep as one of the city's first luxe hotels and has the finest seafood restaurant in the country. The higher up you go, the better the views, but the high ceilings and period appointments make every room a classic. Lobby jazz bar, concierge, gym and no-smoking floors are further draws.

U Šuterů
Palackého 4 (224 948 235/www. usuteru.cz). Metro Můstek. **$**.
A winner for seekers of small and cosy, if basic. The building dates to 1383, but rooms were last renovated in 2004. Yet the whole interior is a time trip back to pre-World War II days, and the formal but solid service highlights this. The pub restaurant downstairs is popular throughout the city for its cheap and classic Czech fare and venison goulash.

Vinohrady & Žižkov

Arcotel Hotel Teatrino
Bořivojova 53, Žižkov (221 422 211/www.arcotel.at). Metro Jiřího z Poděbrad. **$$$**.
Rough and ready Žižkov is rapidly being turned into Prague's Greenwich Village, largely down to places like this big shrine to nationalist art. Austrian designer, architect and painter Harald Schreiber is to blame for the interiors – the lobby sports his epic rendering of Czech heroes. It contributes to the odd mix that is meant to 'animate the hotel's guests for a journey through the art and history of the city'.

Clown & Bard
Bořivojova 102, Žižkov (222 716 453/ www.clownandbard.com). Metro Jiřího z Poděbrad. **$**.
Noisy, cheap and friendly, this hostel's bar is well known in Prague with the party-hearty set. Located in the always colourful Žižkov district, it's a good choice if you're after some after-dark action. No lock-out, no reservations, no hassles. Free vegetarian breakfast, laundry, no credit cards.

Courtyard by Marriott
Lucemburská 46, Žižkov (236 088 088/ www.marriott.com). Metro Flora. **$$**.
Adjacent to a green line metro stop and one of the city's trendiest shopping malls, this surprisingly solid-value spot is a good option for families or those on biz trips, with the usual Marriott service standards. With 161 rooms, it's a good backup if there's no room at the inn. Disabled access and non-smoking rooms.

Czech Inn
Francouzska 76, Vinohrady (267 267 600/www.czech-inn.com). Metro Náměstí Míru. **$**.
It almost seems wrong to call this spotless, designer accommodation a hostel, but that it is. Certainly private en suite rooms are available and no membership is required (don't even ask about curfews), but so are dorms. With a glitzy cocktail bar, tasty breakfasts, internet café and free booking of your next hostel down the road, word's spreading fast about Czech Inn.

Hotel Abri
Jana Masaryka 36, Vinohrady (222 515 124/www.abri.cz). Metro Náměstí Míru. **$$**.
This small but lovely hotel is well-situated in a quiet Vinohrady neighbourhood, about five minutes from the metro station, and two minutes from a tram stop. The staff are unflappable, rooms are large, the lobby is spacious and the terrace entices in warm weather. A modern Czech restaurant is on site.

Hotel Anna

*Budečská 17, Vinohrady (222 513 111/
www.hotelanna.cz). Metro Náměstí
Míru/tram 4, 10, 16, 22, 23.* **$$**.
On a quiet, leafy street in Vinohrady, the
Anna, with modernised amenities but
an art nouveau interior is a Prague vet-
eran-visitor trump card. Simply but
classily furnished, these 24 rooms feature
Wi-Fi internet access.

Hotel Tříska

*Vinohradská 105, Žižkov (222 727
313/www.hotel-triska.cz). Metro Jiřího
z Poděbrad.* **$**.
Whitewashed baroque meets Czech
murals, art deco and imperial, but it's
a bargain and the owners have lovingly
designed each room. It's located in the
heart of the district, with great bars and
clubs nearby. Try to book a courtyard-
facing room; the street gets noisy.

Miss Sophie's Prague

*Melounova 3, Vinohrady (296 303
530/www.miss-sophies.com). Metro
IP Pavlova.* **$**.
Dorms, private rooms and apartments,
exude an uptempo style. Recently
opened, Miss Sophie's has fitted its
apartments with full kitchens, the dorm
rooms with wooden floors and private
rooms with elegant marble bathrooms.
A helpful vibe prevails. The more ele-
gant end of the budget hotel scale, with
a terrace and a cellar lounge.

Le Palais

*U Zvonařky 1, Vinohrady (234 634 111/
www.palaishotel.cz) Metro IP Pavlova/
Náměstí míru/tram 4, 16, 22, 23.* **$$$$**.
This gorgeous belle époque palace
beckons from its idyllic corner of the
city. It was originally decorated by 19th-
century Czech artist Luděk Mařold in
exchange for rent, and many of his
touches remain, such as the frescoed
ceilings and staircase. Service is excel-
lent and the rooms are sophisticated. A
well-equipped fitness centre, a buzzing
restaurant and a lovely summer terrace,
plus massage services, add appeal.

Prague Hilton

*Pobřežní 1, Karlín (224 841 111/www.
hiltonprague.cz). Metro Florenc.* **$$$$**.
This glass box behemoth is very un-
Prague like from the outside but hides
an airy atrium and five-star luxury
inside. You won't want for much,
except for Prague charm, but it's just
east of the old centre. The lauded Czech
House restaurant is another plus, and
there are disabled-adapted rooms.

Holešovice & north

Diplomat Hotel Praha

*Evropská 15, Dejvice (296 559 111/
www.diplomatpraha.cz). Metro
Dejvická.* **$$$$**.
On the city end of the airport road (20
minutes from Ruzyně), the Diplomat is
still close to the centre. Business-like,
with serious meeting rooms, it's also
big with families and has regular spe-
cials. Helpful staff plus disabled-
adapted rooms, a gym, no-smoking
floors and interpreting services are
further draws.

Hotel Schwaiger

*Schwaigerova 3, Bubeneč (233 320
271/www.villaschwaiger.cz). Metro
Hradčanská.* **$$$**.
The former villa of a 19th-century
Bohemian painter, the Schwaiger
stands in a leafy part of town close to
Stromovka park, but a ten-minute cab
ride from downtown. Recently redone
in what could be described as Tuscan-
meets-Zen style, it has an Argentine
steakhouse restaurant. Staff are pleasant and there's a garden and sauna.

Sir Toby's Hostel

*Dělnická 24, Holešovice (283 870 635/
www.sirtobys.com). Metro Vltavská or
Nádraží Holešovice.* **$**.
Friendly staff make Sir Toby's a winner, with 70 beds in an art nouveau
building that's so stylishly redone you
may forget you're in a hostel. It lies in
the heart of a vibrant neighbourhood,
close to galleries and buzzy nightlife.

ESSENTIALS

Getting Around

Arriving & leaving

By air

Ruzyně Airport
*239 007576/www.czechairlines.com/en.
About 20 km (12.5 miles) north-west
of central Prague, off Evropská.*
There's no metro access to Ruzyně; the
quickest way into town is by **ČEDAZ**
shuttle (220 114 296, www.cedaz.cz)
to the Dejvická metro station and
Náměstí Republiky, which takes 20
minutes and runs from 6am to 9pm
daily. Singles cost 90 Kč to Dejvická,
and 120 Kč to Náměstí Republiky.

The **Prague Airport Shuttle**
(602 395 421, www.prague-airport-
shuttle.com), with English-speaking
staff, runs daily, providing door-to-
door transport. Transport to your
hotel is 550 Kč for up to four people,
900 Kč for 5-8 passengers, 1,500 Kč
for 9-12 passengers. Book online.

The **Public bus** (www.dp-praha.cz)
service runs between Ruzyně and the
Dejvická metro, with the 119 running
every 20 minutes from 4.16am to midnight daily. It takes about 15 minutes
and costs 26 Kč for a single, with
tickets available from the bus stop
machine but not onboard.

AAA Taxi (14014, www.aaa
taxi.cz) charges about 450 Kč to
the centre and has a rank outside
the arrivals hall. Avoid other taxis
waiting at the airport, which are
likely to rip you off.

By rail

Czech Rail
Trains run everywhere and are
affordable; they're threadbare but
reliable. For info in English on train
times, call 221 111 122 or visit www.
cd.cz. For ticket prices, call 840 112

113. The website www.idos.cz also
gives timetable info for all buses.
You cannot buy tickets online but
station staff speak English. All the
major stations are served by metro.

Mainline stations

Hlavní nádraží
*Main Station, Wilsonova, Nové Město
(840 112 113/www.idos.cz). Metro
Hlavní nádraží.*
Most international trains arrive at
Hlavní nádraží, two blocks north of
Wenceslas Square, on red metro line C.

Nádraží Holešovice
*Holešovice Station, Vrbenského,
Holešovice (220 806 790/www.
idos.cz). Metro Nádraží Holešovice.*
A few international trains stop only
at Nádraží Holešovice, in the Holešovice
district and on the red metro line C,
a ten-minute metro ride north of the
centre of Prague. Many more stop at
Nádraží Holešovice then continue on
to the main station, Hlavní nádraží,
so be sure not to hop off early.

Smíchovské nádraží
*Smíchov Station, Nádražní (221 111
122/www.idos.cz).Metro Smíchovské
nádraží/tram 12.*
Some trains arriving from the west
stop at Smíchovské nádraží, which is
situated on the yellow metro line B,
but usually also at Hlavní nádraží.

By coach

Florenc station
*Křižíkova 4, Prague 8 (infoline 900
144 144/www.csad.cz). Metro Florenc.*
International buses arrive at Florenc,
a grimy and unprepossessing station.
But it lies a ten-minute walk east of
hotels on the much more civilised Na
Poříčí street on the edge of Old Town.

Public transport

Prague public transport – its metro, trams, buses and funicular – is run by Prague Public Transit, or **Dopravní podnik**, whose website (www.dpp.cz) provides maps and information that can be downloaded and printed. Services generally run from 5am to midnight daily, with night trams and buses running at other times. At the information offices below, employees usually have at least a smattering of English and German and provide free information, night transport booklets and individual tram and bus schedules and sell tickets (cash only). You can also find maps for sale from agents and the routes posted in metro stations. Tram stops, meanwhile, have posted schedules but not handy route maps for the taking. At tram stops, the times posted apply to the stop where you are – which is highlighted in on the schedule. If your destination is listed below the highlighted stop, you're in the right place. Call 800 191 817 for more information, 7am-9pm daily, or check www.dpp.cz.

Information offices

Anděl metro station *Smíchov* *(222 646 055)*. **Open** 7am-9pm Mon-Fri; 9.30am-5pm Sat.
Můstek metro station *Nové Město* *(222 646 350)*. **Open** 7am-6pm Mon-Fri; 9.30am-5pm Sat.
Muzeum metro station *Nové Město* *(222 623 778)*. **Open** 7am-9pm daily.
Nádraží Holešovice metro station *Holešovice (222 646 055)*. **Open** 7am-6pm Mon-Fri.
Ruzyně Airport *(220 115 404)*. **Open** 7am-10pm daily.
Ruzyně Airport Terminal North *(296 669 652)*. **Open** 7am-10pm daily.

Prague Card

The **Prague Card** is a four-day sightseeing admissions card that comes with an optional transport pass good for all modes of public transit for the same period. The Prague Card (www.praguecard.biz), sold at the offices of Čedok (p183), the state tourism company, covers entrance to some 55 museums and attractions, including Prague Castle and the Astronomical Clock in Old Town, for a fee of 790 Kč for adults or 530 Kč for students. Add on the transport card for a further 330 Kč for three days. If you're planning to take in several museums and galleries it's worth the price, but note that the Jewish Museum and some excellent galleries like the Rudolfinum are not covered. The travel pass is good no matter how many journeys you make and valid for the entire centre. The Prague Card is available at travel information centres and at the office of the Prague Information Service on Old Town Square (www.pis.cz), though not at metro stations.

To use the transport pass with your Prague Card, fill out your name and sign it (they're non-transferable), and just keep it with you while you ride – no need to pass it through card readers.

Travelcards

Day or multi-day travelcards are also available from the metro stations. Rates are 100 Kč for a 24-hour pass, 330 Kč for a 72-hour pass and 500 Kč for a 120-hour pass, and they cover all travel on public transport in the centre of the city, including metro, trams, buses and the funicular on Petřín hill in Malá Strana. They're good for any time of day or night and also cover night trams and night buses.

Travelcards start to save you money with the three-day version, if you plan to be on the road a lot. One-day and three-day travelcards come as standard printed tickets that you insert into the slot in

ESSENTIALS

metro station entry gates, or in the yellow ticket boxes on trams or buses, which time-stamp your pass. To validate a short-term pass, fill in your full name and date of birth on the reverse. The dates go into effect from the time you first put down. Once that's done, you can ride any bus or tram and only need show your pass to a driver or inspector if asked.

Metro

The Prague metro, constructed under the Soviet programme of 'normalisation', is one of the regime's best achievements. It is fast, clean, reliable and roomier than most in Europe, probably because it was built so late in the city's history. Stations are deep underground and the city's three colour-coded lines are a cinch to navigate. The heavily subsidised system is also cheap, with a 26 Kč ticket getting you anywhere you'd need to go, including transfers – just remember to stamp it as you enter the metro or board surface transport, lest you face the wrath of the city's generally unpleasant inspectors, who may fine you 950 Kč, cash only, on the spot.

Using the system

A one-day travelcard or **Prague Card** is the best way to pay for your metro transport if you're going to make more than four round trips, or travel on an unpredictable schedule. Otherwise, single tickets can be purchased from a ticket office or machine in the metro station (annoyingly, they're almost never installed at tram or bus stops).

Metro timetable

The metro runs daily from around 5am. Generally, you won't have to wait more than ten minutes, and during peak times services run every six to eight minutes. They can slow to every 20 minutes on weekends and holidays. Last trains are usually around midnight daily.

Fares

A 26 Kč ticket is valid for 75 minutes at any time or on any day of the year, allowing unlimited travel throughout Prague, including transfers between metros, buses and trams.

Buses & trams

The Prague bus and tram systems require you to buy a ticket before boarding. Do so: there are inspectors about, who can fine you 400 Kč. You can buy one (or a one-day pass) from ticket machines, though, frustratingly, they're usually only located in metro stations.

Night buses & trams

The latest-running regular trams and buses operate only until about 20 minutes after midnight, so night trams and buses, which are popular with a party-loving crowd, can be a lifesaver. They generally run from around 11.30pm to 5am, seven days a week, but come less frequently on weekends and holidays. Night trams have numbers in the 50s and night buses are numbered in the 500s. Most services run every 30 to 45 minutes so it's worth checking the schedule before going out for the night, especially in winter.

Taxis

Prague taxis have a well-deserved reputation for rip-offs and, despite frequent campaigns announced to clean them up, you still face a pretty good risk of being ripped off if you use any but a handful of reputable companies. Fortunately you can now find these drivers at taxi ranks in central areas of town, which until recently were considered the turf of the opportunists. Taxis with a yellow rooftop sign switched on are available but you really should call an established company and order a cab, which will generally be able to fetch you in five minutes or so. Starting rates are 40 Kč plus 28 Kč per kilometre and 6 Kč per minute waiting.

To book an honest taxi, call **AAA** (14014), **ProfiTaxi** (844 700 800) or **Halo Taxi** (244 114 411). They generally do not accept credit cards, but you'll pay nothing extra for the call-out service.

Water transport

There are no commuter boat services in Prague, but for leisure cruises, see Jazz Boat (p122).

Driving

Parking

Driving can be a nightmare in Prague. The city has one of Europe's highest accident rates, combined with narrow, cobbled streets, trams (which always have right of way and use special traffic signals of their own) and frequent rain, ice and snow. Street parking in the centre without a residents' permit is not permitted either, and is likely to end up getting you clamped with one of Prague's infamous yellow boots (call the number on the boot or 158 to pay up and get yourself freed).

Blue zones are reserved for local residents and companies. Orange zones are reserved for stops of up to two hours and cost a minimum of 10 Kč for 15 minutes and 40 Kč for one hour; and green zones are for stays of up to six hours and cost 15 Kč for 30 minutes, 30 Kč for an hour and 120 Kč for six hours.

You'll need to pay at coin-operated parking meters, which dispense tickets that must be displayed face up on the dashboard, visible through the windscreen.

There are increasing numbers of private underground car parks in central Prague but they are pricey, usually short-term and often full.

Vehicle removal

If your (illegally parked) car has mysteriously disappeared, chances are it's been taken to a car pound. Penalty and release fees are stiff. To find out where your car has been taken and how to retrieve it, call 158, 24hrs daily.

Vehicle hire

Alimex (800 150 170, www. alimex.eu) offers competitive rates, just so long as you don't mind driving a branded car around town. Otherwise, try **Europcar** (224 811 290, www.europcar.cz), **Czechocar** (800 321 321, www. czechocar.cz) or **Budget** (235 325 713, www.budget.cz).

Cycling

Pedalling in Prague is hellish: no cycle lanes, drivers oblivious to your presence and pedestrians who yell at you if you ride on the pavement. If you must, bikes can be hired, and tours taken, from the following organisation:

City Bike

Králodvorská 5, Staré Město (mobile 776 180 284, www.citybike-prague. com). Metro Náměstí Republiky. **Open** *Apr-Oct* 9am-7pm daily. *Hire* 300-540 Kč for two hours.
Cycle tours of the city, leaving from this address three times a day (10.30am, 1.30pm and 4.30pm), and with reasonable bike rental fees.

Resources A-Z

Accident & emergency

Prague's general emergency telephone number is 112. The following hospitals have 24-hour emergency facilities.

Canadian Medical Care *Veleslavínská 1, Dejvice (235 360 133/ emergency 724 300 301). Metro Dejvická.*

Medicover Clinic *Pankrác House, Lomnického 1705, Pankrác (234 630 111/emergency 603 555 006). Metro Pražského povstání.*

Motol Hospital *(Fakultní nemocnice v Motole) V Úvalu 84, Smíchov, Prague 5 (224 431 111/emergency 224 438 590). Anděl Metro, then tram 7, 9, 10, 58, 59.*

Na Homolce Hospital *(Nemocnice Na Homolce) Roentgenova 2, Smíchov, Prague 5 (257 271 111, emergencies 257 273 191). Anděl Metro, then tram 7, 9, 10, 58, 59.*

Credit card loss

American Express *222 412 241*
Diners Club *267 197 450*
JCB *0120 500 544*
MC/Eurocard/Visa *800 111 055.*

Customs

For allowances, see www.cs.mfcr.cz.

Dental emergencies

Dental Emergencies *Spálená 12, Nové Město (224 946 268). Metro Můstek.* **Open** 7pm-7am Mon-Fri; 24 hours Sat, Sun.

European Dental Center *Václavské náměstí 33, Nové Město (224 228 994). Metro Můstek.* **Open** 8.30am-8pm Mon-Fri; 9am-6pm Sat. Sunday and later hours at a premium.

Disabled

Prague is difficult for disabled visitors, although legislation is gradually improving things. Buses and trams with wheelchair access are being phased in, but the metro is mostly escalator-dependent. A free guide to stations with lifts is available from ticket offices.

Electricity

The Czech Republic uses the standard European 220-240V, 50-cycle AC voltage through continental three-pin plugs.

Embassies & consulates

See also the *Zlaté stránky* (or *Yellow Pages*), which has an English index.

American Embassy *Tržiště 15, Malá Strana (257 022 000/www. usembassy.cz). Metro Malostranská.*

Australian Trade Commission & Consulate *Klimentská 10, Nové Město (251 018 350). Metro Náměstí Republiky.*

British Embassy *Thunovská 14, Malá Strana (257 402 111/www. britain.cz). Metro Malostranská.*

Canadian Embassy *Muchova 6, Dejvice (272 101 800/www.canada.cz). Metro Hradčanská.*

Irish Embassy *Tržiště 13, Malá Strana (257 530 061/www.embassyofireland.cz). Metro Malostranská.*

New Zealand Consulate *Dykova 19, Vinohrady (222 514 672). Metro Náměstí Míru.*

Internet

There are many cybercafés and lots of bars, such as Jáma (p133), have free Wi-Fi. See www.cybercafes.com.

For particular hot spots, check out www.wi-fihotspotlist.com.
Internet Café Pl@neta *Vinohradska 102, Vinohrady (267 311 182/www. planeta.cz). Metro Jiřího z Poděbrad.* **Open** 8am-11pm daily. **Terminals** 60.

Opening hours

Banks 8am-5pm Mon-Fri.
Businesses 9am-5pm Mon-Fri.
Shops 10am-6pm Mon-Sat; some to 8pm. Many are also open on Sunday, usually 11am-5pm or noon-6pm.

Pharmacies (Lekárna)

Belgická 37 *Vinohrady (222 519 731). Metro Náměstí Míru.* **Open** 24hrs daily.
Palackého 5 *Nové Město (224 946 982). Metro Můstek.* **Open** 24 hrs daily.

Police

The main police station (Na Perštýně and Bartolomějská streets, Staré Město, Metro Náměstí Republiky) should have an English-speaking person available to help, but many visitors have found this lacking. The emergency number is 158.

Post

Post offices are usually open 9am to 5.30pm Monday to Friday and 9am to noon Saturday, although the main Post Office on Jindřišská street is open from 2am-midnight daily. For general enquiries, call the central information line on 800 104 410 or consult www.ceskaposta.cz.

Main post offices

Hybernska 15 *Nové Město (224 219 714). Metro Náměstí Republiky.*
Jindřišská 14 *Nové Město (221 131 111). Metro Můstek.* **Kaprova 12** *Staré Město (224 811 587). Metro Staroměstská.*

Public phones

Public payphones take coins or pre-paid cards, available at newsstands in denominations of 50-100 units, or credit cards (sometimes both). Local calls cost 10 Kč for five minutes during peak hours. Most public phones in the city centre are in a poor state of repair, as Czechs have embraced mobile phones with a passion.

Operator services

Call 800 123 456 for the operator if you have difficulty in dialling or for help with international person-to-person calls. Dial 155 for the international operator if you need to reverse the charges (call collect) or if you can't dial direct.

Directory enquiries

For help in finding a number, dial 1188 or the international operator at 1181. Online, you can access many useful contacts at www.expats.cz and www.prague.tv.

Safety

Prague is not a particularly dangerous city for visitors, but its crowded spots – buses, busy streets, metro trains and stations – attract the usual petty crooks. Keep valuables in your hotel or room safe, and ensure the cash and cards you carry with you are well tucked away.

Smoking

In 2006, a law banned smoking in restaurants during peak times, but permitted it at others. It also bars smoking at tram stops, the area of which the law fails to define. At press time, the scuffle to amend the vague law was continuing. Many hotels offer smoking rooms.

ESSENTIALS

Telephones

The Czech Republic's dialling code is 420. If you are calling from outside the country, dial your international access code, followed by this number, then the full Prague number. When phoning abroad from the Czech Republic, dial 00, then the country code.

Tickets

With the exception of the major cultural institutions, which have in-house box offices and offer phone and web ticketing services at no significant premium, most venues subcontract their ticket sales out to agencies. To find out which ones to purchase tickets from, consult the venue's website. Between them, **Ticketpro** and **Bohemia Ticket International** represent most cultural venues. However, note that Bohemia Ticket doesn't accept credit cards.

Bohemia Ticket International

Malé náměstí 13, Staré Město (224 227 832/www.ticketsbti.cz). Metro Můstek. **Open** 9am-5pm Mon-Fri; 9am-1pm Sat.

Ticket Pro

Old Town Hall, Staré Město (224 223 613/www.ticketpro.cz). Metro Staroměstská. **Open** 9am-6pm Mon-Fri; 9am-5pm Sat-Sun.

Time

The Czech Republic operates on Central European time, which is one hour later than Greenwich Mean Time (GMT), and six hours ahead of the United States' Eastern Standard time. In the spring, clocks go forwards by one hour, whereas in the autumn they go back to CET.

Tipping

Tip in taxis, restaurants, hotels, hairdressers, bars and pubs. Ten per cent is normal, but some restaurants can add 15 per cent.

Tourist information

Čedok is the city's official tourist information company. There is also a Prague Information Service office on Old Town Square.

Čedok

Na Příkopě 18, Nové Město (800 112 112/www.cedok.cz). Metro Náměstí Republiky. **Open** 9am-7pm Mon-Fri; 9.30am-1pm Sat.

Prague Information Service

Staroměstké Náměstí, Staré Město (no phone/www.pis.cz). Metro Staroměstská. **Open** *Nov-Mar* 9am-6pm daily. *Apr-Oct* 9am-7pm daily. **Other locations** *Main Station (Hlavní nádraží)*

Visas

EU citizens do not require a visa to visit the Czech Republic, nor do those of Australia, Canada, New Zealand or the USA. Other nationals should visit their government website or contact their country's Czech embassy to find out information about visa requirements. Check www.ukvisas.gov.uk to see your visa status well before you travel.

What's on

Numerous free listings magazines are distributed around town and with newspapers, but *The Prague Post* (www.praguepost.com), out on Wednesdays, is the best reference. Good online sources are www.expats.cz and www.prague.tv. For gay listings, see www.gayguide.net.

Vocabulary

Pronunciation

a – as in gap; **á** – as in father;
e – as in let; **é** – as in air;
i, y – as in lit; **í, ý** – as in seed;
o – as in lot; **ó** – as in lore;
u – as in book; **ú, ů** – as in loom;
c – as in its; **č** – as in chin;
ch – as in loch; **ď** – as in duty;
ň – as in onion; **ř** – as a standard
r, but with a forceful buzz like ž;
š – as in shin; **ť** – as in stew;
ž – as in pleasure; **dž** – as in George

The basics

Czech words are always stressed
on the first syllable.
hello/good day *dobrý den*
good evening *dobrý večer*
good night *dobrou noc*
goodbye *nashledanou*
yes *ano* (often *o* or just *jo*)
no *ne*
please *prosím*
thank you *děkuji*
excuse me *promiňte*
sorry *pardon*
help! *pomoc!*
attention! *pozor!*
I don't speak Czech
Nemluvím česky
I don't understand *Nerozumím*
Do you speak English?
Mluvíte anglicky?
sir *pán*
madam *paní*
open *otevřeno*
closed *zavřeno*
I would like... *Chtěl bych...*
How much is it? *Kolik to stojí?*
May I have a receipt, please?
Účet, prosím?
Can we pay, please?
Zaplatíme, prosím?
Where is...? *Kde je...?*
go left *doleva*
go right *doprava*

straight *rovně*
far *daleko*
near *blízko*
good *dobrý*
bad *špatný*
big *velký*
small *malý*
No problem *To je v pořádku*
rip-off *zlodějina*

Street names etc

avenue *třída*
bridge *most*
church *kostel*
embankment *nábřeží* or *nábř*
gardens *sady* or *zahrada*
monastery, convent *klášter*
square *náměstí* or *nám*
station *nádraží* or *nádr*
street *ulice* or *ul*

Numbers

0 *nula*; 1 *jeden*; 2 *dva*; 3 *tři*; 4 *čtyři*;
5 *pět*; 6 *šest*; 7 *sedm*; 8 *osm*; 9 *devět*;
10 *deset*; 20 *dvacet*; 30 *třicet*;
40 *čtyřicet*; 50 *padesát*; 60 *šedesát*;
70 *sedmdesát*; 80 *osmdesát*;
90 *devadesát*; 100 *sto*; 1,000 *tisíc*

Days & months

Monday *pondělí*; **Tuesday** *úterý*;
Wednesday *středa*; **Thursday**
čtvrtek; **Friday** *pátek*; **Saturday**
sobota; **Sunday** *neděle*

Pick-up lines

What a babe! *To je kost!*
What a stud! *Dobrej frajer!*
Hezké oči! *Nice eyes!*

Put-down lines

Sneak off! *Táhni!*
Kiss my arse! *Polib mi prdel!*

Menu Glossary

Czech menus in the more traditional restaurants generally list two categories of main dishes: *minutky*, cooked to order (which may take ages), and *hotová jídla*, ready-to-serve fare. The usual accompaniments to these are rice, potatoes, *knedlíky* (dumplings), or the fried béchamel dough known as *krokety*, all of which should be ordered separately. When dining in pubs, the closest thing to fresh vegetables is often *obloha*, a garnish of pickles, or a tomato on a single leaf of cabbage. Tasty appetisers are Prague ham with horseradish or rich soups (*polévka*), and a dessert staple is *palačinky*, filled pancakes.

Meals (jídla)

snídaně *breakfast*; **oběd** *lunch*; **večeře** *dinner*.

Preparation (příprava)

bez masa/bezmasá jídla *without meat*; **čerstvé** *fresh*; **domácí** *homemade*; **dušené** *steamed*; **grilované** *grilled*; **míchaný** *mixed*; **na roštu** *roasted*; **pečené** *baked*; **plněné** *stuffed*; **smažené** *fried*; **špíz** *grilled on a skewer*; **uzené** *smoked*; **vařené** *boiled*.

Basics (základní)

chléb *bread*; **cukr** *sugar*; **drůbež** *poultry*; **karbanátek** *patty*; **máslo** *butter*; **maso** *meat*; **ocet** *vinegar*; **olej** *oil*; **omáčka** *sauce*; **ovoce** *fruit*; **pepř** *pepper*; **rohlík** *roll*; **ryby** *fish*; **smetana** *cream*; **sůl** *salt*; **sýr** *cheese*; **vejce** *eggs*; **zelenina** *vegetables*.

Drinks (nápoje)

čaj *tea*; **káva** *coffee*; **mléko** *milk*; **pivo** *beer*; **pomerančový džus** *orange juice*; **sodovka** *soda*; **víno** *wine*; **voda** *water*; **slivovice** *plum brandy*; **Becherovka** *herbal liqueur*; **Fernet** *bitters*; **červené víno** *red wine*; **bílé víno** *white wine*; **perlová** *carbonated*; **neperlová** *still*.

Appetisers (předkrmy)

boršč *Russian beetroot soup (borscht)*; **chlebíček** *meat open-sandwich*; **hovězí vývar** *beef broth*; **kaviár** *caviar*; **paštika** *pâté*; **polévka** *soup*; **uzený losos** *smoked salmon*.

Meat (maso)

biftek *beefsteak*; **hovězí** *beef*; **játra** *liver*; **jehně** *lamb*; **jelení** *venison*; **kančí** *boar*; **klobása, párek, salám, vuřt** *sausage*; **králík** *rabbit*; **ledvinky** *kidneys*; **slanina** *bacon*; **srnčí** *roebuck*; **šunka** *ham*; **telecí** *veal*; **tlačenka** *brawn*; **vepřové** *pork*; **zvěřina** *game*.

Poultry & fish (drůbež a ryby)

bažant *pheasant*; **husa** *goose*; **kachna** *duck*; **kapr** *carp*; **křepelka** *quail*; **krocan** *turkey*; **kuře** *chicken*; **losos** *salmon*; **pstruh** *trout*.

Main meals (hlavní jídla)

guláš *goulash*; **řízek** *schnitzel*; **sekaná** *meat loaf*; **smaženýsýr**

fried cheese; **svíčková** *beef served in a cream sauce;* **vepřová játra na cibulce** *pig's liver stewed with onion;* **vepřové koleno** *pork knee;* **vepřový řízek** *fried breaded pork.*

Side dishes (přílohy)

brambor *potato;* **bramborák** *potato pancake;* **bramborová kaše** *mashed potatoes;* **hranolky** *chips;* **kaše** *mashed potatoes;* **knedlíky** *dumplings;* **krokety** *potato or béchamel dough croquettes;* **obloha** *small lettuce and tomato salad;* **rýže** *rice;* **salát** *salad;* **šopský salát** *cucumber, tomato and curd salad;* **tatarská omáčka** *tartar sauce;* **zelí** *cabbage.*

Cheese (sýr)

balkán a saltier *feta;* **eidam** *hard white cheese;* **hermelín** *soft, similar to bland brie;* **Madeland** *Swiss cheese;* **niva** *blue cheese;* **pivní sýr** *beer-flavoured semi-soft cheese;* **primátor** *Swiss cheese;* **tavený sýr** *packaged cheese spread;* **tvaroh** *soft curd cheese.*

Vegetables (zelenina)

česnek *garlic;* **chřest** *asparagus;* **cibule** *onion(s);* **čočka** *lentils;* **fazole** *beans;* **feferonky** *chilli peppers;* **hrášek** *peas;* **kukuřice** *corn;* **květák** *cauliflower;* **mrkev** *carrot;* **okurka** *cucumber;* **petržel** *parsley;* **rajčata** *tomatoes;* **salát** *lettuce;* **špenát** *spinach;* **žampiony** *mushrooms;* **zelí** *cabbage.*

Fruit (ovoce)

ananas *pineapple;* **banány** *banana;* **borůvky** *blueberries;* **broskev** *peach;* **hrozny** *grapes;* **hruška** *pear;* **jablko** *apple;* **jahody** *strawberries;* **jeřabina** *rowanberries;* **mandle** *almonds;* **meruňka** *apricot;* **ořechy** *nuts;* **pomeranč** *orange;* **rozinky** *raisins;* **švestky** *plums;* **třešně** *cherries.*

Desserts (moučník)

buchty *traditional curd-filled cakes;* **čokoláda** *chocolate;* **dort** *layered cake;* **koláč** *cake with various fillings;* **ovocné knedlíky** *fruit dumplings;* **palačinka** *crêpe;* **pohár** *ice-cream sundae;* **šlehačka** *whipped cream;* **zákusek** *cake;* **závin** *strudel;* **žemlovka** *bread pudding with apples and cinnamon;* **zmrzlina** *ice-cream.*

Useful phrases

May I see the menu? *Mohu vidět jídelní lístek?* **Do you have…?** *Máte…?* **I am a vegetarian** *Jsem vegetarián/vegetariánka (m/f).* **How is it prepared?** *Jak je to připravené?* **Did you say 'beer cheese'?** *Říkal jste 'pivní sýr'?* **Wow, that smells!** *Páni, to smrdí!* **Can I have it without…?** *Mohu mít bez…?* **What did you do to this beef?** *Co jste dělal s tím hovězím?* **I didn't order this** *Neobjednal jsem si to.* **How much longer will it be?** *Jak dlouho to ještě bude?* **The bill, please** *Účet, prosím.* **I can't eat this and I won't pay for it!** (use with extreme caution) *Nedá se to jíst a nezaplatím to.* **Take-away/to go** *S sebou.* **A beer, please** *Pivo, prosím.* **Two beers, please** *Dvě piva, prosím.* **Same again, please** *Ještě jednou, prosím.* **What'll you have?** *Co si dáte?* **Not for me, thanks** *Pro mě ne, děkuji.* **No ice, thanks** *Bez ledu, děkuji.* **He's really smashed** *Je totálně namazaný*

ESSENTIALS

Index

Sights & Areas

ESSENTIALS

ESSENTIALS

ESSENTIALS